THE SMOKER BIBLE & GRILL COOKBOOK

A Must-Have Guide to Get the Master of Grilling and Smoking Food.

Impress Your Friends and Family Each Time with 1000-Days of Succulent and Creative Recipes

Adam Rockwell

Table of Contents

Introduction

It all starts with quality meat. Let's say that today, thanks to the traceability of meat, we can know where it comes from and how it was raised, and this allows us to choose with peace of mind and awareness.

For optimal grilling, it is very important that the meat does not go from the refrigerator to the grill in one step. This is because the temperature range between the cold meat and the hot grill would only lower the temperature of the grill and the sealing of the meat fibers (the famous Maillard reaction) would not be achieved. This would result in losing all the juices that are inside and the meat would be tough when you go to eat it. In addition, a layer of condensation would quickly form on the surface of the meat, causing it to become moist: if you throw moist meat on a hot grill, a steam pad will form and the meat will begin to boil, turning gray and boiling.

The solution? Remove the meat from the refrigerator about two hours before grilling to bring it to room temperature. If the pieces of meat are large, such as rib-eye steak or tenderloin, then you can take them out of the refrigerator even three hours earlier. You must remember that the meat must be brought to room temperature before it meets the coals.

After waiting for the meat to be at room temperature, if it is still a little wet, you also need to dry it well before putting it to cook.

MARINADE

The purpose of marinating is to flavor the meat and tenderize it. For the game, it is also used to remove the "wild" flavor. But it is also recommended to use it to prevent the meat from burning during cooking, as it will limit the production of carcinogens released when burned.

The meat should be marinated in the refrigerator and, depending on the degree of acidity present in the marinade itself and according to the type of meat, you will then have to determine its duration. Remember that since marinating is an acidic compound, if you leave the meat in the liquid for too long, you may get the opposite effect. That is, loss of juices and thus tougher meat.

But let's get a little more technical.

The best way to add flavor to meat is to do so through the use of fatty substances emulsified in an acidic substance.

By emulsifying oil (or another fatty element) in an acid, which instead penetrates the fibers of the meat very easily, you can use the latter to carry the former. Wine, beer, vinegar, yogurt, lemon or orange juice, or any other acidic substance that affects the meat protein can be used as the acidic substance.

In this way, the acidic substance will affect the protein and thus open the entrance to the fatty substance that will carry the flavor of the spices with it.

In addition, it is necessary to add an ingredient that has the job of glue to hold the fatty and the acid parts together. This is because otherwise the 2 substances would tend to separate and you would not be able to give much flavor to the meat. As an emulsifier to hold the mixture together, you can use mustard or soy lecithin, for example.

So, to achieve a good marinade, you need:

- One fatty and one acidic substance emulsified through a third ingredient that will act as a glue

- Flavors and spices to taste

- Marinate the meat in a vacuum to achieve a truly professional result. This is because, by doing so, you will speed up the seasoning of the meat, decreasing both the marinating time and the amount of ingredients needed.

TRICKS DURING COOKING

Cooking on the grill is quite simple, but some precautions are needed. For example, large pieces of meat need a longer cooking time but at a lower temperature, while smaller pieces such as sliced chicken breast, skewers and sausages need a higher temperature and a relatively short cooking time.

Also, to prevent the meat from sticking, be sure to have the grill hot and the meat well drained from the marinade.

Do not poke holes in the meat or squish it on the grill. Meat is a juicy food and loses some juice during cooking. If you puncture or crush the meat against the grill, you will only make it lose more juices and make it tough. The only holes allowed are in the sausage, which, being composed of a good amount of fat, will lose some with the holes while remaining soft and flavorful.

COOKING TIMES AND TEMPERATURE

Cooking times vary depending on the size and type of meat. For example, chicken and pork need to be well cooked before being eaten, so their cooking time is longer than a beef chop.

Because chicken and pork need to cook long enough, they need a more moderate temperature, so I recommend that you do not put them in the center of the grill, which is the spot with the highest heat. It is better to put them slightly off-center, so they will cook without losing too much of their juices and will be softer.

For a medium-rare tenderloin, consider about 4 minutes per side. For a well-marinated chicken breast, about 6 minutes per side. For sausage about 15 minutes, and for a regular-sized hamburger, it might take about 7 to 8 minutes.

Once you remove the meat from the grill, do not serve it right away: you will need to let the meat rest a few minutes on a plate so the juices can redistribute throughout the piece.

Cook at two temperatures: "very hot" to do the Maillard; "moderate" to cook the inside evenly.

The Maillard reaction requires 350°/360°F. Higher temperatures cause the carbonization of sugars first and proteins later. But in this regard, the speed of heat transfer from the environment to the meat plays a key role. The fastest and most efficient transfer of heat is by "conduction," that is, by contact, and so if you cook in a pan or plancha, contact times must be very short. That's why if you use ribbed-bottom steak pans or cast-iron grills, it's a good idea not to overdo the temperature.

For transfers by radiation or convection, it is good to go higher as a temperature, and place between 475°F and 530°F. Here the distance of the meat from the heat source plays a key role: If you bring your grill to 530°F and cook in an "indirect" manner with the heat shield, you will easily have a perfect Maillard.

The "moderate temperature," on the other hand, ranges from 210°F to 275°F: the lower it is, the more even the internal temperature will be. But again without overdoing it, otherwise you will risk drying out the meat too much.

SMOKING

Since time immemorial, fish have been smoked to keep longer. Today, there is no need to dig holes in the ground to give meat or fish an aromatic smoky flavor. A smoker is not even needed. You can smoke food with an ordinary charcoal or gas grill, provided these are equipped with a lid.

Smoking is not difficult, as long as you follow a few simple rules.

WHAT IS SMOKING?

With smoking, foods are exposed to hot smoke, so-called charcoal smoke, released by the dry wood burning without any flame. The smoke penetrates meat, fish, cheese or even vegetables, making them dry and changing their color, smell and taste. In this way, food subjected to smoking not only acquires an unmistakable aroma, but will keep longer.

The intensity of this smoked aroma depends on the smoking time and the wood used. For example, hickory wood gives a strong, sour smell, while maple and alder are much more subtle. Fruit tree wood is mild and leaves a fruity note. Softwood is not suitable for smoking, and even less so are wood residues or bark: in addition to having a negative effect on taste, resin and pesticide residues pose a health risk.

It is possible to distinguish between two smoking methods: hot smoking and cold smoking. With cold smoking, food is smoked for several days or weeks in high humidity conditions at a temperature of 60-68°F. In hot smoking, temperatures are so high (up to 210°F) that food is cooked at the same time. Those who want to smoke with a grill usually use the hot method, because the cold method really takes a long time.

When you decide to take the path that leads to smoking foods, you must embrace an important concept: smoke represents a real ingredient, just as salt, pepper or oil can be.

1 - DON'T BE IN A HURRY

Smoking does not tolerate haste. Slow, low-temperature cooking is necessary to give that aromatic note to your foods. Chicken and pork, and some cuts of beef (such as brisket), require a slow approach.

However, you can also flavor with wood, foods that need only a few minutes of cooking time, such as steaks and shrimp. In these cases the aromatic note will be less pronounced.

2 - CHECK THE TEMPERATURE OF THE GRILL

During smoking, the internal temperature should range between 190° and 210°F. This is the range that will allow the meat to cook slowly without drying out: if the temperature changes, the food will be tough and inedible.

For cooking that takes longer than 60 minutes, remember to use an aluminum tray filled with water to keep the heat and humidity constant (the latter will not be necessary if using a water smoker).

Ventilation valves on barbecues with lids help maintain, raise or lower the temperature. Good ventilation will ensure quality smoke and the right temperature.

3 - CHECK THE COLOR OF THE SMOKE

If the smoke is perfectly white, take action because it will cover the meat with the toxic fumes emitted by the burning wood. On the other hand, the appliance is not sufficiently ventilated, or if the wood is too damp, a blackish smoke will deposit soot on the food.

The correct color of the smoke is a soft gray. Never use resinous or freshly cut wood because it produces acrid smoke.

4 - DO NOT ALWAYS OPEN THE LID

Every time you open the lid, you will lose smoke and lower the temperature. Avoid lifting the lid unless it is strictly necessary, such as filling the water pan, putting in smoked chips, or maintaining the coals.

5 - THE IMPORTANCE OF THE CRUST

The meat should be covered with a dark, black crust when preparing food on the grill using the original American smoking technique. This is due to the embers' heat, smoke intervention, and the natural process of caramelization. The black crust is essential, and it does not mean burnt food or improper cooking.

6 - EQUIP YOURSELF WITH A FOOD THERMOMETER

Your pulled pork or Brisket will be ready when it reaches the right temperature. To monitor it, you will need to have a probe thermometer that will allow you to always have the temperature under control.

DIRECT OR INDIRECT SMOKING

Smoking meat, fish, and vegetables do not require a particular smoker. You can also smoke on a charcoal or gas grill, if these are equipped with a lid. Only in this way will the smoky aroma penetrate the food. Smoking on the grill should not be confused with indirect cooking, a particularly delicate grilling method that takes longer than 30 minutes.

In indirect cooking, the food is not placed directly above the heat source. This allows lower temperatures to be maintained and the meat to sizzle under the lid as in an evenly heated oven. This makes it possible to cook large pieces of meat, roasts, chickens, or whole fish longer without drying them out. Foods that need to be browned briefly over high heat, such as steaks, shellfish, and vegetable slices, should be grilled by the direct way, that is, by placing them on the coals at a temperature between 390° and 570°F.

If you want a smoky aroma to grilled meat, you need to add the appropriate wood chips. With direct cooking, the smoky smell is not particularly intense because the smoke does not have enough time to develop. The indirect method is therefore the most suitable for smoking, because the food will remain in contact with the smoke longer.

SMOKING

Smoking is a true art, and smoke is considered an ingredient. So are spices, vinegar, oil and salt.

Chicken, pork, salmon, and cod are foods that have a natural predisposition to being smoked. But also oysters, shrimp, and of course there is no shortage of beef (brisket especially).

SMOKING WITH A CHARCOAL GRILL

Although you have to wait a while before you start grilling with the charcoal grill, this remains the most popular method because it is considered the most authentic. The ball grill allows both direct and indirect cooking. Decisive is the addition of wood chips.

How to smoke properly:

1.   First, soak the wood chips in water for 30-60 minutes. Impregnated with water, the chips will then tend to burn without flame, rather than burn.

2.   Heat the grill: as soon as the coals are burning and covered with a layer of ash, close the lid and wait until the desired temperature is reached.

3.   Now it is time for the wood chips. Drain them well and scatter them over the coals. The rule of thumb is: a handful of chips for every pound of meat. Immediately afterward, close the lid again.

4.   It takes a few minutes for the chips to reach the required temperature. When the smoke comes out of the vent, it is time to put the meat on the grill.

5.   When grilling directly, the food should be placed on top of the chips so that it can absorb as much of the smoky aroma as possible during the short cooking time. Then keep the lid closed until the meat is cooked unless you need to turn it over.

Compared to the direct method, cooking with the indirect method requires a different basic setting. The coals (and therefore also the wood chips) should not be in the center of the grill, but should be distributed around the edges, so that the food in the center of the grill is not directly over the coals. The same procedure applies to smoking. Just as with a smoker, when smoking with an indirect grill, the key is to keep the temperature constantly low. To do this, you need to use little charcoal or put a water tray under the food.

Grill professionals recommend smoking for only half the cooking time, because if food is exposed to smoke for too long, it can turn out bitter.

SMOKING WITH A GAS GRILL

Smoking with the gas grill is also possible without any problems, with the added advantage that this type of appliance is immediately ready to use. The key difference, compared to the charcoal grill, is that you cannot put wood chips directly on the fire. For smoking with a gas grill, it is advisable to use a smoking box, which should be filled with chips and placed near the food to be grilled. Alternatively, the chips can be wrapped in aluminum foil with ventilation holes.

First, before you start using the smoking box, bring the grill to the desired temperature and then be sure to cook the food only when the chips are burning. Only in this way will the smoky aroma be optimally absorbed. In the case of indirect cooking, simply place the food on an unlit heating element.

WATER SMOKER

Recommended for those who already have experience behind them and want to up their game, this type of appliance allows you to maintain a temperature between 190° and 240°F for at least 4 hours (sometimes even longer depending on the type of charcoal used).

Compared to the traditional charcoal barbecue on the temperature maintenance front, this device is much more reliable and allows for long and more elaborate smoking.

BBQ SMOKER

Recommended for those who like the old style, this smoker derives from early devices consisting of simple barrels cut in half lengthwise, fitted with a cooking grate and tipped on one side so that the coals and wood burned on one side and the food cooked on the other.

With this type of smoking, the charcoal and wood chips burn in a compartment (the combustion chamber) located on the side of the cooking chamber. This device prevents the temperature of the cooking chamber from rising too high. An adjustable ventilation valve on the combustion chamber and another on the chimney above the cooking chamber reliably control the air supply and the amount of smoke.

VERTICAL SMOKER

This type of industrial smoker is recommended for professionals who wish to smoke up to 10-15 pounds of food.

Some digital models allow you to control the temperature, smoking time, and amount of smoke. In addition, the chamber is automatically fed with briquettes, without needing to put your hand in it. Initially, these smokers were installed in old refrigerators with well-insulated walls.

Beef Recipes

1. Smoked and Pulled Beef

Preparation Time: 10 minutes **Cooking Time: 6 hours**
Servings: 6

Ingredients:
- 4 lb. beef sirloin tip roast
- 1/2 cup BBQ rub
- 2 bottles of amber beer
- 1 bottle barbecues sauce

Directions: Turn your wood pellet grill on smoke setting then trim excess fat from the steak.
Coat the steak with BBQ rub and let it smoke on the grill for 1 hour.
Continue cooking and flipping the steak for the next 3 hours. Transfer the steak to a braising vessel. Add the beers.
Braise the beef until tender then transfer to a platter reserving 2 cups of cooking liquid.
Use a pair of forks to shred the beef and return it to the pan. Add the reserved liquid and barbecue sauce. Stir well and keep warm before serving.
Enjoy.

Nutrition: Calories: 828.7; Fat: 45.7g; Carbs: 3.9g; Protein: 86.2g; Fiber: 0g

2. Reverse Seared Flank Steak

Preparation Time: 10 minutes **Cooking Time: 10 minutes**
Servings: 2

Ingredients:
- 1.5 lb. Flanks steak
- 1 tbsp. salt
- 1/2 onion powder
- 1/4 tbsp. garlic powder
- 1/2 black pepper, coarsely ground

Directions: Preheat your wood pellet grill to 225 F.
Mix salt, onion powder, garlic powder, and pepper in a mixing bowl. Generously rub the steak with the mixture.
Put the steaks on the grill, close the lid, and let the steak cook.
Crank up the grill to high then let it heat. The steak should be off the grill and tented with foil to keep it warm.
Once the grill is heated up to 450°F, place the steak back and grill for 3 minutes per side.
Remove from heat, pat with butter, and serve. Enjoy.

Nutrition: Calories: 111.8; Fats: 4.9g; Carbs: 0.9g; Protein: 16.2g; Fiber: 0g

3. Grilled Butter Basted Porterhouse Steak

Preparation Time: 10 minutes **Cooking Time: 40 minutes**
Servings: 4

Ingredients:
- 4 tbsp. butter, melted
- 2 tbsp. Worcestershire sauce
- 2 tbsp. Dijon mustard
- Griller Prime rib rub

Directions: Set your wood pellet grill to 225°F with the lid closed for 15 minutes.
Mix butter, sauce, and Dijon mustard in a mixing bowl until smooth. Brush the mixture on the meat then season with the rub. Arrange the meat on the grill grate and cook for 30 minutes.
Transfer the meat to a pattern then increase the heat to high.
Return the meat to the grill grate to grill until your desired doneness is achieved.
Baste with the butter mixture again if you desire and let rest for 3 minutes before serving. Enjoy.

Nutrition: Calories: 725.7; Fats: 61.9g; Carbs: 4.8g; Protein: 36.1g; Sugar 0.9g; Fiber 0.9g

4. Wood Pellet Grill Prime Rib Roast

Preparation Time: 10 minutes **Cooking Time: 4 hours**

Servings: 10
Ingredients:

- *7 lb. bone prime rib roast*
- *Griller prime rib rub*

Directions: Coat the roast generously with the rub then wrap in a plastic wrap. Let sit in the fridge for 24 hours to marinate.

Set the temperatures to 500°F.to to preheat with the lid closed for 15 minutes.

Place the rib directly on the grill fat side up and cook for 30 minutes.

Make the temperature 300°F and cook for 4 hours or until the internal temperature is 120°F-rare, 130°F-medium rare, 140°F-medium, and 150°F-well done.

Remove from the grill and let rest for 30 minutes then serve and enjoy.

Nutrition: Calories: 289.8; Fats: 22.8g; Protein: 19.2g

5. Teriyaki Beef Jerky

Preparation Time: 10 minutes　　　　　　　　　　　　　**Cooking Time: 5 hours**
Servings: 6

Ingredients:

- *3 cups soy sauce*
- *2 cups brown sugar*
- *3 garlic cloves*
- *2-inch ginger knob, peeled and chopped*
- *1 tbsp. sesame oil*
- *4 lb. beef, skirt steak*

Directions: Except the meat, place all other ingredients in a food processor. Pulse until well mixed.

Trim any excess fat from the meat and slice into 1/4-inch slices. Add the steak with the marinade into a zip lock bag and let marinate for 12-24 hours in a fridge.

Set the wood pellet grill to smoke and let preheat for 5 minutes.

Arrange the steaks on the grill leaving a space between each. Let's smoke for 5 hours.

Remove the steak from the grill and serve when warm.

Nutrition: Calories: 79.9; Fats: 0.9g; Carbs: 6.9g; Protein: 11.2g; Sugar: 5.9g; Fiber 0g

6. Smoked Brisket

Preparation Time: 20 minutes　　　　　　　　　　　　　**Cooking Time: 9 hours**
Servings: 10

Ingredients:

- *2 tbsp. garlic powder*
- *2 tbsp. onion powder*
- *2 tbsp. paprika*
- *2 tbsp. chili powder*
- *1/3 cup salt*
- *1/3 cup black pepper*
- *12 lb. whole packer brisket, trimmed*
- *1-1/2 cup beef broth*

Directions: Set your wood pellet temperature to 225°F. Let preheat for 15 minutes with the lid closed.

Meanwhile, mix garlic, onion, paprika, chili, salt, and pepper in a mixing bowl.

Season the brisket generously on all sides.

Place the meat on the grill with the fat side down and let it cool until the internal temperature reaches 160°F.

Remove the meat from the grill and double wrap it with foil. Return it to the grill and cook until the internal temperature reaches 204°F. Remove from the grill, unwrap the brisket, and let sit for 15 minutes.

Slice and serve.

Nutrition: Calories: 269.8; Fats: 19.8g; Carbs: 2.8g; Protein: 20.1g; Sugar 0.9g; Fiber 0g

7. Grilled New York Strip

Preparation Time: 5 minutes　　　　　　　　　　　　　**Cooking Time: 15 minutes**
Servings: 6

Ingredients:

- *3 New York strips*
- *Salt and pepper*

Directions: If the steak is in the fridge, remove it 30 minutes before cooking.

Prepare the Griller to 450°F.

Season the steak generously with salt and pepper. Put it on the grill and let it cook for 5 minutes per side or until the internal temperature reaches 1280F.
Remove the steak. For 10 minutes, let it rest.

Nutrition: Calories: 197.9; Fats: 13.8g; Protein: 17.2g

8. Rib Roast

Preparation Time: 10 minutes   **Cooking Time: 2 hours**
Servings: 8

Ingredients:

- 5 lb. rib roast, boneless
- 4 tbsp. salt
- 1 tbsp. black pepper
- 1-1/2 tbsp. onion powder
- 1 tbsp. granulated garlic
- 1 tbsp. rosemary
- 1 cup chopped onion
- 1/2 cup carrots, chopped
- 1/2 cup celery, chopped
- 2 cups beef broth

Directions: Remove the beef from the fridge 1 hour before cooking.
Preheat the Griller to 250°F.
Mix salt, pepper, onion, garlic, and rosemary in a small mixing bowl to create your rub.
Generously coat the roast with the rub and set it aside.
Combine chopped onions, carrots, and celery in a cake pan then place the bee on top.
Place the cake pan in the middle of the Griller and cook for 1 hour.
Pour the beef broth at the bottom of the cake pan and cook until the internal temperature reaches 1200F.
Remove the cake pan from the Griller and let rest for 20 minutes before slicing the meat.
Pour the cooking juice through a strainer, and then skim off any fat at the top.
Serve the roast with the cooking juices.

Nutrition: Calories: 720.8; Fats: 59.8g; Carbs: 2.9g; Protein: 43.1g; Sugars: 0.9g; Fiber 0.9g

9. The South Barbacoa

Preparation Time: 15 minutes   **Cooking Time: 3 hours**
Servings: 10

Ingredients:

- 1 and ½ teaspoon pepper
- 1 tablespoon dried oregano
- 1 and ½ teaspoon cayenne pepper
- 1 and ½ teaspoon chili powder
- 1 and ½ teaspoon garlic powder
- ·1 teaspoon ground cumin
- 1 teaspoon salt
- 3 pounds boneless beef chuck roast

Directions: Add dampened hickory wood to your smoker and preheat to 200 degrees Fahrenheit
Take a small bowl and add oregano, cayenne pepper, black pepper, garlic powder, chili powder, cumin, salt, and seasoned salt. Mix well. Dip the chuck roast into your mixing bowl and rub the spice mix all over
Transfer the meat to your smoker and smoker for one and a ½ hours
Make sure to turn the meat after every 30 minutes, if you see less smoke formation, add more Pellets after every 30 minutes as well.
Once the meat shows a dark red color with darkened edges, transfer the meat to a roasting pan and seal it tightly with an aluminum foil. Preheat your oven to 325 degrees Fahrenheit.
Transfer the meat to your oven and bake for one and a ½ hours more.
Shred the meat using two forks.

Nutrition: Calories: 558.8; Fats: 4.8g; Carbs: 56.9g; Fiber: 0.9g

10. Korean Beef Rib Eye

Preparation Time: 10 minutes   **Cooking Time: 15 minutes**
Servings: 6

Ingredients:

- ½ cup of soy sauce
- ¼ cup scallions, chopped
- 2 tablespoons garlic, minced

- 2 tablespoons Korean chili paste
- 1 tablespoon honey
- 2 teaspoons ground ginger
- 2 teaspoons onion powder

- 2 boneless rib-eye steaks, 8-12 ounces
- Smoked coleslaw
- 12 flour tortillas

Directions: Preheat the smoker to 200 degrees Fahrenheit with peach or pearwood

Take a small bowl and whisk in soy sauce, garlic, scallion, honey, ginger, onion powder, and mix to make the paste. Spread the paste on both sides of the steak.

Transfer the steak to your smoker and smoke for 15 minutes per pound

Remove the steak when the internal temperature reaches 115 degrees Fahrenheit

Cut the steak into strips and serve with coleslaw wrapped in tortillas. Enjoy!

Nutrition: Calories: 239.9; Fats: 10.8g; Carbs: 7.9g; Fiber: 0.9g

11. Mustard Beef Ribs

Preparation Time: 15 minutes
Servings: 6

Cooking Time: 3 hours

Ingredients:

For mustard sauce:
- 1 cup of prepared yellow mustard
- ¼ cup of red wine vinegar
- ¼ cup of dill pickle juice
- 2 tablespoons of soy sauce

- 2 tablespoons of Worcestershire sauce
- 1 teaspoon of ground ginger
- 1 teaspoon of granulated garlic

For the spice rub:
- 2 tablespoons of salt
- 2 tablespoons of freshly ground black pepper

- 1 tablespoon of white cane sugar

- 1 tablespoon of granulated garlic

For ribs:
- 6 (14-ounce) (4-5-inch long) beef short ribs

Directions: Preheat the Griller & Smoker on smoke setting to 230-250 degrees F, using charcoal.

For the sauce: take a bowl and mix together all ingredients.

For the rub: take a small bowl and mix together all ingredients.

Coat the ribs with sauce generously then sprinkle with spice rub evenly.

Put the ribs onto the grill over indirect heat, bone side down.

Cook for about 1-1½ hours. Flip the side and cook for 45 minutes.

Flip the side and cook for 45 minutes more.

Remove the ribs from the grill and put them onto a chopping board for about 10 minutes before serving.

With a pointy knife, cut the ribs into equal sized individual pieces and serve.

Nutrition: Calories: 866.8; Fats: 37.2g; Carbs: 7.5g; Fiber: 1.9g; Sugar: 3.5g; Protein: 117.3g

12. Herbed Rib Roast

Preparation Time: 10 minutes
Servings: 10

Cooking Time: 3 hours 50 minutes

Ingredients:
- 1 (5-pound) prime rib roast
- Salt, as required
- 5 tablespoons of olive oil
- 2 teaspoons of dried thyme, crushed

- 2 teaspoons of dried rosemary, crushed
- 2 teaspoons of garlic powder
- 1 teaspoon of onion powder
- 1 teaspoon of paprika
- ½ teaspoon of cayenne pepper

- Ground black pepper, as required

Directions: Season the roast with salt generously.

With a plastic wrap, cover the roast and refrigerate for 24 hours.

In a bowl, mix the remaining ingredients and put them aside for about 1 hour.

Rub the roast with oil mixture from each side evenly.

Arrange the roast on a large baking sheet and refrigerate for about 6-12 hours.

Preheat the Griller & Smoker on the smoke setting to 225-230 degrees F, using pecan wood chips.

Put the roast onto the grill and cook for 3-3½ hours.

Meanwhile, preheat the oven to 500 degrees F.

Remove the roast from the grill and place it on a large baking sheet.

Put the baking sheet in the oven and roast for about 15-20 minutes.

Remove the roast from the oven and put it on a chopping board for about 10-15 minutes before serving.

With a pointy knife, cut the roast into desired-sized slices and serve.

Nutrition: Calories: 604.8; Fats: 47.5g; Carbs: 3.5g; Fiber: 0.3g; Sugar: 0.3g; Protein: 38.2g

13. Beef Rump Roast

Preparation Time: 10 minutes   **Cooking Time: 6 hours**
Servings: 8

Ingredients:

- *1 teaspoon of smoked paprika*
- *1 teaspoon of cayenne pepper*
- *1 teaspoon of onion powder*
- *1 teaspoon of garlic powder*
- *Salt and ground black pepper, as required*
- *3 pounds of beef rump roast*
- *¼ cup of Worcestershire sauce*

Directions: Preheat the Griller & Smoker on the smoke setting to 200 degrees F, using charcoal.

In a bowl, mix together all spices.

Coat the roast with Worcester sauce evenly then, rub with spice mixture generously.

Put the roast onto the grill and cook for 5-6 hours.

Remove the roast from the grill and put it on a chopping board for about 10-15 minutes before serving.

With a pointy knife, cut the roast into desired-sized slices and serve.

Nutrition: Calories: 251.8; Fats: 8.8g; Carbs: 2.1g; Fiber: 0.2g; Sugar: 1.5g; Protein: 37.9g

14. Beef Tenderloin

Preparation Time: 10 minutes   **Cooking Time: 1 hour 19 minutes**
Servings: 12

Ingredients:

- *1 (5-pound) beef tenderloin, trimmed*
- *Kosher salt, as required*
- *¼ cup of olive oil*
- *Freshly ground black pepper, as required*

Directions: Tend the tenderloin at 7-8 places with kitchen strings.

Season tenderloin with kosher salt generously.

With a plastic wrap, cover the tenderloin and keep aside at room temperature for about 1 hour.

Preheat the Griller & Smoker on grill setting to 225-250 degrees F.

Now, coat tenderloin with oil evenly and season with black pepper.

Arrange tenderloin onto the grill and cook for about 55-65 minutes.

Now, place cooking grate directly over hot coals and sear tenderloin for about 2 minutes per side.

Remove the tenderloin from the grill and place onto a chopping board for about 10-15 minutes before serving.

With a pointy knife, cut the tenderloin into desired-sized slices and serve.

Nutrition: Calories: 424.8; Fats: 21.3g; Carbs: 0g; Fiber: 0g; Sugar: 0g; Protein: 54.9g

15. Smoked Pulled Beef

Preparation Time: 15 minutes   **Cooking Time: 9 hours**
Servings: 10

Ingredients:

- *1 (6-pound) of chuck roast*
- *2 ½ tablespoons of salt*
- *2 ½ tablespoons of black pepper*
- *2 ½ tablespoons of garlic powder*

- ½ cup of chopped onion
- 3 cups of beef broth

Directions: Preheat the smoker to 225°F (107°C). Let the lid closed and await 45 minutes.

Mix garlic powder with black pepper and salt until combined.

Rub the chuck roast with the spice mixture then using your hand massage the roast until it is thoroughly seasoned.

Place the seasoned roast on the grill then cook the roast for 3 hours. Spray the roast with beef stock once every hour.

After 3 hours, sprinkle chopped onion on the bottom of a pan then pours the remaining beef stock over the onion—about 2 cups.

Transfer the cooked roast to the pan then place the pan on the grill.

Increase the smoker's temperature to 250°F (121°C) then cooks for 3 hours more.

After 3 hours, cover the pan with aluminum foil then lower the temperature to 165°F (74°C).

Cook the roast for an additional 3 hours until done.

Once it is done, transfer the smoked beef to a flat surface and let it cool.

Once it is cold, use a fork to shred the meat and place it on a dish.

Serve and enjoy!

Nutrition: Calories: 103.8; Carbs: 5.8g; Fats: 1.9g; Protein: 16.2g

16. Blackened Steak

Preparation Time: 10 minutes
Servings: 4

Cooking Time: 60 minutes

Ingredients:
- 2 steaks, each about 40 ounces
- 4 tablespoons of blackened rub
- 4 tablespoons of butter, unsalted

Directions: Turn on the Pellet grill fill the grill hopper with hickory flavored wood pellets, power the grill on by using the instrument panel, select 'smoke' on the temperature dial, or set the temperature to 225 degrees F and let it preheat for at least 45 minutes.

Transfer steaks to a dish then repeat with the remaining steak.

Let seared steaks rest for 10 minutes, then slice each steak across the grain and serve.

Nutrition: Calories: 184.2; Fats: 8.5g; Carbs: 0g; Protein: 23.4g

17. Honey Glazed Smoked Beef

Preparation Time: 10 minutes
Servings: 10

Cooking Time: 8 hours

Ingredients:
- 1 (6-pound) beef brisket
- 2 ½ tablespoons of salt
- 2 ½ tablespoons of pepper
- ¾ cup of barbecue sauce
- 3 tablespoons of red wine
- 3 tablespoons of raw honey

Directions: Preheat the smoker to 225°F (107°C). Spread the charcoal on one side.

Meanwhile, rub the meat brisket with salt, pepper, and barbecue sauce.

When the smoker has reached the specified temperature, place the brisket on the grill with the fat side up. Splash wine over beef brisket.

Smoke the meat brisket for 8 hours. Check the smoker every 2 hours and add more charcoal if it is necessary.

Once it is done, take the smoked beef brisket from the smoker, then transfer it to a dish.

Drizzle raw honey over the meat and let it sit for about an hour before slicing.

Serve with roasted or sautéed vegetables according to your desire.

Nutrition: Calories: 89.8; Carbs: 7.9g; Fats: 0.9g; Protein: 11.2g

18. Grilled Steak

Preparation Time: 60 minutes
Servings: 2

Cooking Time: 15 minutes

Ingredients:

- 2 USDA Choice or Prime 1¼-1½ Inch New York Strip Steak (Approx. 12-14 ounces Each) Extra Virgin Olive Oil
- 4 teaspoons of Western Love or Salt and Pepper

Directions: Remove the steak from the refrigerator, loosely cover with wrap about 45 minutes before returning to room temperature.
Polish both sides with olive oil, when the steak reaches room temperature
Season from each side of the steak with a teaspoon of rub or salt and pepper and let absorb at room temperature for at least 5 minutes before grilling.
Configure a wood pellet smoker and grill for direct cooking using a baking grate, set the temperature high, and preheat to at least 450 ° F using the pellets. Put the steak on the grill and cook for about 2-3 minutes.
On the same side, rotate the steak 90 degrees to mark the cross grill and cook for another 2-3 minutes. Turn the steak over and bake until the desired finish is achieved.
Put the steak on a platter, loosen the tent with foil and leave for 5 minutes before serving.

Nutrition: Calories: 239.8; Carbs: 0g; Fats: 14.8g; Protein: 19.2g

19. Texas Style Brisket Flat

Preparation Time: 45 minutes (Additional Marinade)   **Cooking Time: 5-6 hours**
Servings: 8

Ingredients:

- 6 ½ lbs. beef brisket flat
- ½ cup of roasted garlic flavored extra virgin olive oil
- ½ Cup Texas Style Brisket Love or Favorite Brisket Love

Directions: Cut off the fat cap of the brisket and remove the silver skin.
Rub all sides of the trimmed meat with olive oil. Put the rub to all sides of the brisket so it completely covers it.
Twice wrap the brisket with plastic wrap and cool overnight to allow the meat to penetrate. Or, if needed, you can cook the brisket immediately.
Remove the brisket from the refrigerator, insert a wood pellet smoker, and grill or remote meat probe in the thickest part of the meat.
Set wood pellet smoker and grill for indirect cooking using mesquite or oak pellets and preheat to 250 ° F.
Smoke the brisket at 250 ° F until the internal temperature reaches 160 ° F (about 4 hours).
Take out the brisket from the grill, wrap it twice in sturdy aluminum foil, keep the meat probe in place and return to the smoking grill.
Raise the pit temperature to 325 ° F and cook the brisket for another 2 hours until the internal temperature reaches 205 ° F.
Remove the brisket with foil, wrap it with a towel and put it in the cooler. Let sit in the cooler for 2-4 hours before slicing into cereals and serving.

Nutrition: Calories: 179.9; Carbs: 1.8g; Fats: 8.8g; Protein: 23.4g

20. Smoked Tri-Tip

Preparation Time: 25 minutes   **Cooking Time: 5 hours**
Servings: 4

Ingredients:

- 1½ pounds tri-tip roast
- Salt
- Freshly ground black pepper
- 2 teaspoons garlic powder
- 2 teaspoons lemon pepper
- ½ cup apple juice

Directions: Supply your smoker with wood pellets and follow the manufacturer's specific start-up procedure.
Allow your grill to prepare with the lid closed, to 180°F.
Season the tri-tip roast with lemon pepper, salt, pepper, and garlic powder. Using your two hands, work on the seasoning into the meat.
Put the meat to roast directly on the grill grate and smoke for 4 hours.
Pull the tri-tip from the grill and place it on enough aluminum foil to wrap it completely.
Increase the grill's temperature to 375°F.
Fold in three sides of the foil around the roast and add the apple juice. Fold in the last side, completely enclosing the tri-tip and liquid. Return the wrapped tri-tip to the grill and cook for 45 minutes more.
Remove the tri-tip roast from the grill and let it rest for 10 to 15 minutes, before unwrapping, slicing, and serving.

Nutrition: Calories: 154.8; Carbs: 0g; Fats: 6.8g; Protein: 23.4g

21. Smoked Roast Beef

Preparation Time: 10 minutes
Servings: 5 to 8

Cooking Time: 12 to 14 hours

Ingredients:

- 1 (4-pound) top round roast
- 1 batch Espresso Brisket Rub
- 1 tablespoon butter

Directions: Supply your smoker with wood pellets and follow the manufacturer's specific start-up procedure. Let the grill pre-heat with the lid closed, to 180°F.
Season the top round roast with the rub. Using your two hands, work the rub into the meat.
Put the meat to roast directly on the grill grate and smoke until its internal temperature reaches 140°F. Remove the roast from the grill.
Put a cast-iron skillet on the grill grate and increase the grill's temperature to 450°F. Put the roast in the skillet, add the butter, and cook until its internal temperature reaches 145°F, flipping once after about 3 minutes. (If your grill has that option, reverse-searing the meat over an open flame rather than in the cast-iron skillet.)
Remove the food you roast from the grill and let it rest for 10 to 15 minutes, before slicing and serving.

Nutrition: Calories: 289.8; Carbs: 2.8g; Fats: 8.8g; Protein: 50.2g

22. Almond Crusted Beef Fillet

Preparation Time: 15 minutes
Servings: 4

Cooking Time: 55 minutes

Ingredients:

- ¼ cup chopped almonds
- 1 tablespoon Dijon mustard
- 1 Cup chicken broth
- Salt
- 1/3 cup chopped onion
- ¼ cup olive oil
- Pepper
- 2 tablespoons curry powder
- 3 pounds beef fillet tenderloin

Directions: Rub the pepper and salt into the tenderloin.
Put the mustard, almonds, curry, chicken broth, onion, and olive oil into a bowl. Mix well to combine.
Take this mixture and rub the tenderloin generously with it.
Add wood pellets to the smoker and follow your cooker's startup procedure. Preheat the smoker, with your lid closed, until it reaches 450. Lay on the grill, cover, and smoke for ten minutes on both sides.
Continue to cook until it reaches your desired doneness.
Take it all the grill and let it rest for at least ten minutes.

Nutrition: Calories: 117.9; Carbs: 2.8g; Fats: 2.8g; Protein: 20.3g

23. Herbed Beef Eye Fillet

Preparation Time: 15 minutes
Servings: 6

Cooking Time: 8 hours

Ingredients:

- Pepper
- Salt
- 2 tablespoons chopped rosemary
- 2 tablespoons chopped basil
- 2 tablespoons olive oil
- 3 cloves crushed garlic
- ¼ cup chopped oregano
- ¼ cup chopped parsley
- 2 pounds beef eye fillet

Directions: Use salt and pepper to rub in the meat before placing it in a container.
Put the rosemary, garlic, oil, basil, oregano, and parsley in a bowl. Mix well to combine.
Rub the fillet generously with this mixture on all sides. Let the meat sit on the counter for 30 minutes and then, add wood pellets to your smoker and follow your cooker's startup procedure. Pre-heat your smoker, with the lid closed, until it reaches 450F.
Lay the meat on the grill, cover, and smoke for ten minutes per side or your preferred tenderness.
Once it is done to your likeness, allow it to rest for ten minutes. Slice and enjoy.

Nutrition: Calories: 201.8; Carbs: 0g; Fats: 7.9g; Protein: 33.2g

24. Herbed Steaks

Preparation Time: 10 minutes
Servings: 4

Cooking Time: 5 hours

Ingredients:
- Pinch red pepper flakes
- ½ teaspoon coriander seeds
- 2 teaspoons green peppercorns
- 2 teaspoons black peppercorns
- 2 tablespoons chopped mint leaves
- ¼ cup olive oil
- 2 tablespoons peanut oil
- 3 pounds flank steak

Directions: Sprinkle the flank steak with salt and rub generously. Place the meat in a large zip-top bag.
Mix together the peppercorns, red pepper flakes, olive oil, coriander, mint leaves, and peanut oil.
Pour this mixture over the flank steak. Place into the refrigerator for four hours.
Add wood pellets to the smoker and follow your cooker's startup procedure. Pre-heat your smoker, with your lid closed, until it reaches 450F.
Take the flank steak out of the refrigerator 30 minutes before you are ready to grill it.
Place the flank steak onto the grill and grill ten minutes on each. You can grill longer if you want the steak more well-done. After removing it from the grill and set it for about ten minutes. Slice before serving.

Nutrition: Calories: 239.8; Carbs: 11.8g; Fats: 10.8g; Protein: 23.1g

25. La Rochelle Steak

Preparation Time: 10 minutes
Servings: 4

Cooking Time: 5 hours

Ingredients:
- 1 tablespoon red currant jelly
- ½ teaspoon salt
- 3 teaspoon curry powder
- 8 ounces pineapple chunks in juice
- 1 ½ pounds flank steak
- ¼ cup olive oil

Directions: Place the flank steak into a large bag.
Mix the pepper, red currant jelly, salt, pineapple chunks with juice, curry powder, and olive oil together.
Pour this mixture over the flank steak. Refrigerate for four hours.
Add wood pellets to the smoker and follow your cooker's startup procedure. Preheat the smoker, with your lid closed, until it reaches 350F.
Then you are ready to cook the steak, remove the steak from the refrigerator 30 minutes before ready to cook.
Lay the steaks on the grill, cover, and smoke for ten minutes on both sides, or done to your liking.
Remove your roasted food from the grill and allow it to cool for about ten minutes.

Nutrition: Calories: 199.8; Carbs: 0g; Fats: 6.9g; Protein: 33.2g

26. Lemony Mustard Crusted Veal

Preparation Time: 10 minutes
Servings: 2

Cooking Time: 2 hours 30 minutes

Ingredients:
- Pepper
- Salt
- ¼ cup breadcrumbs
- 2 tablespoons water
- 1 teaspoon basil
- 1 pound veal round roast
- 1 tablespoon Dijon mustard
- 1 tablespoon lemon juice

Directions: Lay the roast in a shallow roasting pan on a rack.
Combine together the basil, pepper, mustard, thyme, lemon juice, water, and breadcrumbs.
Spread this mixture over the roast being sure to get all sides.
Add wood pellets to the smoker and follow your cooker's startup procedure. Pre-heat your smoker, with your lid closed, until it reaches 450F.
Put the roast onto the grill and cook for ten minutes per side until it is to your desired doneness.
Take off from the grill and allow to set for ten minutes.

Nutrition: Calories: 389.8; Carbs: 0g; Fats: 14.8g; Protein: 40.2g

27. Green Burgers

Preparation Time: 10 minutes
Servings: 4

Cooking Time: 35 minutes

Ingredients:
- Pepper
- 2 pounds ground beef
- 1 tablespoon chopped cilantro
- 1 egg
- 1 pound frozen spinach, thawed and drained
- 3 cloves garlic
- 3 tablespoons olive oil
- 1 tablespoon chopped tarragon
- Salt
- 2 chopped green onions

Directions: Wash and chop the green onion. Combine the onion and spinach together.
Put the salt, garlic, cilantro, pepper, oil, tarragon, egg, and ground beef.
Use your two hands and mix all the ingredients until everything is thoroughly combined. Shape into six burgers.
Add wood pellets to the smoker and follow your cooker's startup procedure. Preheat the smoker, with your lid closed, until it reaches 380F.
Cover the burgers after placing on the grill. Both sides should be cooked for 5 minutes.
Serve with toppings of choice.

Nutrition: Calories: 189.8; Carbs: 2.9g; Fats: 9.9g; Protein: 21.3g

28. T-Bone with Blue Cheese Butter

Preparation Time: 10 minutes
Servings: 4

Cooking Time: 1 hour

Ingredients:
- 2 tablespoons garlic, minced
- 2 tablespoons salt
- 4 ounces T-bone steaks
- ½ cup crumbled blue cheese
- 1 tablespoon pepper
- 4 tablespoons room temperature butter

Directions: Combine the butter and the blue cheese together and set to the side. Do not refrigerate the butter unless you are making it way in advance.
Add wood pellets to the smoker and follow your cooker's startup procedure. Preheat the smoker, with your lid closed, until it reaches 165F. Rub the steaks with pepper, garlic, and salt.
Cover the steaks after putting them on. For about 30 minutes, allow it to smoke.
Turn the heat up to 450F and let the steaks smoke for 15 minutes if you like them medium-rare. Cook longer to reach your desired doneness.
Take the steaks out off of the grill and let them rest for 3-5 minutes. Serve them topped with some of the blue cheese butter.

Nutrition: Calories: 266.8; Carbs: 0g; Fats: 15.8g; Protein: 29.3g

29. Roast Beast

Preparation Time: 5 minutes
Servings: 4

Cooking Time: 8 hours

Ingredients:
- 2 tablespoons steak seasoning
- EVOO
- 4 pound rump roast
- 1 tablespoon garlic, minced

Directions: Add wood pellets to your smoker and follow your cooker's startup procedure. Preheat the smoker, with your lid closed, until it reaches 425F.
Rub the roast all over with a good amount of olive oil and then season with the steak seasoning and garlic.
Put the meat on the grill and then sear every side for about two to five minutes. Set it off of the grill.
Turn the heat of the smoker to 225F.
Put the roast back on the grill, cover, and allow it to smoke for three to four hours. Depending on your desired doneness, it should reach a temperature of 120° to 155°F.

Use some foil for tenting the roast after removing it from the heat. Allow it to roast, rest for ten minutes, and slice against the grain.

Nutrition: Calories: 399.8; Carbs: 20.8g; Fats: 7.9g; Protein: 22.3g

30. Prime Rib Roast

Preparation Time: 24 hours   **Cooking Time: 4 hours and 30 minutes**
Servings: 8

Ingredients:
- *1 prime rib roast, containing 5 to 7 bones*
- *Rib rub as needed*

Directions: Season rib roast with rib rub until well coated, put it in a large plastic bag, seal it and let it marinate for a minimum of 24 hours in the refrigerator.
When ready to cook, switch on the Traeger grill, fill the grill hopper with cherry flavored wood pellets, power the grill on by using the control panel, select 'smoke' on the temperature dial, or set the temperature to 225 degrees F and let it pre-heat for a minimum of 15 minutes.
When the grill has preheated, place rib roast on the grill grate fat-side up, change the smoking temperature to 425 degrees F, shut the grill, and smoke for 30 minutes.
Then change the smoking temperature to 325 degrees F and continue cooking for 3 to 4 hours until the roast has cooked to the desired level, rare at 120 degrees F, medium rare at 130 degrees F, medium at 140 degrees F, and well done at 150 degrees F.
When done, transfer roast rib to a cutting board, let it rest for 15 minutes, then cut it into slices and serve.

Nutrition: Calories: 247.9; Fats: 20.9g; Carbs: 0g; Protein: 28.3g

31. Kalbi Beef Ribs

Preparation Time: 15 minutes   **Cooking Time: 23 minutes**
Servings: 6

Ingredients:
- *Thinly sliced beef ribs - 2 ½ lbs*
- *Soy sauce - ½ cup*
- *Brown sugar - ½ cup*
- *Rice wine or mirin - ⅛ cup*
- *Minced garlic - 2 tbsp*
- *Sesame oil - 1 tbsp*
- *Grated onion - ⅛ cup*

Directions: Take a medium-sized bowl, mix the soy sauce, mirin, brown sugar, sesame oil, garlic, and grated onion then, put the ribs to the bowl to marinate and cover it properly with cling wrap. Put it in the refrigerator for up to 6 hours.
Once you remove the marinated ribs from the refrigerator, immediately put them on the grill. Cover the grill quickly so no heat is lost. Also, make sure the grill is preheated well before you place the ribs on it.
Cook on one side for 4 minutes and then flip it. Cook the other side for 4 minutes.
Pull it out once it looks fully cooked. Serve it with rice or any other side dish.

Nutrition: Calories: 354.8; Carbs: 21.9g; Protein: 28.3g; Fats: 5.9g

32. Homemade Meatballs

Preparation Time: 15 minutes   **Cooking Time: 1 hour 20 minutes**
Servings: 12

Ingredients:
- *Ground beef - 2 lbs*
- *White bread - 2 slices*
- *Whole milk - ½ cup*
- *Salt - 1 tbsp*
- *Onion powder - ½ tbsp*
- *Italian seasoning - 2 tbsp*
- *Ground black pepper- ¼ tbsp*
- *Minced garlic - ½ tbsp*

Directions: Mix the whole milk, minced garlic, white bread, Italian seasoning, onion powder, and black pepper. Put the ground beef and mix well.
Prepare your wood pellet grill on the 'smoke' option and leave the lid open for 4-5 minutes.
Line a baking sheet and start placing small balls on the sheet. Smoke for 35 minutes and then flip the balls.
Let it stay for 35 more minutes. Once it turns golden brown, serve hot!

33. Grilled Hanger Steak

Preparation Time: 10 minutes

Cooking Time: 50 minutes

Servings: 6

Ingredients:

- Hanger Steak - 1
- Salt
- Pepper

- For Bourbon Sauce
- Bourbon whiskey - ⅛ cup
- Honey - ⅛ cup

- Sriracha - 1 tbsp
- Garlic - ½ tbsp
- Salt - ¼ tbsp

Directions: Prepare the grill to 225 degrees. Use pepper and salt to season the steak liberally.
Put the steak on the grill and close the lid. Cook until the temperature goes down to the finish.
Take an iron skillet and place it on the stove. Add some butter to the pan and place the steak on it.
Cook on both sides for 2 minutes each. Remove the steak from the stove.
Put the bourbon sauce ingredients to the pan. Cook and whisk for 3-4 minutes. Pour it over your steak.
Serve with your favorite side dish or simply have it with the bourbon sauce.

Nutrition: Calories: 132.8; Carbs: 5.8g; Protein: 10.2g; Fats: 6.9g

34. Slow Roasted Shawarma

Preparation Time: 25 minutes

Cooking Time: 4 hours 55 minutes

Servings: 6-8

Ingredients:

- Top sirloin - 5.5 lbs
- Lamb fat - 4.5 lbs
- Boneless, skinless chicken thighs- 5.5 lbs

- Pita bread
- Traeger rub - 4 tbsp
- Double skewer - 1
- Large yellow onions - 2

- Variety of topping options such as tomatoes, cucumbers, pickles, tahini, Israeli salad, fries, etc.
- Cast iron griddle

Directions: Prepare the stack of shawarma the night before you wish to cook it.
Slice all the meat and fat into ½-inch slices. Put them into three bowls.
Season the bowl with the rub, massaging it thoroughly into the meat.
Put half a yellow onion on the bottom of the skewers to ensure a firm base. Add two layers at a time from each bowl. Try to make the entire stack symmetrical. Place the other two onions on top. Wrap them in plastic wrap and refrigerate them overnight.
When the meat is ready to cook, pre-heat the pellet grill for about 15 minutes with the lid closed at a temperature of 275 degrees Fahrenheit.
Lay the shawarma directly on the grill grate and cook it for at least 3-4 hours. Rotate the skewers at least once.
Remove them from the grill and increase their temperature to 445 degrees Fahrenheit. When the grill is preheating, place a cast iron griddle directly on the grill grate and brush it with some olive oil.
Once the griddle is hot enough, place the shawarma directly on the cast iron. Sear it on each side for 5-10 minutes. Remove it from the grill and slice off the edges. Repeat the process with the remaining shawarma.
Serve in pita bread along with your favorite toppings, such as cucumbers, tomatoes, fries, Israeli salad, pickles, or tahini.

Nutrition: Calories: 376.8; Carbs: 4.4g; Protein: 30.5g; Fats: 26.1g

35. Spicy Grilled Beef Steak

Preparation Time: 15 minutes

Cooking Time: about 1 hour and 22 minutes

Servings: 6

Ingredients:

- Chili powder—2 tbsps.
- Beef rib eye—4 steaks
- Brown sugar—1 tsp.

- Worcestershire sauce—2 tbsps.
- Garlic cloves—2, minced
- Ground cumin—1 tsp.

- Olive oil—2 tbsps.
- Salt—1 tsp.

Directions: Combine salt and mashed garlic in a small mixing bowl.
Add brown sugar, olive oil, chili powder, Worcestershire sauce, chili powder, and cumin.
Use this mixture to coat the steaks.
Place the coated steaks and the rest of the rub in a large zip seal bag. Let it marinate in the refrigerator for about 5–24 hours.

Prepare your Wood Pellet Smoker-Grill by preheating it to about 225°F. Close the top lid and leave for 12–18 minutes.

Smoke the steaks for about 50–60 minutes. Then, remove.

Increase the temperature to about 350°F and cook the steaks again to get an internal temperature of about 135°F. Remove and allow the meat to cool and serve.

Nutrition: Calories: 633.8; Carbs: 33.8g; Protein: 67.2g; Fats: 12.9g

36. Corned Beef with Cabbage

Preparation Time: 10 minutes   **Cooking Time: 30 minutes**
Servings: 4

Ingredients:
- A cut of corned beef
- 2 cups of water
- 5 to 6 red potatoes
- 1 head of cabbage
- 3 teaspoons of garlic salt
- 1 teaspoon of ground black pepper
- 3 to 4 tablespoons of whole grain mustard
- 3 Tablespoons of melted butter

Directions: Rinse the two sides of the corned beef under cold water for about 2 minutes in order to exceed any excess salt.

Coat both sides of the corned beef with two tablespoons of mustard.

Put the water and the corned beef in an aluminum pan and smoke it at a temperature of about 220° F.

Remove the stem, remove the cabbage's core, and then quarter it.

Melt the butter; then stir in about one tablespoon of mustard and about one teaspoon of garlic salt.

Put the cabbage quarters into the aluminum pan in each corner and core it side up so it looks like bowls.

Chop the potatoes in half and season it with about two teaspoons garlic salt and about ½ teaspoon pepper.

Put the potatoes along the edges of the aluminum pan between the quarters of the cabbage.

Cover with the aluminum foil; then turn up your wood pellet grill to about 280°F and cook for about two additional hours until the internal temperature of the meat reaches about 200 to 205° F.

Remove the aluminum foil and cook for about 15 minutes. Slice the meat then serve.

Nutrition: Calories: 212.9; Fats: 14.8g, Carbs: 7.9g; Protein: 8.2g; Fiber: 0.9g

37. Corned Beef Pastrami

Preparation Time: 1 hours   **Cooking Time: 5 hours**
Servings: 5-6 Serving

The Meat:
- Pre-packed corned beef (silverback) (6 lbs.)

The Mixture:
- Coarse ground pepper – 3 tbsp.
- Garlic (very fine grains) – 2 tbsp.
- Onion Flakes – 2 tbsp.
- Chili Powder – 2 tbsp.
- Expresso rub – 2 tbsp.
- The Fire:
- Wood pellet smoker, pecan wood pellets.

Directions: Rinse the cut of beef thoroughly then, let it soak in cold water for a whole day. Change the water every six hours.

After it has been soaking for a whole day, take the beef out of the water. Dry it thoroughly with a paper towel.

Mix the rub ingredients in a bowl and then apply them to the beef. Set the beef aside while you preheat your smoker.

Put the beef in the smoker with a temperature up to 250 degrees. Cook until the internal temperature is 150 degrees. The beef should be cooked for about 3-4 hours to reach this temperature.

Now wrap the beef cut in foil. Keep cooking until the internal temperature goes up to 185 -195 degrees. It should take about two more hours to reach this internal temperature.

The corned beef pastrami is ready.

Burger Recipes

38. Mushroom Beef Burgers

Preparation Time: 10 minutes
Serving: 4

Cooking Time: 10 minutes

Ingredients:

- 4 oz. button mushrooms
- 1 lb. ground sirloin (90% lean)
- 2 tbsp. olive oil
- 1/8 tsp. black pepper
- ¾ tsp. salt
- 1/3 cup chopped cucumber
- ¼ cup plain Greek yogurt (full fat)
- 2 tbsp. roasted minced garlic
- 1 tbsp. lemon juice
- 1 tbsp. chopped parsley
- 8 large butter lettuce leaves
- 4 heirloom tomatoes
- 4 onions, sliced

Directions: Until it hits medium-high pressure, preheat your grill. In the food processor, put the mushrooms and blend them for about 1 minute.

In a small cup, combine the mushrooms, ground syrup, oil, pepper and a pinch of salt. Shape four patties out of the mixture carefully and put them on a baking sheet. The sheet must be lined with parchment paper.

Combine the garlic, cucumber, milk, chopped parsley, lemon juice, and salt together in a shallow cup. Set aside this mixture.

Place the burgers over the grill and wait until fully cooked, which should take approximately 3 minutes to cook each side.

On each plate, placed three lettuce leaves. Using a burger patty, several tomato slices, sliced red onions, and one tablespoon of the yogurt mixture to coat each and serve.

Nutrition: Fats: 18.8g; Carbs: 6.8g; Protein: 26.3g

39. Lamb Burgers

Preparation Time: 15 minutes
Servings: 5

Cooking Time: 16 minutes

Ingredients:

- 2 pounds ground lamb
- 9 ounces Halloumi cheese, grated
- 2 eggs
- 1 tablespoon fresh rosemary, chopped finely
- 1 tablespoon fresh parsley, chopped finely
- 2 teaspoons ground cumin
- Salt and ground black pepper, as required

Directions: Put the ingredients into a large bowl and blend until well mixed.

From the mixture, produce ten equal-sized patties. Place the bottom of the electric grill on the water tray.

Into the water tray, put around 2 cups of lukewarm water.

Place the drip pan and position the heating element over the water tray.

Now, place the grilling pan over the heating element.

To turn it on, plug in the electric grill and press the 'Fuel' button. Click the 'Fan' button then.

Set the temperature settings according to instructions from the manufacturer.

Cover the lid with the grill and allow it to preheat.

Remove the lid after preheating and grease the grilling pan. Cover the grilling pan with the burgers.

Cover the lid and cook on each side for about 15-8 minutes. Serve hot

Nutrition: Calories: 553.8; Fats: 30.2g; Carbs: 2.1g; Fiber: 0.4g; Sugar: 1.2g; Protein: 64.7g

40. Stuffed Burgers

Preparation Time: 15 minutes
Servings: 10

Cooking Time: 20 minutes

Ingredients:

For Filling:

- 2 cups cooked ham, chopped
- 2 cups fresh mushrooms, chopped
- 2 cups onion, chopped

- *3 cups cheddar cheese, shredded*

For Patties:
- *5 pounds lean ground beef*
- *1/3 cup Worcestershire sauce*
- *2 teaspoons hickory seasoning*
- *Salt and ground black pepper, as required*

Directions: For the filling: Combine all ingredients together in a dish. Only set aside.
For patties: Add all the ingredients to another large bowl and mix until well mixed.
Split the mixture into 20 equal parts of beef. Make patties of equal size out of each part.
Place ten patties on a smooth surface. Place the cheese mixture uniformly over each patty.
Cover with the remaining patties by pressing the edges to protect the filling.
Place the bottom of the electric grill on the water tray. Into the water tray, put around 2 cups of lukewarm water.
Place the drip pan and position the heating element over the water tray.
Now, place the grilling pan over the heating element.
To turn it on, plug in the electric grill and press the 'Fuel' button.
Click the 'Fan' button then. Set the temperature settings according to instructions from the manufacturer.
Cover the lid with the grill and allow it to preheat.
Remove the lid after preheating and grease the grilling pan. Cover the grilling pan with the burgers.
Cover the lid and cook on each side for approximately 8-10 minutes. Serve it wet.

Nutrition: Calories: 622.8; Fats: 27.5g; Carbs: 5.7g; Fiber: 0.8g; Sugar: 2.9g; Protein: 82.7g

41. Turkey Burger

Preparation Time: 5 minutes
Servings: 4

Cooking Time: 13 minutes

Ingredients:
- *1 pound ground turkey*
- *½ red onion, minced*
- *1 jalapeño pepper, seeded, stemmed, and minced*
- *3 tablespoons bread crumbs*
- *1½ teaspoons ground cumin*
- *1 teaspoon paprika*
- *½ teaspoon cayenne pepper*
- *½ teaspoon sea salt*
- *½ teaspoon freshly ground black pepper*
- *4 burger buns, for serving*
- *Lettuce, tomato, and cheese, if desired, for serving*
- *Ketchup and mustard, if desired, for serving*

Directions: Insert and close the hood with the Grill Grate. Choose GRILL, set the heat to HIGH, and set the time to 13 minutes. To commence preheating, click START/STOP.
Meanwhile, mix the ground turkey, red onion, jalapeño pepper, bread crumbs, cumin, paprika, cayenne pepper, salt, and black pepper with your hands in a wide cup. Mix until just mixed; be careful not to overwork the mixture of burgers.
Dampen your hands with cool water and form four patties of the turkey mixture.
Place the burgers on the Grill Grate when the unit beeps to signal it has preheated. Close the hood and take 11 minutes to cook.
After 11 minutes, check the thickness of the burgers. When the internal temperature on a food thermometer reaches at least 165 ° F, cooking is done. Close the hood if necessary and continue cooking for up to 2 more minutes.
Place each patty on a bun until the burgers are finished cooking. Top with lettuce, tomato, cheese, ketchup, and/or mustard, for example, with your favorite fixings.

Nutrition: Calories: 320.8; Fats: 11.8g; Carbs: 26.9g; Fiber: 1.8g; Protein: 25.3g

42. Feta Spinach Turkey Burgers

Preparation Time: 10 minutes
Servings: 4

Cooking Time: 10 minutes

Ingredients:
- *1 lb. of ground turkey*
- *1 tablespoon of Breadcrumbs*
- *1/4 teaspoon of crushed red pepper*
- *1 teaspoon of parsley*
- *1 teaspoon of oregano*
- *1 teaspoon of garlic powder*
- *1/3 cup. Of sun-dried tomatoes*
- *1/2 cup of crumbled Feta cheese*
- *1/2 cup of chopped Baby spinach*
- *1/2 teaspoon of pepper*
- *1/2 teaspoon of sea salt*

Directions: In the mixing tub, add all the ingredients and blend until just blended.
From the mixture, make four equally formed patties. Preheat to elevated heat on the barbecue.
On a hot grill, put the patties and cook on all sides for 3-5 minutes or until the internal temperature reaches 165 F and serve

Nutrition: Calories: 214.8; Fats: 5.8g; Carbs: 8.8g; Protein: 30.2g

43. BBQ Burgers

Preparation Time: 5 minutes   **Servings: 6**

Ingredients:

- *6 Buns for Ground beef*
- *6 Ground beef patties, Kobe*
- *Beef Rub Seasoning Toppings you like*

Directions: Set to high, and pre-heat the griller. Close the lid.
Season the ground beef and place on the grill. Cook for 10 minutes on one side, flip and cook the other side for 5 minutes. Set the temperature to 150F. Toast the buns.
Place the patties on one half the buns, add the topping you wish and place the other half the bun.
Serve and enjoy.

Nutrition: Calories: 319.8; Protein: 15.2g; Carbs: 29.8g; Fats: 10.9g

44. Asian Barbecue Burger

Preparation Time: 10 minutes   **Cooking Time: 7 minutes**
Servings: 6

Ingredients:

- *1 Chicken Breast, cut into chunks*
- *½ cup Szechwan Cabbage (or cabbage of your choice)*
- *1 egg white*
- *¼ tsp. pepper*
- *2 slices of smoked bacon, optional for topping*
- *1 pound ground beef*
- *¼ cup chopped green onion*

Directions: Stack these ingredients: The 1st topping – top bun The 2nd topping – half of the iceberg lettuce The 3rd topping – ¼ - ½ cup barbecue sauce The 4th topping – chicken breast (you can use leftover chicken or I used store bought rotisserie chicken) The 5th topping – ¼ - ½ cup chopped onions.
Prepare the grill for medium heat and lightly oil the grate. Cut cabbage into ¼ inch strips and set aside.
Shape ground beef into four patties and press into the ground pepper. 3. Cook meat over medium heat until the desired doneness; drain grease.
Take a bowl and beat the egg white with a fork until foamy. Brush each burger with egg white to create a crust and cook about 5 minutes more, or until the desired doneness.
Whisk together honey and soy sauce in another small bowl and brush over cooked burgers (only if using bacon).

Nutrition: Calories: 152.8; Fats: 3.9g; Protein: 12.3g; Sugar: 2.9g

45. Grilled Beef Burgers

Preparation Time: 5 minutes   **Cooking Time: 15 minutes**
Servings: 4

Ingredients:

- *2 pounds beef, grounded*
- *4 hamburger buns*
- *4 slices pepper jack cheese*
- *2 jalapeno peppers, seeded, stemmed and minced*
- *1/2 cup shredded cheddar cheese*
- *1/2 teaspoon chili powder*
- *4 ounces cream cheese*
- *4 slices bacon, cooked and crumbled*
- *1/4 teaspoon paprika*
- *1/4 teaspoon black pepper, ground*
- *Lettuce, sliced tomato and red onion, optional*

Directions: Combine bacon, cream cheese, cheddar cheese and pepper in a mixing bowl.
Divide the ground beef into eight patties.

Add the cheese mixture onto four patties and arrange a second patty on the top of each burger, then press gently Combine all ingredients well.

Prepare four patties from the mixture. Take a pot, arrange the reversible rack and place the crisping basket over the rack. Put the patties in the basket. Seal your Griller lid.

Pre-heat Griller by pressing the "GRILL" option and setting it to "MED" and timer to 6 minutes.

Let it pre-heat until you hear a beep. Arrange the shrimps over the grill grate, lock lid and cook for 3 minutes.

Flip the salmon and cook for 3 minutes more and serve.

Nutrition: Calories: 252.8; Carbs: 22.3g; Fats: 7.3g; Protein: 36.7g

46. Americans Burger

Preparation Time: 10 minutes   **Cooking Time: 20 minutes**
Servings: 4

Ingredients:
- 1 pound ground beef
- 4 seed hamburger buns, cut in half
- 1 tablespoon olive oil
- 1/2 cup breadcrumbs
- 1 large egg, whisked
- 1/2 teaspoon salt
- 1/2 teaspoon pepper

Directions: Take all the ingredients for the burger except oil and the bun in a bowl.

Mix them and then make 4 of the ½ inch patties out of it. Brush these patties with olive oil.

Pre-heat Griller by pressing the "GRILL" option and setting it to "HIGH".

Once it pre-heat until you hear a beep, open the lid. Place two patties in the grill grate and cook for 5 minutes.

Grill the remaining patties in the same way and serve.

Nutrition: Calories: 300.8; Carbs: 19.8g; Fats: 15.4g; Protein: 28.4g

47. Steakhouse Burgers

Preparation Time: 10 minutes   **Cooking Time: 20 minutes**
Servings: 8

Ingredients:
- 1/3 cup milk
- 2-1/2 teaspoons kosher salt
- 3 garlic cloves, minced
- 1-1/2 tablespoons Worcestershire sauce
- 2 tablespoons ketchup
- 1 teaspoon freshly ground black pepper
- 3 pounds 85% lean ground beef
- 2 pieces sandwich bread
- 3 scallions, very finely sliced (optional)
- 8 hamburger buns

Directions: Prepare the grill to high heat.

Mash the bread and milk using a fork in a wide bowl until it forms a chunky paste. Mix well and apply the salt, pepper, garlic, Worcestershire sauce and ketchup.

Attach the ground beef and scallions and use your hands to split the meat up. Mix all until it's just mixed. Divide the mixture and shape balls into 8 equal parts. Flatten the balls, about 4-1/2 inches long, into 3/4-inch patties. Do not let the burgers puff up from the grill. You can prevent this by forming a slight depression in the center of each patty. Put on oil in the grilling grates. Grill the burgers, wrapped, till the first side is well browned, 2 to 4 minutes. Flip the burgers and continue cooking until the desired doneness is achieved for a few more minutes. Toast the buns on the cooler side of the grill before serving, if needed.

Nutrition: Calories: 516.8; Fats: 26.9g; Carbs: 27.9g; Sugar: 4.8g; Fiber: 0.9g; Protein: 37.2g

48. Asian Sriracha Burger

Preparation Time: 20 minutes   **Cooking Time: 8 minutes**
Servings: 4

Ingredients:

For the Burgers:
- 1 1/2 lb lean ground beef
- 2tsp onion powder
- 1/4 tsp white pepper

- 1/4 cup Panko bread crumbs
- 2 TB Asian oyster sauce
- 1 TB granulated sugar
- 1 tsp sesame oil (caramel brown in color)
- 2 TB regular soy sauce
- 1/4 tsp kosher salt
- 1/2 tsp ground ginger
- 1 egg
- 2 tsp garlic powder

Sriracha Mayo:
- 2 TB Dijon mustard
- 4 tsp Sriracha
- 1/2 cup whole mayo

For Serving:
- 4 buns or ciabatta rolls
- 8 oz bag cabbage cole slaw

Directions: Take a bowl, and combine mayo, Sriracha, and Dijon mustard in a bowl. You can add or reduce Sriracha depending on your desired kick.
Mix the burger ingredients and mix well to thoroughly in a large bowl. Form into four even patties.
Grill on preheated grill until patties are cooked to your liking. Medium is recommended. Serve with cabbage slaw, cilantro, and plenty of Sriracha mayo on buns.

Nutrition: Calories: 497.9; Fats: 10.7g; Carbs: 48.2g; Sugar: 4.3g; Protein: 50.6g

49. Ground Turkey Burgers

Preparation Time: 15 minutes
Servings: 6

Cooking Time: 50 minutes

Ingredients:
- 1 beaten egg
- 2/3 cup of breadcrumbs.
- 1/2 cup of chopped celery
- 1/4 cup of chopped onion
- 1 tbsp. of minced parsley
- 1 tsp. of Worcestershire sauce
- 1 tsp. of dried oregano
- 1/2 tsp. of salt to taste
- 1/4 tsp. of pepper
- 1 - 1/4 pounds of lean ground turkey
- 6 hamburger buns

Optional toppings:
- 1 sliced tomato
- 1 sliced onion
- Lettuce leaves

Directions: Using a small mixing bowl, add all the ingredients on the list aside from the turkey and buns, then mix properly to combine. Add in the ground turkey, and then mix everything to combine. Feel free to use clean hands for this. Make about six patties of the mixture, and then set aside.
Preheat your Wood Pellet Smoker and Grill to 375 degrees F.
Put the turkey patties on the grill and grill for about forty-five minutes until its internal temperature reads 165 degrees F. To assemble, use a knife to split the bun into two, top with the prepared burger and your favorite topping, then close with another half of the buns, serve.

Nutrition: Calories: 165.8; Protein: 13.9g; Fats: 8.1g; Carbs: 8.8g

50. Grilled Pork Burgers

Preparation Time: 15 minutes
Servings: 4 – 6

Cooking Time: 1 hour

Ingredients:
- 1 beaten egg
- 3/4 cup of soft breadcrumbs
- 3/4 cup of grated parmesan cheese
- 1 tbsp. of dried parsley
- 2 tsp. of dried basil
- 1/2 tsp. of salt to taste
- 1/2 tsp. of garlic powder
- 1/4 tsp. of pepper to taste
- 2 pounds of ground pork
- 6 hamburger buns

Toppings:
- Lettuce leaves
- Sliced tomato
- Sliced sweet onion

Directions: Take a large mixing bowl and, add in the egg, breadcrumbs, cheese, parsley, basil, garlic powder, pepper and salt, to taste, then mix properly to combine. Add in the ground pork, then mix properly to combine using clean hands. Form about six patties out of the mixture, then set aside.

Next, set a Wood Pellet smoker and grill to smoke (250 degrees F), then let it fire up for about five minutes. Place the patties on the grill and smoke for about thirty minutes. Flip the patties over, increase the grill's temperature to 300 degrees F, and then grill the cakes for a few minutes until an inserted thermometer reads 160 degrees F. Serve the pork burgers on the buns, lettuce, tomato, and onion.

Nutrition: Calories: 654.8; Protein: 49.3g; Fats: 39.2g; Carbs: 23.9g

51. Chicken Sandwich

Preparation Time: 15 minutes   **Cooking Time: 50 minutes**
Servings: 4

Ingredients:

- ¼ cup of mayonnaise
- 1 tbsp. of Dijon mustard
- 1 tbsp. n of honey
- 4 boneless and skinless chicken breasts
- ½ tsp. of steak seasoning
- 4 slices of American Swiss cheese
- 4 hamburger buns
- 2 bacon strips
- Lettuce leaves and tomato slices

Directions:
Using a small mixing bowl, add in the mayonnaise, mustard, and honey, then mix properly to combine. Use a meat mallet to pound the chicken into even thickness, then slice into four parts. Season the chicken with the steak seasoning, then set aside.
Preheat the Smoker and Grill to 350 degrees F for about ten to fifteen minutes with its lid closed. Put the seasoned chicken on the grill and grill for about twenty-five to thirty minutes until it reads an internal temperature of 165 degrees F. Grill the bacon until crispy, then crumble.
Add the cheese to the chicken and cook for about one minute until it melts completely. Simultaneously, grill the buns for about one to two minutes until it is toasted as desired. Put the chicken on the buns, top with the grilled bacon, mayonnaise mixture, lettuce, and tomato, then serve.

Nutrition: Calories: 332.8; Protein: 35.2g; Fats: 13.9g; Carbs: 14.6g

52. Grilled Lamb Burgers

Preparation Time: 15 minutes   **Cooking Time: 25 minutes**
Servings: 5

Ingredients:

- 1 ¼ pound of ground lamb.
- 1 egg
- 1 tsp. of dried oregano
- 1 tsp. of dry sherry
- 1 tsp. of white wine vinegar
- ½ tsp. of crushed red pepper flakes
- 4 minced cloves of garlic
- ½ cup of chopped green onions
- 1 tbsp. of chopped mint
- 2 tbsp. of chopped cilantro
- 2 tbsps. of dry breadcrumbs
- 1/8 tsp. of salt to taste
- ¼ tsp. of ground black pepper to taste
- 5 hamburger buns

Directions: Prepare the Smoker or Grill to 350-450 degrees F, then grease it grates. Using a large mixing bowl, add all the ingredients on the list aside from the buns, then mix properly to combine with clean hands. Make about five patties out of the mixture, then set aside.
Place the lamb patties on the preheated grill and cook for about seven to nine minutes, turning only once until an inserted thermometer reads 160 degrees F. Serve the lamb burgers on the hamburger, add your favorite toppings, and enjoy.

Nutrition: Calories: 375.8; Fats: 18.2g; Fiber: 1.4g; Carbs: 25.1g; Protein: 25.8g

53. Tuna Burgers

Preparation Time: 30 minutes   **Cooking Time: 15 minutes**
Servings: 4-6

Ingredients:

- 2 lbs. Tuna steak, ground
- 2 Eggs
- 1 Bell pepper, diced
- 1 tsp. Worcestershire or soy sauce
- 1 Onion, Diced
- 1 tbsp. Salmon rub seasoning
- 1 tbsp. Saskatchewan Seasoning

Directions: Take a large bowl and combines the salmon seasoning, Saskatchewan seasoning, bell pepper, onion, soy/Worcestershire sauce, eggs, and tuna. Mix well. Oil the hands and make patties.
Preheat the grill to high. Grill the tuna patties for 10 - 15 min. Flip after 7 minutes.
Serve with the topping you like.

Nutrition: Calories: 235.8; Protein: 18.2g; Carbs: 0.9g; Fats: 4.9g

Poultry Recipes

54. Greek Chicken and Veggie Kebabs

Preparation Time: 45 minutes
Servings: 4

Cooking Time: 14 minutes

Ingredients:

- 2 tablespoons plain Greek yogurt
- ¼ cup extra-virgin olive oil
- Juice of 4 lemons
- Grated zest of 1 lemon
- 4 garlic cloves, minced
- 2 tablespoons dried oregano
- 1 teaspoon sea salt
- ½ teaspoon freshly ground black pepper
- 1 pound chicken breasts that is boneless and skinless, cut into 2-inch cubes
- 1 red onion, quartered
- 1 zucchini, sliced

Directions: Whisk in a bowl the Greek yogurt, oil, lemon juice, zest, garlic, oregano, salt, and pepper until well combined.
Put the chicken and half of the marinade into a large resealable plastic bag or container. Move the chicken around to coat evenly. Refrigerate for at least 30 minutes.
Close the hood after inserting the grill grate. Start pre-heating for 14 minutes.
While the unit is preheating, assemble the kebabs by threading the chicken on the skewers, alternating with the red onion and zucchini. Ensure the ingredients are pushed almost completely down to the end of the skewers.
Place the skewers on the Grill Grate when the device beeps to signal that it has preheated.
Close hood and cook for 10 to 14 minutes, occasionally basting the kebabs with the remaining marinade while cooking.
The chicken is now ready when the internal temperature of the meat exceeds 165 ° F.

Nutrition: Calories: 282.9; Fats: 1.9g; Carbs: 7.9g; Fiber: 1.8g; Protein: 26.3g

55. Fajita Chicken Kebabs

Preparation Time: 45 minutes
Servings: 4

Cooking Time: 14 minutes

Ingredients:

- 1 tablespoon ground cumin
- 1 tablespoon garlic powder
- 1 tablespoon chili powder
- 2 teaspoons paprika
- ¼ teaspoon sea salt
- ¼ teaspoon freshly ground black pepper
- 1 pound skinless chicken breasts, (also boneless) cut in 2-inch cubes
- 2 tablespoons extra-virgin olive oil, divided
- 2 red bell peppers, seeded and cut into 1-inch cubes
- 1 red onion, quartered
- Juice of 1 lime

Directions: Take a small mixing bowl and combine the cumin, garlic powder, chili powder, paprika, salt, and pepper, and mix well.
Place the chicken, one tablespoon oil, and half of the spice mixture into a large resealable plastic bag or container. Toss to coat evenly.
Place the bell pepper, onion, remaining one tablespoon of oil, and remaining spice mixture into a large resealable plastic bag or container. Toss to coat evenly. For at least 30 minutes, refrigerate the chicken and vegetables.
Close the hood after inserting the grill grate. Start pre-heating for 14 minutes.
While the unit is preheating, assemble the kebabs by threading the chicken onto the skewers, alternating with the peppers and onion. Ensure the ingredients are pushed almost completely down to the end of the skewers.
Place the skewers on the Grill Grate when the device beeps to signal that it has preheated. Close the hood and cook for 10 to 14 minutes.
The chicken is now ready when the internal temperature of the meat exceeds 165 ° F. Remove from the heat, and drizzle with lime juice.

Nutrition: Calories: 230.8; Fats: 10.8g; Carbs: 8.8g; Fiber: 1.8g; Protein: 25.3g

56. Zesty Garlic Grilled Chicken

Preparation Time: 40 minutes
Servings: 4

Cooking Time: 18 minutes

Ingredients:

- 1½ tablespoons extra-virgin olive oil
- 3 garlic cloves, minced
- ¼ teaspoon ground cumin
- Sea salt
- Freshly ground black pepper
- Grated zest of 1 lime
- Juice of 1 lime
- 4 boneless, skinless chicken breasts

Directions: Stir the oil, garlic, cumin, salt, pepper, zest, and lime juice together in a large shallow cup. Attach the breasts of the chicken and coat well. Cover and marinate for 30 minutes in the refrigerator.

Insert and close the hood with the Grill Grate. Choose a GRILL, set the MEDIUM temperature, and set the time to 18 minutes. To commence preheating, click START/STOP.

When the unit has beeped to signify it has preheated, place the chicken breasts on the Grill Grate. Close the hood and cook for 7 minutes. After 7 minutes, flip the chicken, close the hood, and cook for an additional 7 minutes. Check the chicken for doneness. If needed, cook up to 4 minutes more. When the internal temperature of the chicken meat reaches 165F, that is when cooking is complete.

Remove from the grill, and position for 5 minutes on a cutting board or platter to rest. Just serve.

Nutrition: Calories: 168.7; Fats: 6.8g; Carbs: 0.8g; Fiber: 0g; Protein: 26.3g

57. Maple-Glazed Chicken Wings

Preparation Time: 5 minutes   **Cooking Time: 14 minutes**
Servings: 4

Ingredients:

- 1 cup maple syrup
- 1/3 cup soy sauce
- ¼ cup teriyaki sauce
- 3 garlic cloves, minced
- 2 teaspoons garlic powder
- 2 teaspoons onion powder
- 1 teaspoon freshly ground black pepper
- 2 pounds bone-in chicken wings (drumettes and flats)

Directions: Insert and close the hood with the Grill Grate. Choose a GRILL, set the MEDIUM temperature, and set the time to 14 minutes. To commence preheating, click START/STOP.

Meanwhile, in a large bowl, whisk together the maple syrup, soy sauce, teriyaki sauce, garlic, garlic powder, onion powder, and black pepper. Add the wings, and use tongs to toss and coat.

When the unit has beeped to signify it has preheated, place the chicken wings on the Grill Grate. Close the hood and cook for 5 minutes. After 5 minutes, flip the wings, close the hood, and cook for an additional 5 minutes. Check the wings for doneness. Cooking is complete when, on a food thermometer, the internal temperature of the meat reaches at least 165 °F. If needed, cook for up to 4 minutes more.

Remove from the grill and serve.

Nutrition: Calories: 721.8; Fats: 35.8g; Carbs: 58.7g; Fiber: 0.9g; Protein: 41.2g

58. Spicy Barbecue Chicken Drumsticks

Preparation Time: 10 minutes   **Cooking Time: 20 minutes**
Servings: 4

Ingredients:

- 2 cups barbecue sauce
- Juice of 1 lime
- 2 tablespoons honey
- 1 tablespoon hot sauce
- Sea salt
- Freshly ground black pepper
- 1 pound chicken drumsticks

Directions: In a large bowl, combine the barbecue sauce, lime juice, honey, and hot sauce. Season with salt and pepper. Set aside ½ cup of the sauce. Add the drumsticks to the bowl, and toss until evenly coated.

Insert the Grill Grate and close the hood. Select GRILL, set the temperature to MEDIUM, and set the time to 20 minutes. Select START/STOP to begin preheating.

When the unit beeps to signify it has preheated, place the drumsticks on the Grill Grate. Close the hood and cook for 18 minutes, often basting during cooking.

Cooking is complete when the internal temperature of the meat reaches at least 165°F on a food thermometer. If necessary, close the hood and continue cooking for 2 minutes more.

Nutrition: Calories: 432.8; Fats: 13.9g; Carbs: 54.8g; Fiber: 0.9g; Protein: 21.3g

59. Grilled Chicken Cutlets

Preparation Time: 20 minutes
Servings: 4

Cooking Time: 10 minutes

Ingredients:

- 3 medium cloves garlic, minced (about 1 tablespoon)
- 3 tablespoons minced fresh rosemary
- 2 tablespoons fresh juice from 2 lemons
- 2 teaspoons kosher salt
- 1 teaspoon freshly ground black pepper
- 1/4 cup olive oil
- 4 chicken cutlets, about 1 1/2 pounds total weight, halved
- crosswise if necessary to make even thicknesses

Directions: Take a small bowl, and stir together the garlic, rosemary, lemon juice, salt and pepper. Gradually whisk in the oil until blended.
Put chicken pieces between 2 pieces of plastic wrap. Pound to an even thickness using a meat mallet or small heavy skillet.
Take a large zip-top plastic bag and combine the chicken pieces and marinade. Seal and toss to coat. Let stand at room temperature for 15 minutes, turning once. Marinate longer if possible, turning occasionally.
Prepare the grill for direct grilling over medium-high heat (350° to 450°). Meanwhile, oil the grill rack or spray with nonstick spray. Lightly grease the chicken pieces on both sides with oil from a spray bottle before grilling. Prepare the chicken on the grill rack, brushing with any remaining marinade, and turning occasionally. Grill until done, turning once and brushing with more of the marinade as necessary to prevent sticking and drying out.

Nutrition: Calories: 186.9; Fats: 6.9g; Carbs: 4.8g; Fiber: 0.8g; Protein: 25.3g

60. Glazed Chicken Drumsticks

Preparation Time: 15 minutes
Servings: 12

Cooking Time: 25 minutes

Ingredients:

- 1 (10-ounce) jar red jalapeño pepper jelly
- ¼ cup fresh lime juice
- 12 (6-ounce) chicken drumsticks
- Salt and ground black pepper, as required

Directions: Add jelly and lime juice over medium heat in a small saucepan and cook for about 3-5 minutes or until melted. Remove from the heat and set aside.
Sprinkle the chicken drumsticks with salt and black pepper.
Put the water tray at the bottom of Electric Grill.
Place about 2 cups of lukewarm water into the water tray.
Place the drip pan over the water tray and then arrange the heating element.
Now, place the grilling pan over the heating element.
Plugin the Electric Grill and press the 'Power' button to turn it on.
Then press 'Fan" button. Set the temperature settings according to manufacturer's directions.
Cover the grill with lid and let it preheat. After preheating, remove the lid and grease the grilling pan.
Place the chicken drumsticks over the grilling pan.
Cover with the lid and cook, flipping periodically, for around 15-20 minutes.
Baste the chicken thighs with the jelly mixture during the last 5 minutes of cooking.
Serve hot.

Nutrition: Calories: 358.7; Fats: 9.5g; Carbs: 16.8g; Fiber: 0g; Sugar: 11.3g; Protein: 46.9g

61. Spiced Chicken Breasts

Preparation Time: 15 minutes
Servings: 4

Cooking Time: 14 minutes

Ingredients:

- 2 scallions, chopped
- 1 (1-inch) piece fresh ginger, minced
- 2 garlic cloves, minced
- ¼ cup olive oil
- 2 tablespoons fresh lime juice
- 2 tablespoons low-sodium soy sauce
- 1 teaspoon ground cinnamon
- 1 teaspoon ground cumin
- 1 teaspoon ground turmeric

- Ground black pepper, as required
- 4 (5-ounce) boneless, skinless chicken breasts

Directions: Add all the ingredients in a large Ziploc bag and seal them.
Shake the bag to coat the chicken with marinade well. Refrigerate to marinate for about 20 minutes to 1 hour.
Put the water tray at the bottom of Electric Grill. Place about 2 cups of lukewarm water into the water tray.
Place the drip pan over the water tray and then arrange the heating element.
Now, place the grilling pan over the heating element.
Plugin the Electric Grill and press the 'Power' button to turn it on.
Then press the 'Fan" button. Set the temperature settings according to the manufacturer's directions.
Cover the grill with a lid and let it preheat. After preheating, remove the lid and grease the grilling pan.
Place the chicken breasts over the grilling pan.
Cover the lid and cook on each side for about 6-7 minutes. Serve hot.

Nutrition: Calories: 390.8; Fats: 23.1g; Carbs: 2.5g; Fiber: 0.6g; Sugar: 0.6g; Protein: 42.1g

62. Spicy Chicken Thighs

Preparation Time: 15 minutes   **Cooking Time: 18 minutes**
Servings: 3

Ingredients:
- 2 tablespoons fresh lime juice
- 1 tablespoon ground chipotle powder
- 1 tablespoon paprika
- 1 tablespoon dried oregano, crushed
- ½ tablespoon garlic powder
- Salt and ground black pepper, as required
- 6 (4-ounce) skinless, boneless chicken thighs

Directions: Take a bowl and add the ingredients except chicken thighs and mix until well combined.
Coat the thighs with spice mixture generously. Put the water tray at the bottom of Electric Grill.
Place about 2 cups of lukewarm water into the water tray.
Place the drip pan over the water tray and then arrange the heating element.
Now, place the grilling pan over the heating element.
Plugin the Electric Grill and press the 'Power' button to turn it on. Then press the 'Fan" button.
Set the temperature settings according to the manufacturer's directions.
Cover the grill with a lid and let it preheat.
After preheating, remove the lid and grease the grilling pan.
Place the chicken thighs over the grilling pan. Use the lid to cover and cook for about 8 minutes.
Carefully change the side and grill for 8-10 minutes more. Serve hot.

Nutrition: Calories: 299.8; Fats: 8.3g; Carbs: 3.2g; Fiber: 1.4g; Sugar: 0.5g; Protein: 51.6g

63. Chicken Drumsticks

Preparation Time: 10 minutes   **Cooking Time: 40 minutes**
Servings: 5

Ingredients:
- 2 tablespoons avocado oil
- 1 tablespoon fresh lime juice
- 1 teaspoon red chili powder
- 1 teaspoon garlic powder
- Salt, as required
- 5 (8-ounce) chicken drumsticks

Directions: Take a mixing bowl, mix avocado oil, lime juice, chili powder and garlic powder and mix well.
Add the chicken drumsticks and coat with the marinade generously.
Cover the bowl and refrigerate to marinate for about 30-60 minutes.
Place the water tray at the bottom of Electric Grill.
Place about 2 cups of lukewarm water into the water tray.
Place the drip pan over the water tray and then arrange the heating element.
Now, place the grilling pan over the heating element.
Plugin the Electric Grill and press the 'Power' button to turn it on. Then press the 'Fan" button.
Set the temperature settings according to the manufacturer's directions.
Cover the grill with lid and let it preheat. After preheating, remove the lid and grease the grilling pan.
Place the chicken drumsticks over the grilling pan.
Cover and cook with the lid for about 30-40 minutes, flipping every 5 minutes afterward. Serve hot.

64. Meatballs Kabobs

Preparation Time: 15 minutes
Servings: 4

Cooking Time: 14 minutes

Ingredients:

- 1 yellow onion, chopped roughly
- ½ cup lemongrass, chopped roughly
- 2 garlic cloves, chopped roughly
- 1½ pounds lean ground turkey
- 1 teaspoon sesame oil
- ½ tablespoons low-sodium soy sauce
- 1 tablespoon arrowroot starch
- 1/8 teaspoons powdered stevia
- Salt and ground black pepper, as required

Directions: In a food processor, add the onion, lemongrass and garlic and pulse until chopped finely.
Transfer the onion mixture into a large bowl. Add the remaining ingredients and mix until well combined.
Make 12 equal sized balls from the meat mixture. Thread the balls onto the presoaked wooden skewers.
Place the water tray in the bottom of the Electric Grill, then put about 2 cups of lukewarm water into the water tray. Place the drip pan over the water tray and then arrange the heating element.
Now, place the grilling pan over the heating element.
Plugin the Electric Grill and press the 'Power' button to turn it on. Then press the 'Fan" button.
Set the temperature settings according to the manufacturer's directions.
Cover the grill with a lid and let it preheat. After preheating, remove the lid and grease the grilling pan.
Place the skewers over the grilling pan.
Cover the lid and cook on each side for approximately 6-7 minutes. Serve hot.

Nutrition: Calories: 275.8; Fats: 13.2g; Carbs: 5.3g; Fiber: 0.5g; Sugar: 1.2g; Protein: 34.5g

65. Lemon Mustard Chicken

Preparation Time: 5 minutes
Servings: 6

Cooking Time: 30 minutes

Ingredients:

- 6 chicken thighs
- Salt and pepper to taste
- 3 teaspoons dried Italian seasoning
- 1 tablespoon oregano, dried
- ½ cup Dijon mustard
- ¼ cup of vegetable oil
- 2 tablespoons lemon juice

Directions: Take a bowl and add all listed ingredients except chicken.
Mix everything well. Brush both sides of the chicken with the mixture, and transfer the chicken to the cooking basket. Set your Griller Smart XL to roast mode and 350 degrees F.
Select chicken mode and start; let it cook until the timer runs out. Serve and enjoy!

Nutrition: Calories: 796.8; Fats: 51.8g; Carbs: 44.8g; Fiber: 8.7g; Protein: 42.3g

66. Lemon Pepper Chicken

Preparation Time: 5 minutes
Servings: 4

Cooking Time: 20 minutes

Ingredients:

- 1 tablespoon lemon pepper
- 4 boneless skinless chicken breasts
- 1 teaspoon table salt
- 1½ teaspoons granulated garlic

Directions: Press the "Grill" button on the Griller and adjust the time to 20 minutes at Medium.
Season the chicken breasts with salt, granulated garlic, and lemon pepper.
Place the chicken in the Griller when it shows "Add Food."
Grill for about 20 minutes, flipping halfway through.
Dish out on a platter and serve warm.

Nutrition: Calories: 283.8; Fats: 24.8g; Carbs: 34.8g; Fiber: 1.8g; Protein: 26.3g

67. Sweet Tangy Orange Chicken

Preparation Time: 5 minutes

Cooking Time: 15 minutes

Servings: 4

Ingredients:

- 2 teaspoons ground coriander
- ½ teaspoons garlic salt
- ¼ teaspoon ground black pepper
- 12 chicken wings
- 1 tablespoon canola oil
- ¼ cup butter, melted
- 3 tablespoons honey
- ½ cup of orange juice
- 1/3 cup Sriracha chili sauce
- 2 tablespoons lime juice
- ¼ cup cilantro, chopped

Directions: Take the chicken and coat them well with oil.
Season with spices, let them sit for 2 hours in the fridge.
Add remaining ingredients to a saucepan and cook over low heat for 3-4 minutes.
Set your Griller to GRILL and MED mode. Set timer to 10 minutes.
Add chicken to grill grate, cook for 5 minutes, flip and cook for 5 minutes more
Serve and enjoy once done!

Nutrition: Calories: 319.8; Fats: 13.9g; Carbs: 18.9g; Fiber: 0.9g; Protein: 25.3g

68. Juicy BBQ Chicken

Preparation Time: 5 minutes
Servings: 4

Cooking Time: 12 minutes

Ingredients:

- 6 chicken drumsticks
- ½ tablespoon Worcestershire sauce
- 2 teaspoons BBQ seasoning
- 1 tablespoon brown sugar
- 1 teaspoon dried onion, chopped
- 1/3 cup spice seasoning
- 1 tablespoon bourbon
- 1 pinch teaspoon salt
- ½ cup ketchup

Directions: Add all ingredients into a saucepan except drumsticks.
Stir cook for 8-10 minutes. Keep them aside and let it cool.
Pre-heat the Griller by pressing the "GRILL" option and setting it to "MED."
Set the timer to 12 minutes. Let it pre-heat until you hear a beep.
Arrange drumsticks over grill grate, and brush with remaining sauce.
Lock lid and cook for 6 minutes. flip and brush with more sauce
Cook for 6 minutes more. Serve and enjoy!

Nutrition: Calories: 299.8; Fats: 7.9g; Carbs: 9.8g; Fiber: 1.4g; Protein: 12.7g

69. Apple Flavored Alfredo Chicken

Preparation Time: 5 minutes
Servings: 4

Cooking Time: 20 minutes

Ingredients:

- 1 large apple, wedged
- 1 tablespoon lemon juice
- 4 chicken breast, halved
- 4 teaspoons chicken seasoning
- 4 slices provolone cheese
- ¼ cup blue cheese, crumbled
- ½ cup alfredo sauce

Directions: Take a mixing bowl and add seasoning.
Take another bowl and toss the apple with lemon juice.
Set your Ninja Foodi Smart XL to Grill and MED mode, and set timer to 16 minutes.
Transfer chicken over grill grate, lock lid and cook for 8 minutes.
Flip and cook for 8 minutes more. Similarly grill the apple, 2 minutes per side.
Serve the cooked chicken with sauce, grilled apple, and cheese.

Nutrition: Calories: 246.8; Fats: 18.8g; Carbs: 28.8g; Fiber: 1.9g; Protein: 14.2

Pork Recipes

70. Simple Smoked Pork Ribs

Preparation Time: 15 minutes
Servings: 7

Cooking Time: 5 hours

Ingredients:

- Three rack baby back ribs
- 3/4 cup pork and poultry rub
- 3/4 cup Que BBQ Sauce

Directions: Peel the membrane from the backside of the ribs and trim any fat.
Season the pork generously with the rub.
Set the grill to 180°F and preheat for 15 minutes with the lid closed.
Place the pork ribs on the grill and smoke them for 5 hours.
Remove it from the grill and wrap them in foil with the BBQ sauce.
Place back the pork and increase the temperature to 350°F—Cook for 45 more minutes.
When eating, remove the pork from the grill and let it rest for 20 minutes.

Nutrition: Calories: 761.8; Fats: 56.9g; Carbs: 22.9g; Protein: 39.2g; Sugar 17.9g; Fiber: 0.5g

71. Grill Pork Crown Roast

Preparation Time: 5 minutes
Servings: 5

Cooking Time: 60 minutes

Ingredients:

- 13 ribs pork
- 1/4 cup favorite rub
- 1 cup apple juice
- 1 cup Apricot BBQ sauce

Directions: Set the temperature to 375°F to preheat for 15 minutes with the lid closed.
Meanwhile, season the pork with the rub, then let sit for 30 minutes.
Wrap the tips of each crown roast with foil to prevent the burns from turning black.
Place the meat on the grill grate and cook for 90 minutes. Spray apple juice every 30 minutes.
Remove the foils when the meat has reached an interior temperature of 125 ° F.
Spray the roast with apple juice again and let cook until the internal temperature has reached 135°F.
Baste the roast with BBQ sauce in the last 10 minutes of cooking.
Remove from the grill and wrap with foil. Let rest for 15 minutes before serving. Enjoy.

Nutrition: Calories: 239.8; Fats: 15.8g; Protein: 23.4g

72. Cocoa Crusted Pork Tenderloin

Preparation Time: 30 minutes
Servings: 5

Cooking Time: 25 minutes

Ingredients:

- One pork tenderloin
- 1/2 tbsp. fennel, ground
- 2 tbsp. cocoa powder, unsweetened
- 1 tbsp. smoked paprika
- 1/2 tbsp. kosher salt
- 1/2 tbsp. black pepper
- 1 tbsp. extra virgin olive oil
- Three green onions

Directions: Remove the pork loin's silver skin and connective tissues.
Mix the rest of the ingredients in a mixing bowl, and then rub the mixture on the pork. Refrigerate for 30 minutes.
Prepare the grill for 15 minutes with the lid closed.
Sear all sides of the loin at the front of the grill, then reduce the temperature to 350°F and move the pork to the center grill.
Cook for an additional 15 minutes.
Remove from grill and let rest for 10 minutes before slicing.

Nutrition: Calories: 263.8; Fats: 12.9g; Carbs: 4.4g; Protein: 33.2g; Sugar: 0g; Fiber: 3.4g

73. Blackened Pork Chops

Preparation Time: 5 minutes
Servings: 6

Cooking Time: 20 minutes

Ingredients:

- Six pork chops
- 1/4 cup blackening seasoning
- Salt and pepper to taste

Directions: Preheat your grill to 375°F.
Generously season the pork chops with the blackening seasoning, salt, and pepper.
Put the pork chops on the grill and close the lid.
Let grill for 8 minutes, then flip the chops.
Remove the chops from the grill and let rest for 10 minutes before slicing and serve.

Nutrition: Calories: 332.8; Fats: 17.9g; Carbs: 0.9g; Protein: 40.2g; Fiber: 0.9g

74. Grilled Tenderloin with Fresh Herb Sauce

Preparation Time: 10 minutes
Servings: 4

Cooking Time: 15 minutes

Ingredients:

- One pork tenderloin, silver skin removed and dried
- BBQ seasoning
- One handful basil, fresh
- 1/4 tbsp. garlic powder
- 1/3 cup olive oil
- 1/2 tbsp. kosher salt

Directions: Preheat the wood pellet grill to medium heat.
Coat the pork with BBQ seasoning, and then cook on semi-direct heat of the grill. Turn the pork regularly to ensure even cooking.
Remove from the grill and let it rest for 10 minutes.
Make the herb sauce by pulsing all the sauce ingredients in a food processor—pulse a few times or until well chopped. Slice the pork diagonally and spoon the sauce on top and serve.

Nutrition: Calories: 299.8; Fats: 21.8g; Carbs: 12.8g; Protein: 14.3g; Sugar: 9.8g; Fiber: 0.9g

75. Togarashi Pork Tenderloin

Preparation Time: 5 minutes
Servings: 6

Cooking Time: 25 minutes

Ingredients:

- 1 Pork tenderloin
- 1/2tbsp kosher salt
- 1/4 cup Togarashi seasoning

Directions: Cut any excess silver skin from the pork and sprinkle with salt to taste. Rub generously with the togarashi seasoning
Put in a preheated oven at 400°F for 25 minutes or until the internal temperature reaches 145°F.
Remove from the grill and let rest for 10 minutes before slicing and serving.

Nutrition: Calories: 389.8; Fats: 12.8g; Carbs: 3.8g; Protein: 33.2g; Sugar: 0g; Fiber: 2.8g

76. Sausage Hash

Preparation Time: 30 minutes
Servings: 4

Cooking Time: 45 minutes

Ingredients:

- Nonstick cooking spray
- Two finely minced garlic cloves
- One teaspoon basil, dried
- One teaspoon oregano, dried
- One teaspoon onion powder
- One teaspoon of salt
- 4-6 cooked smoker Italian Sausage (Sliced)
- One large-sized bell pepper, diced
- One large onion, diced
- Three potatoes, cut into 1-inch cubes
- Three tablespoons of olive oil
- French bread for serving

Directions: Pre-heat your smoker to 225 degrees Fahrenheit using your desired wood chips
Cover the smoker grill rack with foil and coat with cooking spray

Take a small bowl and add garlic, oregano, basil, onion powder, and season the mix with salt and pepper
Take a large bowl and add sausage slices, bell pepper, potatoes, onion, olive oil, and spice mix
Mix well and spread the mixture on your foil-covered rack
Place the rack in your smoker and smoke for 45 minutes. Serve with your French bread.

Nutrition: Calories: 192.8; Fats: 9.9g; Carbs: 14.8g; Fiber: 1.9g

77. Pulled Pig Pork

Preparation Time: 1 hour   **Cooking Time: 12 hours**
Servings: 8

Ingredients:

- 2 cups of soy sauce
- 1 cup of Worcestershire sauce
- 1 cup of cranberry grape juice
- 1 cup of teriyaki sauce

- One tablespoon of hot pepper sauce
- Two tablespoons of steak sauce
- 1 cup of light brown sugar

- ½ a teaspoon of ground black pepper
- 2 pound of flank steak cut up into ¼ inch slices

Directions: Take a non-reactive saucepan and add cider, salt, vinegar, brown sugar, cayenne pepper, black pepper, and butter. Bring the mix to a boil over medium-high heat.
Add in water and return the mixture to a boil. Carefully rub the pork with the sauce.
Take your drip pan and add water. Cover with aluminum foil.
Pre-heat your smoker to 225 degrees F.
Use water to fill the water pan halfway through and place it over the drip pan. Add wood chips to the side tray.
Smoke meat for about 6-10 hours. Make sure to keep basting it with the sauce every hour or so.
After the first smoking is done, take an aluminum foil and wrap up the meat forming a watertight seal.
Put the meat in the middle of your foil and bring the edges to the top, cupping up the flesh completely.
Pour 1 cup of sauce over the meat and tight it up.
Place the package back into your smoker and smoke for 2 hours until the meat easily pulls off from the bone.
Once done, remove it from the smoker, pull off the pork, and discard the bone and fat.
For every 4 pounds of beef, put the meat chunks in a pan and pour 1 cup of sauce.
Heat until simmering and serve immediately!

Nutrition: Calories: 1097.5; Fats: 85.9g; Carbs: 37.9g; Fiber: 2.6g

78. Smoked Honey - Garlic Pork Chops

Preparation Time: 15 minutes   **Cooking Time: 60 minutes**
Servings: 4

Ingredients:

- 1/4 cup of lemon juice freshly squeezed
- 1/4 cup honey (preferably a darker honey)

- Three cloves' garlic, minced
- Two tablespoons of soy sauce (or tamari sauce)

- Salt and pepper to taste
- 24 ounces center-cut pork chops boneless

Directions: Combine honey, lemon juice, soy sauce, garlic, and salt and pepper in a bowl.
Place the pork and pour the marinade in a jar over the pork.
Cover and marinate in a fridge overnight.
Remove pork from marinade and pat dry on a kitchen paper towel. (Reserve marinade)
Start your pellet on Smoke with the lid open until the fire is established (4 - 5 minutes).
Increase temperature to 450 and preheat, lid closed, for 10 - 15 minutes.
Arrange the pork chops on the grill racks and smoke for about one hour (depending on the thickness)
In the meantime, heat the remaining marinade in a small saucepan over medium heat to simmer.
Transfer pork chops on a serving plate, pour with the marinade, and serve hot.

Nutrition: Calories: 300.9; Carb: 16.8g; Fats: 6.3g; Fiber: 0.2g; Protein: 41.2g

79. Smoked Pork Chops with Tarragon

Preparation Time: 20 minutes   **Cooking Time: 3 hours**
Servings: 4

Ingredients:

- 1/2 cup olive oil
- 4 Tablespoon of fresh tarragon chopped
- Two teaspoon fresh thyme, chopped
- Salt and grated black pepper
- Two teaspoon apple cider vinegar
- Four pork chops or fillets

Directions: Whisk the olive oil, tarragon, thyme, salt, pepper, apple cider, and stir well.

Place the pork chops in a tub and mix them with a mixture of tarragon.

Refrigerate for 2 hours.

Start pellet grill on, lid open, until the discharge is established (4-5 minutes). Increase the temperature to 225 and allow to pre-heat, lid closed, for 10 - 15 minutes.

Remove the marinade chops and pat them dry on a kitchen towel.

Arrange pork chops on the grill rack and smoke for 2 to 3 hours.

Transfer chops on a serving platter and lets it rest 15 minutes before serving.

Nutrition: Calories: 528.3; Carbs: 0.5g; Fats: 34.8g; Fiber: 0.1g; Protein: 51.2g

80. Panko-Breaded Pork Chops

Preparation Time: 5 minutes
Servings: 6

Cooking Time: 12 minutes

Ingredients:

- 5 (3½- to 5-ounce) pork chops (bone-in or boneless)
- Seasoning salt
- Pepper
- ¼ cup of all-purpose flour
- 2 tablespoons panko bread crumbs

Directions: Season the pork chops with the seasoning salt and pepper to taste.

Sprinkle the flour on each side of the pork chops, then cover each side with panko bread crumbs. In an air fryer, put the pork chops. It is okay to stack them.

Spray the pork chops with vegetable oil. Cook for six minutes.

Open the power air fryer and flip the pork chops. Cook for a further 6 minutes Cool before serving.

Typically, bone-in pork chops are juicier than boneless. If you favor juicy pork chops, use bone-in.

Nutrition: Calories: 245.7; Fats: 12.8g; Protein: 26.3g; Fiber: 0g

81. Pork Tenders with Bell Peppers

Preparation Time: 5 minutes
Servings: 4

Cooking Time: 15 minutes

Ingredients:

- 11 Oz Pork Tenderloin
- 1 Bell Pepper, in thin strips
- 1 Red Onion, sliced
- 2 Tsps. Provencal Herbs
- Black Pepper to taste
- 1 Tbsp. Olive Oil
- 1/2 Tbsp. Mustard * Round Oven Dish

Directions: Prepare the power air fryer to 390 degrees.

In the oven dish, mix the bell pepper strips with the onion, herbs, and a few salt and pepper to taste.

Add half a tablespoon of vegetable oil to the mixture.

Cut the tenderloin into four pieces and rub with salt, pepper and mustard.

Thinly coat the pieces with the remaining vegetable oil and place them upright in the oven dish on top of the pepper mixture.

Place the bowl into the power air fryer. Set the timer to fifteen minutes and roast the meat and therefore the vegetables.

Turn the meat and blend the peppers halfway through. Serve with a fresh salad.

Nutrition: Calories: 321.8; Fats: 14.8g; Protein: 23.1g; Fiber: 0g

82. Balsamic Glazed Pork Chops

Preparation Time: 5 minutes
Servings: 4

Cooking Time: 50 minutes

Ingredients:

- ¾ cup of balsamic vinegar
- 1 ½ tablespoons sugar
- 1 tablespoon butter
- 3 tablespoons olive oil
- 3 tablespoons salt
- 3 pork rib chops

Directions: Put the ingredients in a bowl and allow the meat to marinate in the fridge for at least 2 hours.
Prepare the air fryer to 390°F.
Place the grill pan accessory in the air fryer.
Grill the pork chops for 20 minutes ensuring to flip the meat every 10 minutes for even grilling. Meanwhile, pour the balsamic vinegar into a saucepan and permit it to simmer for at least 10 minutes until the sauce thickens. Brush the meat with the glaze before serving.

Nutrition: Calories: 273.7; Fats: 17.9g; Protein: 17.2g

83. Keto Parmesan Crusted Pork Chops

Preparation Time: 10 minutes   **Cooking Time: 15 minutes**
Servings: 8

Ingredients:

- 3 tbsp. grated parmesan cheese
- 1 C. pork rind crumbs
- 2 beaten eggs
- ¼ tsp. chili powder
- ½ tsp. onion powder
- 1 tsp. smoked paprika
- ¼ tsp. pepper
- ½ tsp. salt
- 4-6 thick boneless pork chops

Directions: Ensure your air fryer is preheated to 400 degrees.
With pepper and salt, season each side of pork chops.
In a kitchen appliance, pulse pork rinds into crumbs. Mix crumbs with other seasonings.
Beat eggs and increase to another bowl. Dip pork chops into eggs then into pork rind crumb mixture.
Spray down the air fryer with vegetable oil and add pork chops to the basket. Set temperature to 400°F and set time to fifteen minutes.

Nutrition: Calories: 421.8; Fats: 18.8g; Protein: 38.2g; Sugar: 1.9g

84. Cilantro-Mint Pork BBQ Thai Style

Preparation Time: 5 minutes   **Cooking Time: 15 minutes**
Servings: 3

Ingredients:

- 1 minced hot chili
- 1 minced shallot
- 1-pound ground pork
- 2 tablespoons fish sauce
- 2 tablespoons lime juice
- 3 tablespoons basil
- 3 tablespoons chopped mint
- 3 tablespoons cilantro

Directions: In a shallow dish, mix well all ingredients with hands. Form into 1-inch ovals. Thread ovals in skewers. Place on skewer rack in air fryer.
Air Frying for quarter-hour, cook on 360°F. Halfway through cooking time, turnover skewers. If needed, cook in batches. Serve and luxuriate in.

Nutrition: Calories: 454.8; Fats: 31.2g; Protein: 40.6g

85. Cajun Barbecue Chicken

Preparation Time: 15 minutes   **Cooking Time: 25 minutes**
Servings: 4

Ingredients:

- 2 tablespoons sweet spicy dry rub
- 1/4 teaspoon ground thyme
- 1/2 teaspoon oregano
- 1 tablespoon olive oil
- 1 lb. chicken breast fillet
- 2 cloves garlic clove, minced
- 1/2 cup barbecue sauce
- 1 tablespoon butter
- 1/4 cup beer
- 1 tablespoon Worcestershire sauce
- 1 tablespoon lime juice
- 1 teaspoon hot sauce

Directions: Mix the thyme, the oregano and dry rub in a bowl.
Line the chicken breasts with olive oil and season both sides with the dry rub mixture.
Prepare the wood pellet grill to 350 degrees F.

Put the chicken breast to the grill and cook for 8 minutes, then let rest for 10 minutes.
Mix the rest of the ingredients in a saucepan and bring to a boil. Serve the chicken with the sauce.

Nutrition: Calories: 285.9; Carbs: 13.8g; Fats: 4.9g; Protein: 38.2g

86. Raspberry Pork Ribs

Preparation Time: 5 minutes   **Cooking Time: 3 hours**
Servings: 6

Ingredients:
- 4 lb. baby back ribs
- 3 tablespoons raspberry chipotle dry rub
- 1 cup barbecue sauce

Directions: Season the ribs with the dry rub and cover with foil.
Place in refrigerator for 1 hour.
Prepare grill to 250 degrees F; when ready, add ribs to grill and cook for 2 hours.
Brush with the barbecue sauce and turn up the temperature to 300 degrees F.
Grill for another 1 hour.

Nutrition: Calories: 113.8; Carbs: 5.8g; Fats: 2.9g; Protein: 14.2g

87. Barbecue Kebabs

Preparation Time: 1 hour   **Cooking Time: 25 minutes**
Servings: 6

Ingredients:
- 1 tablespoon olive oil
- 1/8 cup apple cider vinegar
- 1 tablespoon honey
- 2 tablespoons raspberry chipotle rub
- 1 lb. pork loin, sliced into cubes
- 1 red onion, sliced
- 3 green bell peppers, sliced
- 1/2 cup barbecue sauce

Directions: Mix the vinegar, oil, honey, and rub in a mixing bowl.
Marinate the pork slices in this mixture.
Cover it with foil and marinate in the refrigerator for 1 hour.
Stick the pork cubes into skewers alternating with the green bell pepper and red onion.
Prepare the wood pellet grill to 400 degrees F and grill the kebabs for 20 minutes, rotating every 5 minutes.
Brush with the barbecue sauce.

Nutrition: Calories: 164.8; Carbs: 2.9g; Fats: 9.9g; Protein: 10.2g

88. Lemon Pepper Wings

Preparation Time: 10 minutes   **Cooking Time: 30 minutes**
Servings: 4

Ingredients:
- 1 tablespoon barbecue sauce
- 2 tablespoons lemon zest
- 1/4 cup ground black pepper
- 2 teaspoons ground coriander
- 2 teaspoons garlic powder
- 3 teaspoons dried thyme
- Salt to taste
- 4 lb. chicken wings

Directions: Set your wood pellet grill to smoke and set it to 400 degrees F.
Take a bowl and mix all the ingredients except the chicken wings.
Dip the chicken wings in half of the mixture.
Put the wings on the grill and cook for 15 minutes per side.
Brush the chicken with the remaining sauce.

Nutrition: Calories: 210.8; Carbs: 13.8g; Fats: 12.9g; Protein: 9.1g

89. Pork Shoulder

Preparation Time: 10 minutes   **Cooking Time: 7 hours**
Servings: 8

Ingredients:

- 6 lb. pork shoulder
- 2 tablespoons hickory bacon seasoning
- 1 cup apple cider vinegar
- 1 tablespoon sugar

Directions: Prepare the wood pellet grill to 225 degrees F. Drizzle all sides of the pork with the seasoning. Take a bowl and mix the vinegar and sugar.
Mix until the sugar has been dissolved and then, inject the vinegar mixture into the pork shoulder.
Wrap the pork with foil and put on top of the grill. Cover and smoke for 6 hours. Uncover the pork slowly.
Let rest on a cutting board for 30 minutes.

Nutrition: Calories: 259.8; Carbs: 2.8g; Fats: 19.8g; Protein: 16.2g

90. Rosemary Pork Tenderloin

Preparation Time: 10 minutes
Servings: 2

Cooking Time: 1 hour 20 minutes

Ingredients:

- 1.5-pound pork tenderloin, fat trimmed
- 2 tablespoons minced garlic
- ¼ teaspoon ground black pepper
- 1 tablespoon Dijon mustard
- 1 tablespoon olive oil
- 6 sprigs of rosemary, fresh

Directions: Add the dry pallets into the smoker hopper and put the ash container in place then, open the ash damper, turn on the smoker and close the ash damper.
Prepare the smoker to 375 degrees F, and continue preheating for 20 minutes.
Mix together black pepper, garlic, mustard, and oil until the smooth paste comes together and then coat pork with this paste evenly.
Cut a kitchen string into six 10-inch long pieces, then place them parallel to each, about 2-inch apart, lay 3 sprigs horizontally across the kitchen string, place seasoned pork on it, cover the top with remaining sprigs and tie the strings to secure the sprigs around the tenderloin.
Put pork on the smoker grill, cover and smoke for 15 minutes, then flip the pork tenderloin and continue smoking for another 15 minutes.
When cooked, move the pork tenderloin to a cutting board, let rest for 5 minutes, then remove all the strong and cut pork into even slices.

Nutrition: Calories: 479.8; Fats: 22.9g; Protein: 47.2g; Carbs: 12.9g

91. Honey Glazed Ham

Preparation Time: 25 minutes
Servings: 10

Cooking Time: 2 hours and 50 minutes

Ingredients:

- 8 pounds bone-in ham
- 20 whole cloves
- 1/4 cup corn syrup
- 1 cup smoked honey
- 1 stick of butter, unsalted, softened

Directions: Add the dry pallets to the smoker hopper, put the ash container in place, then open the ash damper, turn on the smoker and close the ash damper.
Preheat the smoker to 350 degrees F for 30 minutes, then lower to 325 degrees F and continue preheating for 20 minutes.
Score ham using a sharp knife, then smear the meat with butter, stuff with cloves and place ham in an aluminum foil-lined baking pan.
Mix corn syrup and honey and then, pour some over the ham and place the pan on the smoker.
Cover and smoke the ham for 2 hours until thoroughly cooked and basting ham with the honey mixture every 15 minutes.
Let rest for 15 minutes and then slice to serve.

Nutrition: Calories: 119.9; Fats: 4.8g; Protein: 16.2g; Carbs: 0.9g

92. Sweet Bacon Wrapped Smokes

Preparation Time: 40 minutes
Servings: 6

Cooking Time: 45 minutes

Ingredients:
- 14-ounce cocktail sausages
- 1-pound bacon strips, halved
- 1/2 cup brown sugar

Directions: Roll the bacon strips using a rolling pin until each strip is of even thickness, then wrap the strips of bacon around the sausage and secure with a toothpick.

Put the wrapped sausages in a casserole dish in a single layer, drizzle with sugar until completely covered, and let them rest in the refrigerator for 30 minutes.

Put the dry pallets into the smoker hopper, put the ash container in place, then open the ash damper, turn on the smoker, and close the ash damper.

Preheat the smoker to 350 degrees F, and let preheat for 30 minutes.

Place the wrapped sausages on a cookie sheet lined with baking paper, place the cookie sheet on the smoker grill, cover and smoke for 30 minutes.

Nutrition: Calories: 269.9; Fats: 26.8g; Protein: 9.2g; Carbs: 17.9g

93. Lemon Pepper Pork Tenderloin

Preparation Time: 2 hours 20 minutes   **Cooking Time: 1 hour 10 minutes**
Servings: 6

Ingredients:
- 2 pounds pork tenderloin, fat trimmed
- ½ teaspoon minced garlic
- 1/2 teaspoon salt
- 1/4 teaspoon ground black pepper
- 2 Lemons, zested
- 1 teaspoon minced parsley
- 1 teaspoon lemon juice
- 2 tablespoons olive oil

Directions: For the marinade: put all the ingredients except for pork in a small bowl and mix well.

Put the pork tenderloin in a large plastic bag along with the marinade, seal the plastic bag, then turn it upside down to cover the pork and marinate for at least 2 hours.

Add the dry pallets to the smoker hopper and put the ash container in place, then open the ash damper, turn on the smoker, and close the ash damper.

Prepare the smoker to 375 degrees F, let preheat for 50 minutes.

Remove the pork tenderloin from the marinade, put it on the smoker grill, smoke for 20 minutes, and flip pork halfway through.

When you are done, transfer the pork meat to a cutting board, let rest for 10 minutes, and then slice to serve.

Nutrition: Calories: 144.3; Fats: 8.5g; Protein: 13.6g; Carbs: 2.8g

94. Bacon

Preparation Time: 10 minutes   **Cooking Time: 55 minutes**
Servings: 6

Ingredients:
- 1-pound bacon slices, thick-cut

Directions: Add the dry pallets to the smoker hopper and put the ash container in place, then open the ash damper, turn on the smoker, and close the ash damper.

Prepare the smoker to 375 degrees F for 30 minutes.

In a large baking sheet, line it with parchment paper and put bacon slices on it in a single layer.

Put the baking sheet on the smoker grill, cover and smoke for 20 minutes, then flip the bacon and continue smoking for 5 minutes.

When ready, plate the bacon on a plate lined with paper towels to absorb excess grease and serve.

Nutrition: Calories: 79.8; Fats: 6.9g; Protein: 5.2g; Carbs: 0g

95. Bourbon Honey Glazed Pork Ribs

Preparation Time: 15 minutes   **Cooking Time: 5 hours**
Servings: 10

Ingredients:
- Pork Ribs (4-lbs., 1.8-kg.)
- The Marinade
- Apple juice – 1 ½ cups
- Yellow mustard – ½ cup
- The Rub
- Brown sugar – ¼ cup
- Smoked paprika – 1 tablespoon
- Onion powder – ¾ tablespoon
- Garlic powder – ¾ tablespoon
- Chili powder – 1 teaspoon
- Cayenne pepper – ¾ teaspoon
- Salt – 1 ½ teaspoons
- The Glaze
- Unsalted butter – 2 tablespoons
- Honey – ¼ cup
- Bourbon – 3 tablespoons

Directions: Mix apple juice and yellow mustard in a bowl.

Apply the mixture over the pork ribs then marinate for at least an hour.

Combine brown sugar with onion powder, cayenne pepper, smoked paprika, chili powder, garlic powder, black pepper, and salt then mix well.

After an hour of marinade, sprinkle the dry spice mixture over the marinated pork ribs and let it rest for a few minutes.

Plug the wood pellet smoker then fill the hopper with the wood pellet. Turn the switch on.

Prepare the wood pellet smoker for indirect heat then adjust the temperature to 250°F.

Put the seasoned pork ribs in the wood pellet smoker and smoke for 3 hours.

Put unsalted butter in a saucepan then melt over low heat then, remove from heat and add honey and bourbon to the saucepan. Mix until incorporated and set aside.

After 3 hours of smoking, baste the honey bourbon mixture over the pork ribs and wrap with aluminum foil.

Put the wrapped pork ribs to the wood pellet smoker and continue smoking for to 2 hours.

Unwrap the smoked pork ribs and serve.

Nutrition: Calories: 312.8; Carbs: 4.8g; Fats: 19.8g; Protein: 26.3g

96. Chili Sweet Smoked Pork Tenderloin

Preparation Time: 10 minutes
Servings: 8

Cooking Time: 3 hours 30 minutes

Ingredients:
- Pork Tenderloin (3-lb., 1.4-kg.)
- The Rub
- Apple juice – 1 cup
- Honey – ½ cup
- Brown sugar – ¾ cup
- Dried thyme – 2 tablespoons
- Black pepper – ½ tablespoon
- Chili powder – 1 ½ teaspoon
- Italian seasoning – ½ teaspoon
- Onion powder – 1 teaspoon

Directions: In a container stir in apple juice, chili powder, dried thyme, honey, brown sugar, black pepper, Italian seasoning, and onion powder.

Rub the pork tenderloin with the spice mixture, then let it rest for an hour.

Next, plug the wood pellet smoker then fill the hopper with the wood pellet. Turn the switch on.

Set the wood pellet smoker for indirect heat then adjust the temperature to 250°F (121°C).

When the wood pellet smoker is ready, put the cured pork tenderloin in the wood pellet smoker and smoke for 3 hours.

Allow smoking for 3 hours then, increase the temperature to 350°F (177°C) and continue smoking the pork tenderloin for another 30 minutes.

Once the internal temperature of the smoked pork tenderloin has reached 165°F (74°C), remove it from the wood pellet smoker and transfer it to a serving dish.

Cut the smoked pork tenderloin into thick slices, then serve.

Nutrition: Calories: 317.9; Carbs: 6.9g; Fats: 9.8g; Protein: 8.2g

97. Grilled Pork Chops

Preparation Time: 15 minutes
Servings: 4

Cooking Time: 1 hour 30 minutes

Ingredients:
- 4 pork chops.
- 1/4 cup of olive oil.
- 1 1/2 tablespoons of brown sugar.
- 2 teaspoons of Dijon mustard.
- 1 1/2 tablespoons of soy sauce.
- 1 teaspoon of lemon zest.
- 2 teaspoons of chopped parsley.
- 2 teaspoons of chopped thyme.
- 1/2 teaspoon of salt to taste.
- 1/2 teaspoon of pepper to taste.
- 1 teaspoon of minced garlic.

Directions: For the marinade: take a small mixing bowl and mix all the ingredients aside from the pork chops. Put the chops into a Ziploc bag, pour in the prepared marinade then shake properly to coat. Let the pork chops marinate in the refrigerator for about one to eight hours.

Preheat a Wood Pellet Smoker and Grill to 300 degrees F, put the marinated pork chops on the grill and cook for about eight minutes. Flip the side by the side of the meat over and cook for an additional eight minutes.

Let the pork chops rest for five minutes, slice, and serve.

Nutrition: Calories: 312.8; Carbs: 4.9g; Protein: 30.2g; Fats: 13.9g

98. Baby Back Ribs

Preparation Time: 15 minutes
Servings: 6

Cooking Time: 1 hour 30 minutes

Ingredients:

- 2 racks baby back ribs.
- 3/4 cup of chicken broth.
- 3/4 cup of soy sauce.
- 1 cup of sugar.
- 6 tablespoons of cider vinegar.
- 6 tablespoons of olive oil.
- 3 minced garlic cloves.
- 2 teaspoons of salt to taste.
- 1 tablespoon of paprika.
- 1/2 teaspoon of chili powder.
- 1/2 teaspoon of pepper to taste.
- 1/4 teaspoon of garlic powder.
- A dash of cayenne pepper.
- Barbecue sauce.

Directions: For the marinade: Take a large bowl and mix well the sugar, vinegar, soy sauce, garlic and oil. Put the pork ribs in a Ziploc bag, pour in about 2/3 of the prepared marinade then sake properly to coat. Allow the ribs to marinate in the refrigerator overnight.

Take another bowl, put the rest of the sugar, salt, and seasonings listed, and mix well. Rub the ribs with the mixture, coating them on all sides, then set them aside. Preheat a wood pellet smoking grill to 250 degrees, put the ribs on the preheated grill, and grill for about two hours.

Blast the ribs with the reserved marinade and cook for an additional one hour. Once cooked, let rest for about five to ten minutes, slice, and serve.

Nutrition: Calories: 646.9; Fats: 40.8g; Carbs: 29.8g; Protein: 37.1g

99. Grilled Honey Pork Loin

Preparation Time: 10 minutes
Servings: 8

Cooking Time: 1 hour 15 minutes

Ingredients:

- 1 (3 lbs.) boneless pork loin.
- 2/3 cup of soy sauce.
- 1 teaspoon of ground ginger.
- 3 crushed garlic cloves.
- 1/4 cup of packed brown sugar.
- 1/3 cup of honey.
- 1 1/2 tablespoons of sesame oil.
- Vegetable oil.

Directions: Trim the fat from the pork loin and place it in a Ziploc bag, set aside. Mix the soy sauce, ginger, and garlic in a small bowl. Pour the mixture into the bag containing the pork loin and shake well to coat. Marinate for about 3 hours in the refrigerator. Be sure to turn the meat occasionally.

Mix the sugar, honey, and sesame oil in another bowl. Prepare the Wood Pellet Smoker and Grill to 275 degrees F, put a pan on the griddle, pour in the sugar mixture then cook for a few minutes until the sugar dissolves, set aside. Put the pork loin on the grill and cook for about one hour.

Brush the loin with the sugar mixture and cook for an additional 45 minutes. Let the pork rest for about 5 minutes, slice, and serve.

Nutrition: Calories: 259.5; Fats: 10.9g; Carbs: 13.2g; Protein: 26.1g

100.   Parmesan Roast Pork

Preparation Time: 10 minutes
Servings: 10

Cooking Time: 3 hours 45 minutes

Ingredients:

- 4 chopped garlic cloves.
- 2 tablespoons of olive oil.
- 1 tablespoon of minced dried basil.
- 1 tablespoon of dried and crushed oregano.
- 1 pound of boneless pork loin.

- *1 cup of bread crumbs.*
- *1/4 cup of grated Parmesan cheese.*

Directions: Mix well, in a small bowl, the garlic, olive oil, basil, and oregano. Rub the mixture on the pork loin, coating all sides, then place in the large bowl. Cover the bowl with a plastic wrap, then place in the refrigerator for about two hours.

Take another mixing bowl and mix the bread crumbs and cheese. Dip the pork in the cheese mixture, then set aside. Preheat a Wood Pellet Smoker and Grill to 225 degrees F, put the pork on the grill, cover and smoke the pork for about four hours.

Wrap the pork in aluminum foil and let stand for about ten minutes. Slice and serve.

Nutrition: Calories: 249.9; Fats : 9.9g ; Carbs: 2.9g ; Protein: 34.2g

101.   Grilled Pork Chops

Preparation Time: 10 minutes   **Cooking Time: 20 minutes**
Servings: 6

Ingredients:
- *Pork chops - 6, thickly cut*
- *Barbeque mix*

Directions: Prepare your wood pellet grill to 450 degrees, put the seasoned chops on the grill and cover.
Cook for 6 minutes and then, remove the pork chops.
Let it remain open for 10 minutes and serve with a side dish.

Nutrition: Calories: 299.8; Carbs: 0g; Protein: 23.1g; Fats: 7.5g

102.   Smoked Bacon

Preparation Time: 10 minutes   **Cooking Time: 30 minutes**
Servings: 6

Ingredients:
- *Thick cut bacon - 1 lb.*

Directions: Prepare your wood pellet grill to 375 degrees and line a huge baking sheet. Put a single layer of thick-cut bacon on it. Cook for 20 minutes and then flip it to the other side.
Cook for 10 minutes and take it out.

Nutrition: Calories: 314.8; Protein: 9.2g; Fats: 9.8g

103.   Stuffed Pork Crown Roast

Preparation Time: 1 hour   **Cooking Time: 3 hours 30 minutes**
Servings: 2-4

Ingredients:
- *12-14 ribs or 1 Snake River Pork Crown Roast*
- *Apple cider vinegar - 2 tbsp*
- *Apple juice - 1 cup*
- *Dijon mustard - 2 tbsp*
- *Salt - 1 tsp*
- *Brown sugar - 1 tbsp*
- *Freshly chopped thyme or rosemary - 2 tbsp*
- *Cloves of minced garlic - 2*
- *Olive oil - ½ cup*
- *Coarsely ground pepper - 1 tsp*
- *Your favorite stuffing - 8 cups*

Directions: Put the pork properly in a shallow roasting pan on a flat rack. Cover both ends of the bone with a piece of foil.
For the marinade: boil the apple cider or apple juice on high heat until it reduces to about half its quantity.
Remove the content from the heat and whisk in the mustard, garlic, vinegar, pepper, thyme, brown sugar, and salt. Once all that is properly blended, whisk in the oil slowly.
Use a pastry brush to apply the marinade to the roast. Cover it on all sides using plastic wrap and allow it to sit for about 60 minutes.

Brush the marinade on the roast again, cover it and return it to the refrigerator for 10 minutes. Preheat the grill for 30 minutes, allow the meat to reach room temperature, then put in on the pellet grill.

Cook the meat for 30 minutes, then lower the temperature of the grill. Fill the crown loosely with the stuffing and mound it at the top. Cover the stuffing properly with foil.

Cook the pork for 90 more minutes. Get rid of the foil and continue to roast the stuffing for 30-90 minutes

Let it to rest for around 15 minutes then, remove the foil covering the bones. Leave the butcher's string on until you are ready to carve it. Now, transfer it to a warm platter, and carve between the bones.

Nutrition: Calories: 1010.7; Carbs: 5.1g; Protein: 108.1g; Fats: 58.2g

104.   Smoked Pork Cutlets with Caraway and Dill

Preparation Time: 1 hour and 45 minutes   Cooking Time: 2 hours
Servings: 4

Ingredients:

- 4 pork cutlets
- 2 lemons freshly squeezed
- 2 Tbs fresh parsley finely chopped
- 1 Tbsp of ground caraway
- 3 Tbsp of fresh dill finely chopped
- 1/4 cup of olive oil
- salt and ground black pepper

Directions: Put the pork cutlets in a large resealable bag along with all ingredients and mix well. Refrigerate for at least 4 hours.

Remove the pork cutlets from the marinade and pat dry on a kitchen towel.

Set the pellet grill on SMOKE with the lid open until the fire is established.

Set the temperature to 250 °F and preheat whit the lid closed for 10 to 15 minutes.

Arrange pork cutlets on the grill rack and smoke for about 1 1/2 hours. Allow cooling on room temperature before serving.

Nutrition: Calories: 307.9; Carbs: 2.1g; Fats: 18.3g; Fiber: 0.3g; Protein: 32.1g

105.   Smoked Pork Ribs with Herbs

Preparation Time: 3 hours and 20 minutes   Cooking Time: 3 hours
Servings: 6

Ingredients:

- 1/4 cup olive oil
- 1 Tbs garlic minced
- 1 Tbs crushed fennel seeds
- 1 tsp of fresh basil leaves finely chopped
- 1 tsp fresh parsley finely chopped
- 1 tsp fresh rosemary finely chopped
- 1 tsp fresh sage finely chopped
- Salt and ground black pepper to taste
- 3 lbs. pork rib roast bone-in

Directions: Take a bowl and mix the olive oil, parsley, garlic, fennel seeds, rosemary, sage, salt, and pepper.

Coat each chop on both sides with the herb mixture.

Prepare the pellet grill on SMOKE with the lid open until the fire is established.

Set the temperature to 225 °F and preheat, lid closed, for 10 to 15 minutes. Smoke the ribs for 3 hours.

Transfer the ribs to a serving platter and serve hot.

Nutrition: Calories: 458.9; Carbs: 0.5g; Fats: 31.1g; Fiber: 0g; Protein: 41.2g

106.   Smoked Spicy Pork Medallions

Preparation Time: 1 hour and 45 minutes   Cooking Time: 1 hours 30 minutes
Servings: 6

Ingredients:

- 2 lbs pork medallions
- 3/4 cup chicken stock
- 1/2 cup tomato sauce (organic)
- 2 Tbs of smoked hot paprika (or to taste)
- 2 Tbsp of fresh basil finely chopped
- 1 Tbsp oregano
- Salt and pepper to taste

Directions: Take a bowl, mix together the chicken stock, paprika, tomato sauce, salt, oregano, and pepper. Brush generously over the outside of the tenderloin. Prepare the pellet grill on Smoke with the lid open until the fire is established (4 to 5 minutes).

Set the temperature to 250°F and preheat, lid closed, for 10 to 15 minutes.

Put the pork on the grill grate and smoke for 1 1/2 hours.

Nutrition: Calories: 363.9; Carbs: 3.9g; Fat: 14.2g; Fiber: 1.8g; Protein: 52.6g

107.   Pork Loin Roulade

Preparation Time: 4 hours and 45 minutes   **Cooking Time: 2 hours and 35 minutes**
Servings: 2

Ingredients:

- 1 pork loin, fat trimmed
- 2 cups basil leaves, fresh
- 3 tablespoons garlic powder
- 1 tablespoon salt
- 2 tablespoons ground black pepper
- 3 tablespoons dried thyme
- 3 tablespoons dried oregano
- 1 cup grated mozzarella cheese
- 24 ounces ricotta cheese
- ½ cup grated parmesan cheese
- 24 ounces marinara sauce

Directions: Take a bowl and mix together all the cheeses, black pepper, garlic powder, salt, thyme, and oregano, then cover the bowl and let the mixture cool in the refrigerator for 30 minutes.

Put the pork loin on working space, make some shallow cuts, and roll it using a rolling pin until flat.

Spread the cheese mixture on the pork loin, leaving 1-inch of edge, lay basil leaves to cover cheese spread completely, roll the pork loin very gently, and secure with toothpicks or kitchen twine.

Put the pork loin on a dish and then place it in the refrigerator to chill for 4 hours.

Open the hopper of the smoker, add dry pallets, make sure the ash-can is in place, then open the ash damper, power on the smoker and close the ash damper.

Preheat the smoker to 350 degrees F, then set it to 275 degrees F and continue preheating for 20 minutes.

Put pork loin on the smoker grill, shut with a lid and smoke for 1 hour and 45 minutes.

Transfer pork loin to a dish and let it rest for 10 minutes.

Put a pot over medium heat, pour in marinara sauce, bring it to boil and then remove pot from heat.

Cut pork loin into slices, remove toothpicks or kitchen twine and top pork slices with marinara sauce.

Serve straight away.

Nutrition: Calories: 389.8; Fats: 23.9g; Protein: 21.3g; Carbs: 21.8g; Fiber: 1.9g; Sugar: 1.9g

108.   Pineapple Bourbon Glazed Ham

Preparation Time: 10 minutes   **Cooking Time: 4 hours and 50 minutes**
Servings: 8

Ingredients:

- 4 pounds spiral cut ham, precooked
- ½ cup ham rub
- 1/2 cup brown sugar
- 1 tablespoon ground mustard
- 1/3 cup molasses
- 1 cup honey
- 18-ounce pineapple preserves
- 1 cup bourbon

Directions: Open the hopper of the smoker, add dry pallets, put the ash container in place, then open the ash damper, power on the smoker, and close the ash damper.

Preheat the smoker to 350 degrees F, then set it to 225 degrees F and continue preheating for 20 minutes.

For the glaze: put a pot over low heat, add all the ingredients except for ham, whisk well and cook for 20 minutes or until glaze thickens then, remove the pot from heat and let the glaze cool until required.

Take an aluminum foil tray, take a wire rack on top of it, place ham on it and then place on the smoker grill.

Cover the smoker with a lid and smoke for 4 hours or until thoroughly cooked, brush with prepared glaze every 15 minutes during the last hour.

Transfer ham to a cutting board, let rest for 15 minutes and then slice to serve.

Nutrition: Calories: 146.1; Fats: 0.6g; Protein: 18.2g; Carbs: 14.8g; Fiber: 0.5g; Sugar: 16.8g

109.   Cider Pork Steak

Preparation Time: 2 hours and 40 minutes   **Cooking Time: 3 hours**
Servings: 4

Ingredients:

- 4 pork steaks
- 1/3 cup sea salt
- ¼ cup pork rub
- 2 teaspoons dried thyme
- 1 cup maple syrup
- 2 teaspoons hot sauce
- ¼ cup BBQ sauce
- 1½ cup apple cider
- 1½ cup ice water
- 1 cup water

Directions: For the brine: put a small saucepan over medium heat, pour in 1 cup water, thyme, salt and 1/3 cup maple syrup and cook for 10 minutes.

Then remove pan from the heat, pour in apple cider, one teaspoon hot sauce and ice water, stir well until ice dissolves and let brine chill for 30 minutes.

Put pork steaks in a large plastic bag, pour in brine, seal the bag, turn it upside down to coat steaks with brine and marinate in the refrigerator for 2 hours.

Put remaining maple syrup in a small bowl, add hot sauce and barbecue sauce, whisk until combined and set aside until required.

Open the hopper of the smoker, add dry pallets, make sure the ash-can is in place, then open the ash damper, power on the smoker and close the ash damper.

Preheat the smoker to 300 degrees F and then remove pork steaks from the brine, pat dry with paper towels, place pork steaks on the smoker grill, shut with lid and smoke for 1 hour 30 minutes to 2 hours, brushing pork steaks with maple syrup every 3 minutes during the last 10 minutes, flipping steaks halfway through.

Transfer steaks to a cutting board, let rest for 5 minutes and serve straight away.

Nutrition: Calories: 149.9; Fats: 8.8g; Protein: 14.2g; Carbs: 2.9g; Fiber: 0g; Sugar: 5.8g

110.   Bacon Cheese Fries

Preparation Time: 10 minutes
Servings: 2

Cooking Time: 100 minutes

Ingredients:

- ½-pound bacon slices
- 2 large potatoes
- ¼ cup olive oil
- 3 teaspoons minced garlic
- ½ teaspoon salt
- ¼ teaspoon ground black pepper
- 2 sprigs of rosemary
- ½ cup grated mozzarella cheese

Directions: Open the hopper of the smoker, add dry pallets, put the ash container in place, then open the ash damper, power on the smoker and close the ash damper.

Preheat the smoker to 375 degrees F and meanwhile, in a large baking sheet, line it with parchment paper and put bacon slices on it in a single layer.

Put the baking sheet on the smoker grill, shut it with a lid, smoke for 20 minutes, then flip the bacon and continue smoking for 5 minutes.

Transfer bacon to a dish lined with paper towels to soak excess fat, then cut bacon into small pieces and set aside until required.

Preheat the smoker to 325 degrees F.

For fries: slice each potato into eight wedges, then spread potato wedges on a rimmed baking sheet in a single layer, drizzle with oil, sprinkle with garlic, black pepper, salt and rosemary and toss until good coat.

Put the baking sheet on the smoker grill, cover and smoke for 20 to 30 minutes.

Then remove the baking sheet from the smoker, sprinkle bacon and cheese on top of the fries and continue smoking for 1 minute or until the cheese melt. Serve straight away.

Nutrition: Calories: 387.9; Fats: 21.9g; Protein: 10.1g; Carbs: 37.9g; Fiber: 3.2g; Sugar: 0.4g

111.   Bacon Wrapped Onion Rings

Preparation Time: 10 minutes
Servings: 8

Cooking Time: 2 hours and 30 minutes

Ingredients:

- 1 pack bacon, thick cut
- 2 white onions

Directions: Open the hopper of the smoker, add dry pallets, put the ash container in place, then open the ash damper, power on the smoker and close the ash damper.

Preheat the smoker to 250 degrees F and peel the onions, cut into thirds, separate the onion slices into rings and wrap each onion rings with two bacon slices, securing with a toothpick.
Prepare more bacon wrapped onion rings until all the bacon is used up.
Put onion rings on the smoker grill, cover and smoke for 2 hours or until bacon is cooked, turning halfway through.
Serve straight away.

Nutrition: Calories: 85.9; Fats: 5.9g; Protein: 6.2g; Carbs: 1.9g; Fiber: 0g; Sugar: 0.4g

112.   Cuban Pork

Preparation Time: 20 minutes   **Cooking Time: 12 hours and 30 minutes**
Servings: 10

Ingredients:

- *8 pounds pork shoulder, boneless*
- *2 medium onions, peeled and cut into rings*
- *2 heads of garlic, peeled and chopped*
- *3 tablespoons salt*
- *1 tablespoon ground black pepper*
- *1 tablespoon cumin*
- *2 tablespoons oregano*
- *4 cups orange juice*
- *2 2/3 cups lime juice*

Directions: Mix the ingredients except for salt, black pepper, and pork in a bowl.
Season pork with salt and black, then put in a large plastic bag, pour in prepared orange juice mixture, seal the bag, turn it upside down and let marinate in the refrigerator for a minimum of 1 hour.
Open the hopper of the smoker, add dry pallets, put the ash container in place, then open the ash damper, power on the smoker and close the ash damper.
Preheat the smoker to 205 degrees F, remove pork from marinade, put it in a high-sided baking pan, and strain it on it.
Put a baking pan containing pork on the smoker grill, cover and smoke for 12 hours.
Remove pork from the grill, then shred with two forks, toss until mixed with its liquid, and serve.

Nutrition: Calories: 279.8; Fats: 9.1g; Protein: 42.8g; Carbs: 4.5g; Fiber: 0.8g; Sugar: 0.3g

113.   Pineapple Maple Glaze Fish

Preparation Time: 10 minutes   **Cooking Time: 15 minutes**
Servings: 6

Ingredients:

- *3 pounds of fresh salmon*
- *1/4 cup maple syrup*
- *1/2 cup pineapple juice*
- *Brine Ingredients:*
- *3 cups of water*
- *Sea salt, to taste*
- *2 cups of pineapple juice*
- *½ cup of brown sugar*
- *5 tablespoons of Worcestershire sauce*
- *1 tablespoon of garlic salt*

Directions: Take a large cooking pan and mix all the brine ingredients.
Put the fish into the brine and let it sit for 2 hours for marinating and then, take out the fish and pat dry with a paper towel and set aside. Preheat the smoker grill to 250 degrees Fahrenheit.
Place salmon on the grill and cook for 15 minutes.
In a bowl combine pineapple and maple syrup and baste fish every 5 minutes.
Once the salmon is done, serve and enjoy.

114.   Smoked Sea Bass

Preparation Time: 10 minutes   **Cooking Time: 40 minutes**
Servings: 4

Ingredients:

Marinade:

- *1 tsp. Blackened Saskatchewan*
- *1 tbsp. Thyme, fresh*
- *1 tbsp. Oregano, fresh*

- 8 cloves of Garlic, crushed
- 1 lemon, the juice
- ¼ cup oil

Sea Bass:
- 4 Sea bass fillets, skin off
- Chicken Rub Seasoning
- Seafood Seasoning (like Old Bay)
- 8 tbsp. Gold Butter

For garnish:
- Thyme
- Lemon

Directions: For the marinade: Take a ziplock bag and mix the ingredients then, put the fillets and marinate for 30 min in the fridge. Turn once.
Preheat the grill to 325F with a closed lid.
Take a dish for baking and add the butter. Remove the fish from the marinade and pour it into the baking dish.
Season the fish with chicken and seafood rub. Put it in the baking dish and on the grill. Cook for 30 minutes. Baste 1 - 2 times. Garnish with lemon slices and thyme.

Nutrition: Calories: 219.8; Protein: 32.3g; Carbs: 0.9g; Fat: 7.9g

115. Fish Recipe

Preparation Time: 45 minutes
Servings: 4 - 6

Cooking Time: 10 minutes

Ingredients:
- 4 lbs. fish, cut it into pieces (portion size)
- 1 tbsp. minced Garlic
- 1/3 cup of Olive oil
- 1 cup of Soy Sauce
- Basil, chopped
- 2 Lemons, the juice

Directions: Prepare the grill to 350F with a closed lid.
Mix the ingredients in a bowl and marinate the fish for 45 min.
Grill the fish until it reaches 145F internal temperature. Serve with your favorite side dish.

Nutrition: Calories: 152.9; Protein: 25.3g; Carbs: 0.9g; Fat: 3.9g

116. Seared Tuna Steaks

Preparation Time: 5 minutes
Servings: 2 - 4

Cooking Time: 5 minutes

Ingredients:
- 3 -inch Tuna
- Black pepper
- Sea Salt
- Olive oil
- Sriracha
- Soy Sauce

Directions: Baste the tuna steaks with oil and sprinkle with black pepper and salt.
Prepare the grill to be high with a closed lid. Grill the tuna for 2 ½ minutes per side.
Let it rest for 5 minutes. Cut into thin pieces and serve with Sriracha and Soy Sauce.

Nutrition: Calories: 119.9; Proteins: 34.2g; Carbs: 0; Fat: 1.2g

117. Finnan Haddie Recipe

Preparation Time: 5 minutes

Cooking Time: 35 minutes

Ingredients:
- 2 pounds smoked haddock fillets
- 2 tablespoons all-purpose flour
- 1/4 cup melted butter
- 2 cups warm milk

Directions: Prepare the oven to 325 degrees F and then put smoked haddock into a glass baking dish.
Mix the flour into the melted butter until smooth, then whisk in milk, and pour over the haddock.
Cook in the preheated oven until the sauce has thickened and the fish flakes easily with a fork, about 35 minutes.

118.   Garlic Shrimp Pesto Bruschetta

Preparation Time: 10 minutes
Servings: 12

Cooking Time: 45 minutes

Ingredients:

- 12 slices of baguette bread
- 12 jumbo shrimp, smoked
- ½ teaspoon ground black pepper
- 1 ½ teaspoon salt
- 1/2 teaspoon garlic powder
- 2 teaspoons minced garlic
- 1/2 teaspoon red chili pepper flakes
- 1/4 teaspoon parsley, leaves
- 1/2 teaspoon paprika, smoked
- 2 tablespoons olive oil
- 12 tablespoons basil pesto

Directions: Open the hopper of the smoker, add dry pallets, put ash-can is in place, then open the ash damper, power on the smoker and close the ash damper.
Prepare the smoker to 350 degrees F and then, take a large baking sheet, line it with aluminum foil and place baguette slices on it.
Chop minced garlic and olives together, brush the mixture on both sides of bread slices, then place the baking sheet on smoker grill, shut with a lid, and smoke for 15 minutes.
Take a skillet pan, add shrimps, season with salt, garlic powder, black pepper, paprika, and red chili powder, sprinkle with olive oil and then place the pan on the grill grate to cook for 5 minutes and then set aside until required.
When bread slices are toasted, let them cool for 5 minutes, then spread one tablespoon pesto on each slice and evenly top with shrimp.
Serve straight away.

Nutrition: Calories: 167.9; Fats: 6.9g; Protein: 5.2g; Carbs: 18.8g; Fiber: 0.9g; Sugar: 0.9g

119.   Shrimp Tacos

Preparation Time: 10 minutes
Servings: 4

Cooking Time: 40 minutes

Ingredients:

- 1-pound Shrimp, peeled, deveined
- 3 tablespoons taco seasoning
- 1/2 teaspoon salt
- 2 tablespoons olive oil

Directions: Open the hopper of the smoker, add dry pallets, put ash-can in place, then open the ash damper, power on the smoker and close the ash damper.
Prepare the smoker to 400 degrees F, switch smoker to open flame cooking mode, press the open flame 3, remove the grill grates and the batch, replace batch with direct flame insert, then return grates on the grill in the lower position and let preheat for 30 minutes.
Put shrimps in a large bowl, add oil, toss until well coated, then thread four shrimps per skewer and sprinkle with taco seasoning.
Place the shrimp skewers on the smoker grill, shut with a lid and smoke for 5 minutes per side. Serve straight away.

Nutrition: Calories: 138.8; Fats: 5.9g; Protein: 19.2g; Carbs: 0.9g; Fiber: 0g; Sugar: 0g

120.   Salmon Cakes

Preparation Time: 45 minutes
Servings: 4

Cooking Time: 7 minutes

Ingredients:

For Salmon Cakes:

- 1 cup cooked salmon, flaked
- 1/2 of red pepper, diced
- 1 tablespoon mustard
- 1/2 tablespoon rib rub
- 1 1/2 cups breadcrumb
- 2 eggs
- 1/2 tablespoon olive oil
- 1/4 cup mayonnaise

For the Sauce:

- 1 cup mayonnaise, divided
- 1/2 tablespoon capers, diced
- 1/4 cup dill pickle relish

Directions: Place all the ingredients for the salmon cakes in a bowl, except for oil, mix and then let rest for 15 minutes.

Open the hopper of the smoker, add dry pallets, put ash-can is in place, then open the ash damper, power on the smoker and close the ash damper.

Prepare the smoker to 350 degrees F, switch smoker to open flame cooking mode, press the open flame 3, remove the grill grates and the batch, replace batch with direct flame insert, then return grates on the grill in the lower position, place the sheet pan and let preheat for 30 minutes.

Prepare the sauce and for this, put all the ingredients for the sauce in a bowl and mix, set aside until required then put the salmon mixture on the heated sheet pan, about 2 tablespoons per patty, press with a spatula to form a patty, grill for 5 minutes, then flip the patties, continue smoking for 2 minutes.

Transfer salmon cakes to a dish and serve with prepared sauce.

Nutrition: Calories: 229.5; Fats: 8.8g; Protein: 22.6g; Carbs: 12.9g; Fiber: 0.9g; Sugar: 2.5g

121.   Grilled Red Snapper

Preparation Time: 10 minutes   **Cooking Time: 1 hour and 15 minutes**
Servings: 4

Ingredients:

- 4 fillets of red snapper, large
- 1 lime, juiced, zested, sliced
- 2 medium onions, thinly sliced

For the Baste:

- 1 teaspoon minced garlic
- 3 teaspoon chopped cilantro
- 1 teaspoon ground black pepper
- 1 teaspoon ancho chili powder
- ½ teaspoon lime zest
- 1 teaspoon salt
- ½ teaspoon cumin
- 1/3 cup olive oil
- ¼ cup ponzu sauce

Directions: Open the hopper of the smoker, add dry pallets, put ash-can in place, then open the ash damper, power on the smoker and close the ash damper.

Prepare the smoker to 350 degrees F, switch smoker to open flame cooking mode, press the open flame 3, remove the grill grates and the batch, replace batch with direct flame insert, then return grates on the grill in the lower position and let preheat for 30 minutes. For the baste: mix all its ingredients in a bowl.

Take a heatproof cooking basket, then breakfast onion slices and line them on the bottom of the basket along with lime slices.

Brush both sides of fillets with the baste mixture, put them in the basket, then the basket on the smoker grill, shut with lid and smoke for 30 to 45 minutes, brushing with the baste every 15 minutes. Serve straight away.

Nutrition: Calories: 310.9; Fats: 8.5g; Protein: 45.2g; Carbs: 10.8g; Fiber: 2.8g; Sugar: 1.2g

122.   Shrimp Scampi

Preparation time: 10 minutes   **Cooking time: 45 minutes**
Servings: 4

Ingredients:

- 1 pound shrimp, peeled, deveined
- 1/2 teaspoon salt
- 1/2 teaspoon garlic powder
- 1 tablespoon lemon juice
- 1/2 cup butter, salted, melted
- 1/4 cup dry white wine
- 1/2 teaspoon minced garlic

Directions: Open the hopper of the smoker, add dry pallets, put ash-can in place, then open the ash damper, power on the smoker and close the ash damper.

Preheat the smoker to 400 degrees F, switch smoker to open flame cooking mode, press the open flame 3, remove the grill grates and the batch, replace batch with direct flame insert, then return grates on the grill in the lower position and let preheat for 30 minutes or until the green light on the dial blinks that indicate smoker has reached to set temperature. Mix together minced garlic, wine, lemon juice, and melted butter until combined, then pour the mixture into a cast iron pan, place it over medium heat and cook for 3 to 4 minutes or until heated through; remove the pan from heat.

Season shrimps with salt and garlic powder, then place them carefully in the pan, place it on the smoker grill, shut with lid and smoke shrimps for 10 minutes or until pink. Serve straight away.

Nutrition: Calories: 137.4; Fats: 8.2g; Protein: 13.9g; Carbs: 1.1g; Fiber: 0.1g; Sugar: 0.2g

123.   Jerk Shrimp

Preparation Time: 15 minutes
Servings: 12

Cooking Time: 6 minutes

Ingredients:

- 2 pounds shrimp, peeled, deveined
- 3 tablespoons olive oil

For the Spice Mix:

- 1 teaspoon garlic powder
- 1 teaspoon of sea salt
- ¼ teaspoon ground cayenne
- 1 tablespoon brown sugar
- 1/8 teaspoon smoked paprika
- 1 tablespoon smoked paprika
- ¼ teaspoon ground thyme
- 1 lime, zested

Directions: Switch on the Traeger grill, fill the grill hopper with flavored wood pellets, power the grill on by using the control panel, select 'smoke' on the temperature dial, or set the temperature to 450 degrees F and let it preheat for a minimum of 5 minutes.
For the spice mix, put all its ingredients in a small bowl and mix.
In a large bowl, place shrimps in it, sprinkle with prepared spice mix, drizzle with oil and toss until well coated.
Open the lid, put shrimps on the grill grate, shut the grill and smoke for 3 minutes per side.
Transfer shrimps to a dish and then serve.

Nutrition: Calories: 130.9; Fats: 4.1g; Carbs: 0g; Protein: 22.3g

124.   Lobster Tails

Preparation Time: 10 minutes
Servings: 4

Cooking Time: 35 minutes

Ingredients:

- 2 lobster tails, each about 10 ounces

For the Sauce:

- 2 tablespoons chopped parsley
- ¼ teaspoon garlic salt
- 1 teaspoon paprika
- ¼ teaspoon ground black pepper
- ¼ teaspoon old bay seasoning
- 8 tablespoons butter, unsalted
- 2 tablespoons lemon juice

Directions: Fill the grill hopper with flavored wood pellets, power the grill on by using the control panel, select 'smoke' on the temperature dial, or set the temperature to 450 degrees F and let it preheat for a minimum of 15 minutes.
For the sauce: in a small saucepan, put it over medium-low heat, add butter in it and when it melts, add the remaining ingredients for the sauce and mix, set aside until required.
For the lobster: cut the shell from the middle to the tail by using kitchen shears and then take the meat from the shell, keeping it attached at the base of the crab tail.
Then butterfly the crab meat by making a slit down the middle, then place lobster tails on a baking sheet and pour 1 tablespoon of sauce over each lobster tail, reserve the remaining sauce.
When the grill has preheated, put crab tails on the grill grate, shut the grill and smoke for 30 minutes until opaque.
Done, transfer lobster tails to a dish and then serve with the remaining sauce.

Nutrition: Calories: 289.9; Fats: 21.9g; Carbs: 0.9g; Protein: 20.3g

125.   Halibut in Parchment

Preparation Time: 15 minutes
Servings: 4

Cooking Time: 15 minutes

Ingredients:

- 16 asparagus spears, trimmed, sliced into 1/2-inch pieces
- 2 ears of corn kernels
- 4 ounces halibut fillets, pin bones removed
- 2 lemons, cut into 12 slices
- Salt as needed
- Ground black pepper as needed
- 2 tablespoons olive oil
- 2 tablespoons chopped parsley

Directions: Switch on the Traeger grill, fill the grill hopper with flavored wood pellets, power the grill on by using the control panel, select 'smoke' on the temperature dial, or set the temperature to 450 degrees F and let it preheat for a minimum of 5 minutes.

Cut out 18-inch long parchment paper, put a fillet in the center of each parchment, season with salt and black pepper, and then drizzle with oil.

Cover each fillet with three lemon slices, overlapping slightly, sprinkle one-fourth of asparagus and corn on each fillet, season with some salt and black pepper, and seal the fillets and vegetables tightly to prevent steam from escaping the packet. When the grill has preheated, put fillet packets on the grill grate, shut the grill and smoke for 15 minutes until packets have turned slightly brown and puffed up.

Transfer packets to a dish, let them stand for 5 minutes, then cut 'X' in the center of each packet, carefully uncover the fillets and vegetables, sprinkle with parsley, and then serve.

Nutrition: Calories: 186.3; Fats: 2.5g; Carbs: 13.9g; Protein: 25.9g

126.   Sriracha Salmon

Preparation Time: 2 hours and 10 minutes   **Cooking Time: 25 minutes**
Servings: 4

Ingredients:
- *3-pound salmon, skin on*

For the Marinade:

- *1 teaspoon lime zest*
- *1 tablespoon minced garlic*
- *1 tablespoon grated ginger*
- *Sea salt as needed*
- *Ground black pepper as needed*
- *¼ cup maple syrup*
- *2 tablespoons soy sauce*
- *2 tablespoons Sriracha sauce*
- *1 tablespoon toasted sesame oil*
- *1 tablespoon rice vinegar*
- *1 teaspoon toasted sesame seeds*

Directions: For the marinade: take a small bowl and put all of its ingredients in it, mix well and then, pour the mixture into a large plastic bag.

Put salmon in the bag, seal it, turn it upside down to coat salmon with the marinade and let it marinate for 2 hours in the refrigerator.

Switch on the Traeger grill, fill the grill hopper with flavored wood pellets, power the grill on by using the control panel, select 'smoke' on the temperature dial, or set the temperature to 450 degrees F and let it preheat for a minimum of 5 minutes.

Take a large baking sheet, line it with parchment paper, put salmon on it skin-side down and then brush with the marinade.

Put a baking sheet containing salmon on the grill grate, shut the grill and smoke for 25 minutes until thoroughly cooked. Transfer salmon to a dish and then serve.

Nutrition: Calories: 359.8; Fats: 20.9g; Carbs: 27.9g; Protein: 16.2g

127.   Cider Salmon

Preparation Time: 9 hours   **Cooking Time: 1 hour**
Servings: 4

Ingredients:
- *1 ½ pound salmon fillet, skin-on, center-cut, pin bone removed*

For the Brine:

- *4 juniper berries, crushed*
- *1 bay leaf, crumbled*
- *1 piece star anise, broken*
- *1 ½ cups apple cider*

For the Cure:

- *½ cup salt*
- *1 teaspoon ground black pepper*
- *¼ cup brown sugar*
- *2 teaspoons barbecue rub*

Directions: For the brine: take a large container and add all of its ingredients in it, mix and then, add salmon and let soak for a minimum of 8 hours in the refrigerator.

For the cure: take a small bowl, put all of its ingredients in it and stir until combined.

After 8 hours, remove salmon from the brine, then take a baking dish, place half of the cure in it, top with salmon skin-side down, sprinkle the remaining cure on top, cover with plastic wrap and let it rest for 1 hour in the refrigerator.

Switch on the Traeger grill, fill the grill hopper with oak flavored wood pellets, power the grill on by using the control panel, select 'smoke' on the temperature dial, or set the temperature to 200 degrees F and let it preheat for a minimum of 5 minutes.

Remove salmon from the cure, pat dry with paper towels, and then sprinkle with black pepper.

When the grill has preheated, put salmon on the grill grate, shut the grill, and smoke for 1 hour until the internal temperature reaches 150 degrees F.

Transfer salmon to a cutting board, let it rest for 5 minutes, then remove the skin and serve.

Nutrition: Calories: 232.9; Fats: 13.9g; Carbs: 0g; Protein: 25.3g

128.   Grilled Lobster Tail

Preparation Time: 10 minutes   **Cooking Time: 15 minutes**
Servings: 4

Ingredients:

- 2 (8 ounces each) lobster tails
- 1/4 teaspoon old bay seasoning
- ½ teaspoon oregano
- 1 teaspoon paprika
- Juice from one lemon
- 1/4 teaspoon Himalayan salt
- 1/4 teaspoon freshly ground black pepper
- 1/4 teaspoon onion powder
- 2 tablespoons freshly chopped parsley
- ¼ cup melted butter

Directions: Slice the tail in the middle with a kitchen shear. Pull the shell apart slightly and run your hand through the meat to separate the meat partially, keeping it attached to the base of the tail partially.

Mix the old bay seasoning, , salt, paprika, oregano, pepper and onion powder in a mixing bowl.

Drizzle lobster tail with lemon juice and season generously with the seasoning mixture.

Prepare the wood pellet smoker to 450°F, using apple wood pellets.

Put the lobster tail directly on the grill grate, meat side down. Cook for about 15 minutes.

Remove the tail from the grill and let them rest for a few minutes to cool.

Drizzle melted butter over the tails.

Serve and garnish with fresh chopped parsley.

Nutrition: Calories: 145.8; Fats: 11.4g; Carbs: 1.9g; Protein 9.5g

129.   Grilled Salmon

Preparation Time: 10 minutes   **Cooking Time: 30 minutes**
Servings: 6

Ingredients:

- 2 pounds salmon (cut into fillets)
- 1/2 cup low sodium soy sauce
- 2 garlic cloves (grated)
- 4 tablespoons olive oil
- 2 tablespoons honey
- 1 teaspoon ground black pepper
- ½ teaspoon smoked paprika
- ½ teaspoon Italian seasoning

Garnish:

- 2 tablespoons chopped green onion

Directions: In a huge container, mix the honey, paprika, pepper, soy sauce, Italian seasoning, garlic and olive oil. Put the salmon fillets and toss to combine. Cover the bowl and refrigerate for 1 hour.

Remove the fillets from the marinade and let it sit for about 2 hours.

Start the wood pellet on smoke, leaving the lid open for 5 minutes.

Cover and preheat the grill to 350°F for 15 minutes.

Grease the grill grate with oil and arrange the fillets on the grill grate, skin side up. Close the grill lid and cook for 4 minutes. Flip the fillets and cook for additional 25 minutes or until the fish is flaky.

Remove the fillets from heat and let it sit for a few minutes.

Serve warm and garnish with chopped green onion.

Nutrition: Calories: 316.9; Fats: 18.5g; Carbs: 8.1g; Protein: 30.9g

130. Grilled Tuna

Preparation Time: 5 minutes   **Cooking Time: 4 minutes**
Servings: 4

Ingredients:

- 4 (6 ounce each) tuna steaks (1 inch thick)
- 1 lemon (juiced)
- 1 clove garlic (minced)
- 1 teaspoon chili
- 2 tablespoons extra virgin olive oil
- 1 cup white wine
- 3 tablespoons brown sugar
- 1 teaspoon rosemary

Directions: Take a huge container, mix the chili, white wine, lemon, rosemary, garlic, sugar and olive oil. Add the tuna steaks and toss to combine.
Transfer the tuna and marinade to a zip lock bag. Refrigerate for 3 hours.
Remove the tuna steaks from the marinade and let them rest for about 1 hour.
Start the grill on smoke, leaving the lid opened for 5 minutes. Use hickory or mesquite wood pellet.
Cover the grill lid and preheat the grill on HIGH for 15 minutes.
Grease the grill grate with oil and put the tuna on the grill grate. Grill tuna steaks for 2 minutes per side.
Remove the tuna from the grill and let them rest for a few minutes. Serve and enjoy.

Nutrition: Calories: 454.9; Fats: 17.5g; Carbs: 9.8g; Protein: 51.5g

131. Grilled King Crab Legs

Preparation Time: 10 minutes   **Cooking Time: 25 minutes**
Servings: 4

Ingredients:

- 4 pounds king crab legs (split)
- 4 tablespoons lemon juice
- 2 tablespoons garlic powder
- 1 cup butter (melted)
- 2 teaspoons brown sugar
- 2 teaspoons paprika
- 2 teaspoons powdered black pepper for taste

Directions: Take a mixing bowl, mix the lemon juice, sugar, butter, garlic, paprika and pepper.
Arrange the split crab on a baking sheet, split side up.
Pour ¾ of the butter mixture over the crab legs.
Prepare pellet grill for indirect cooking and preheat it to 225°F, using mesquite wood pellets.
Arrange the crab legs onto the grill grate, shell side down.
Cover the grill and cook for 25 minutes. Remove the crab legs from the grill.
Serve and top with the remaining butter mixture.

Nutrition: Calories: 893.8; Fats: 52.9g; Carbs: 5.8g; Protein: 88.9g

132. Smoked Sardines

Preparation Time: 12 hours   **Cooking Time: 5 hours**
Servings: 5

Ingredients:

- 20 to 30 fresh gutted sardines
- 4 Cups of water
- ¼ Cup of Kosher salt
- ¼ Cup of honey
- 4 to 5 Bay leaves
- 1 Chopped or finely grated onion
- 2 Smashed garlic cloves
- ½ Cup of chopped parsley or cilantro
- 3 to 4 crushed dried or hot chilies
- 2 Tablespoons of cracked black peppercorns

Directions: Start by gutting and washing the sardines, then remove the backbone and the ribs.
Make a brine, place all the ingredients above except for the sardines in a pot; then bring the mixture to a boil and turn off the heat afterward.
Mix ingredients to combine; then cover and let come to the room temperature.
When the brine is perfectly cool, submerge the sardines in a large, covered, non-reactive container.
Let the sardines soak in the refrigerator for about 12 hours or for overnight.
Take the sardines out of the brine; then rinse under the cold water quickly and pat dry.

Let dry over a rack in a cool place for about 30 to 60 minutes.
Be sure to turn the fish over once; then once the sardines look dry to you; put them in a smoker as far away from the heat as possible. Smoke the sardines for about 5 hours over almond wood.

Nutrition: Calories: 179.9; Fats: 9.8g; Carbs: 0g; Protein: 13.2g

133.   Spicy Smoked Shrimp

Preparation Time: 10 minutes
Servings: 4

Cooking Time: 30 minutes

Ingredients:

- 2 pounds of peeled and deveined shrimp
- 6 ounces of Thai chilies
- 6 Garlic cloves
- 2 Tablespoons of chicken rub of your choice
- 1 and ½ teaspoons of sugar
- 1 and ½ tablespoons of white vinegar
- 3 Tablespoons of olive oil

Directions: Put all ingredients besides the shrimp in a blender, then blend until you get a paste.
Put the shrimp in a shallow container; then add in the chili garlic mixture; then put in the refrigerator and let marinate for about 30 minutes
Remove from the fridge and thread the shrimp on metal or bamboo skewers for about 30 minutes
Preheat the Wood pellet smoker to about 225° F.
Put the shrimp on a grill and cook for about 3 minutes per side or until the shrimp are pink

Nutrition: Calories: 205.8; Fats: 9.9g; Carbs: 9.9g; Protein: 16.2g

134.   Smoked Crab Legs

Preparation Time: 5 minutes
Servings: 5

Cooking Time: 15 minutes

Ingredients:

- 1 Pinch of black pepper
- ¾ Stick of butter to the room temperature
- 2 Tablespoons of chopped chives
- 1 Minced garlic clove
- 1 Sliced lemon
- 3 Lobster, tail, about 7 ounces
- 1 Pinch of kosher salt

Directions: Prepare the Wood Pellet Grill on smoke with the lid open for about 3 to 7 minutes
Preheat to about 350°F, then blend the butter, chives, minced garlic and black pepper in a bowl.
Sealed it with a plastic wrapper and set aside
Blend the butter, the minced garlic, the chives, and the black pepper in a bowl; then cover with a plastic wrap and set it aside.
Butterfly the lobster tails into the middle of the soft part of the underside of the shell and don't cut completely through the center of the meat. Rub some olive oil and season it with one pinch of salt
Smoke Grill the lobsters with the cut side down for about 5 minutes
Flip the tails and top with one tablespoon of herbed butter; then grill for an additional 4 minutes
Remove from the smoker grill and serve with more quantity of herb butter
Top with lemon wedges; then serve and enjoy your dish.

Nutrition: Calories: 89.9; Fats: 0.9g ; Carbs: 0g ; Protein: 20.3g

135.   Garlic Salmon

Preparation Time: 10 minutes
Servings: 4

Cooking Time: 55 minutes

Ingredients:

- 3 pounds salmon fillets, skin on
- 2 tablespoons minced garlic
- 1/2 tablespoons minced parsley
- 4 tablespoons seafood seasoning
- 1/4 cup olive oil

Directions: Open the hopper of the smoker, add dry pallets, put ash-can in place, then open the ash damper, power on the smoker and close the ash damper.

Prepare the smoker to 450 degrees F, switch smoker to open flame cooking mode, press the open flame 3, remove the grill grates and the batch, replace batch with direct flame insert, then return grates on the grill in the lower position and let preheat for 30 minutes or until the green light on the dial blinks that indicate smoker has reached to set temperature.

Take a baking sheet, line it with a parchment sheet and place salmon on it, skin-side down, and then season salmon with seafood seasoning on both sides.

Mix the garlic, parsley, and oil until combined and then brush this mixture on the salmon fillets.

Put a baking sheet containing salmon fillets on the smoker grill, shut it with lid and smoke for 25 minutes or until the internal temperature of salmon reach to 140 degrees F.

Transfer salmon fillets to a dish, brush with more garlic-oil mixture and serve with lemon wedges.

Nutrition: Calories: 129.9; Fats: 5.9g; Protein: 13.2g; Carbs: 5.9g

Lamb Recipes

136.   Grilled Aussie Leg of Lamb

Preparation Time: 30 minutes   **Cooking Time: 2 hours**
Servings: 8

Ingredients:

- 5 lb. Aussie Boneless Leg of lamb

Smoked Paprika Rub:

- 1 tablespoon raw sugar
- 1 tablespoon salt
- 1 tablespoon black pepper
- 1 tablespoon smoked paprika
- 1 tablespoon garlic powder
- 1 tablespoon rosemary
- 1 tablespoon onion powder
- 1 tablespoon cumin
- ½ tablespoon cayenne pepper

Roasted Carrots:

- 1 bunch rainbow carrots
- Olive oil
- Salt and pepper

Directions: Prepare the oven to 350°F and trim any excess fat from the meat.
Combine the paprika rub ingredients and generously rub all over the meat.
Place the lamb on the preheated smoker over indirect heat and smoke for 2 hours.
Meanwhile, toss the carrots in oil, salt and pepper.
Add the carrots to the grill after 1 ½ hour or until the internal temperature has reached 900°F.
Cook until the meat's internal temperature reaches 135°F.
Remove the lamb from the smoker and cover it with foil for 30 minutes.
Once the carrots are cooked, serve with the meat and enjoy.

Nutrition: Calories: 256.8; Fats: 7.9g; Carbs: 5.9g; Protein: 37.2g; Sugars: 2.9g; Fiber: 0.9g

137.   Smoked Lamb Shoulder

Preparation Time: 30 minutes   **Cooking Time: 3 hours**
Servings: 7

Ingredients:

- 5 lb. lamb shoulder
- 1 cup cider vinegar
- 2 tablespoons oil
- 2 tablespoons kosher salt
- 2 tablespoons black pepper, freshly ground
- 1 tablespoon dried rosemary

For the Spritz:

- 1 cup apple cider vinegar
- 1 cup apple juice

Directions: Preheat the two at 225°F with a pan of water for moisture.
Trim some of the lamb's excess fat and rinse the meat in cold water. Pat with a paper towel to rinse.
Inject the cider vinegar in the meat, and then pat dry with a clean paper towel.
Rub the meat with oil, salt, black pepper and dried rosemary. Tie the lamb shoulder with a twine.
Put in the smoker for an hour, then spritz after every 15 minutes until the internal temperature reaches 165F.
Remove from the smoker and let rest for 1 hour before shredding and serving.

Nutrition: Calories: 471.9; Fats: 36.9g; Carbs: 2.9g; Protein: 31.2g; Sugars: 0g; Fiber: 0g

138.   Leg of a Lamb

Preparation Time: 30 minutes   **Cooking Time: 2 hours and 30 minutes**
Servings: 10

Ingredients:

- 1 (8-ounce) package softened cream cheese
- ¼ cup cooked and crumbled bacon
- 1 seeded and chopped jalapeno pepper
- 1 tablespoon crushed dried rosemary
- 2 teaspoons garlic powder
- 1 teaspoon onion powder
- 1 teaspoon paprika
- 1 teaspoon cayenne pepper
- Salt, to taste

- *1 (4-5-pound) butterflied leg of lamb*
- *2-3 tablespoons olive oil*

Directions: For filling in a bowl, add all ingredients and mix till well combined.

For spice mixture in another small bowl, mix together all ingredients.

Place the leg of lamb onto a smooth surface. Sprinkle the inside of the leg with some spice mixture.

Place filling mixture over the inside surface evenly. Roll the leg of lamb tightly and with a butcher's twine, tie the roll to secure the filling. Coat the outer side of the roll with olive oil evenly and then sprinkle with spice mixture. Preheat the pallet grill to 225-240°F.

Arrange the leg of lamb in the pallet grill and cook for about 2-2½ hours. Remove the leg of lamb from the pallet grill and transfer it onto a cutting board.

Cover the leg loosely with a piece of foil and transfer onto a cutting board for about 20-25 minutes before slicing. With a sharp knife, cut the leg of lamb in desired sized slices and serve.

Nutrition: Calories: 714.9; Fats: 38.5g; Carbs: 2.1g; Protein: 84.8g; Fiber: 0.1g

139. Spicy Lamb Shoulder

Preparation Time: 30 minutes **Cooking Time: 5¾ hours**
Servings: 6

Ingredients:

- *1 (5-lb.) bone-in lamb shoulder, trimmed*
- *3-4 tablespoons Moroccan seasoning*
- *2 tablespoon olive oil*
- *1 cup water*
- *¼ cup apple cider vinegar*

Directions: Set the temperature of the grill to 275°F and preheat with a closed lid for 15 minutes, using charcoal.

Coat the lamb shoulder with oil evenly and then rub with Moroccan seasoning generously.

Put the lamb shoulder onto the grill and cook for about 45 minutes.

In a food-safe spray bottle, mix together vinegar and water. Spray the lamb shoulder with vinegar mixture evenly.

Cook for about 4-5 hours, spraying with vinegar mixture after every 20 minutes.

Remove the lamb shoulder from the grill and place onto a cutting board for about 20 minutes before slicing.

With a sharp knife, cut the lamb shoulder in desired sized slices and serve.

Nutrition: Calories: 562.9; Carbs: 2.9g; Protein: 77.6g; Fats: 25.1g; Sugar: 1.2g; Fiber: 0g

140. Smoked Rack of Lamb

Preparation Time: 30 minutes **Cooking Time: 1 hour and 15 minutes**
Servings: 4

Ingredients:

- *1 rack of lamb rib, membrane removed*

For the Marinade:

- *1 lemon, juiced*
- *2 teaspoons minced garlic*
- *1 teaspoon salt*
- *1 teaspoon ground black pepper*
- *1 teaspoon dried thyme*
- *¼ cup balsamic vinegar*
- *1 teaspoon dried basil*

For the Glaze:

- *2 tablespoons soy sauce*
- *¼ cup Dijon mustard*
- *2 tablespoons Worcestershire sauce*
- *¼ cup red wine*

Directions: Prepare the marinade and for this, take a small bowl, place all the ingredients in it and whisk until combined.

Place the rack of lamb into a large plastic bag, pour in marinade, seal it, turn it upside down to coat lamb with the marinade and let it marinate for a minimum of 8 hours in the refrigerator.

Switch on the grill, fill the grill hopper with flavored wood pellets, power the grill on by using the control panel, select 'smoke' on the temperature dial, or set the temperature to 300°F and let it preheat for a minimum of 5 minutes.

Prepare the glaze and take a small bowl, place all of its ingredients in it and whisk until combined.

Open the lid, place the lamb rack on the grill grate, shut the grill and smoke for 15 minutes. Brush with glaze, flip the lamb and then continue smoking for 1 hour and 15 minutes until the internal temperature reaches 145°F, basting with the glaze every 30 minutes.

When done, transfer lamb rack to a cutting board, let it rest for 15 minutes, cut it into slices, and then serve.

Nutrition: Calories: 322.8; Fats: 17.9g; Carbs: 12.8g; Protein: 25.3g; Fiber: 0.9g

141.   **Wine Braised Lamb Shank**

Preparation Time: 30 minutes   **Cooking Time: 10 hours**
Servings: 2

Ingredients:
- 2 (1¼-lb.) lamb shanks
- 1-2 cups water
- ¼ cup brown sugar
- ⅓ cup rice wine
- ⅓ cup soy sauce
- 1 tablespoon dark sesame oil
- 4 (1½x½-inch) orange zest strips
- 2 (3-inch long) cinnamon sticks
- 1½ teaspoon Chinese five-spice powder

Directions: Set the grill's temperature to 225-250°F and preheat with a closed lid for 15 minutes, using charcoal and soaked Applewood chips. With a sharp knife, pierce each lamb shank at many places.
Take a bowl and add all remaining ingredients and mix until sugar is dissolved.
In a large foil pan, evenly place the lamb shanks and top with sugar mixture.
Put the foil pan onto the grill and cook for about 8-10 hours, flipping after every 30 minutes.
Remove from the grill and serve hot.

Nutrition: Calories: 1199.9; Carbs: 39.5g; Protein: 162.2g; Fats: 48.1g; Sugar: 28.9g; Fiber: 0.2g

142.   **Leg of Lamb with Salsa**

Preparation Time: 30 minutes   **Cooking Time: 1 hour and 30 minutes**
Servings: 6

Ingredients:
- 6 cloves of garlic, peeled and sliced
- 1 leg of lamb
- Salt and pepper to taste
- 2 tablespoons fresh rosemary, chopped
- Olive oil
- 3 cups salsa

Directions: Set the wood pellet grill to high. Preheat for 15 minutes while the lid is closed.
Make slits all over the lamb leg. Insert the garlic slices.
Drizzle with oil and rub with salt, pepper and rosemary.
Marinate for 30 minutes. Set the temperature to 350°F.
Cook lamb leg for 1 hour and 30 minutes. Serve with salsa.

Nutrition: Calories: 565.8; Fats: 40.9g; Carbs: 3.8g; Protein: 44.2g; Sugar: 2.8g; Fiber: 0g

143.   **Roasted Leg of Lamb**

Preparation Time: 30 minutes   **Cooking Time: 2 hours**
Servings: 12

Ingredients:
- 8 pounds leg of lamb, bone-in, fat trimmed
- 2 lemons, juiced, zested
- 1 tablespoon minced garlic
- Sprigs of rosemary, 1-inch diced
- 4 cloves of garlic, peeled, sliced lengthwise
- Ground black pepper and salt
- 2 teaspoons olive oil

Directions: Switch on the Pellet grill, fill the grill hopper with cherry flavored wood pellets, power the grill on by using the control panel, select smoke on the temperature dial, or set the temperature to 450°F and let it preheat for a minimum of 15 minutes.
Meanwhile, take a small bowl, place minced garlic in it, stir in oil and then rub this mixture on all sides of the lamb leg.
Then make ¾-inch deep cuts into the lamb meat, about two dozen, stuff each cut with garlic slices and rosemary, sprinkle with lemon zest, drizzle with lemon juice, and then season well with salt and black pepper.
Open the lid, place the lamb's leg on the grill grate, shut the grill, and smoke for 30 minutes.

Change the smoking temperature to 350° F and then continue smoking for 1 hour and 30 minutes.
When done, transfer lamb to a cutting board, let it rest for 15 minutes, then cut it into slices and serve.

Nutrition: Calories: 389.9; Fats: 34.9g; Carbs: 0g; Protein: 17.2g; Sugar: 0g; Fiber: 0g

144.   Rosemary Lamb

Preparation Time: 10 minutes   **Cooking Time: 3 hours**
Servings: 2

Ingredients:

- 1 rack of lamb rib, membrane removed
- 12 baby potatoes
- 1 bunch of asparagus, ends trimmed
- Ground black pepper, as needed
- Salt, as needed
- 1 teaspoon dried rosemary
- 2 tablespoons olive oil
- ½ cup butter, unsalted

Directions: Switch on the Pellet grill, fill the grill hopper with flavored wood pellets, power the grill on by using the control panel, select smoke on the temperature dial, or set the temperature to 225 degrees F and let it preheat for a minimum of 5 minutes. Meanwhile, drizzle oil on both sides of lamb ribs and then sprinkle with rosemary. Take a deep baking dish, place potatoes in it, add butter and mix until coated.
When the grill has preheated, open the lid, put lamb ribs on the grill grate along with potatoes in the baking dish, shut the grill, and smoke for 3 hours until the internal temperature reaches 145°F.
Add asparagus into the baking dish in the last 20 minutes and, when done, remove the baking dish from the grill and transfer lamb to a cutting board.
Let lamb rest for 15 minutes, cut it into slices, and then serve with potatoes and asparagus.

Nutrition: Calories: 389.8; Fats: 34.8g; Carbs: 0g; Protein: 17.2g; Sugar: 0g; Fiber: 0g

145.   Middle Eastern Lamb Stew

Preparation Time: 10 minutes   **Cooking Time: 20 minutes**
Servings: 4

Ingredients:

- 2 tablespoons olive oil
- 1½ lb. lamb stew meat, sliced into cubes
- 1 onion, diced
- 6 garlic cloves, chopped
- 1 teaspoon cumin
- 1 teaspoon coriander
- 1 teaspoon turmeric
- 1 teaspoon cinnamon
- Salt and pepper to taste
- 2 tablespoons tomato paste
- ¼ cup red wine vinegar
- 1¼ cups chicken broth
- 15 oz. chickpeas, rinsed and drained
- ¼ cup raisins

Directions: Add the oil. Cook the onion for 3 minutes.
Add the lamb and seasonings. Cook for 5 minutes, stirring frequently.
Stir in the rest of the ingredients. Cover the pot. Set it to Pressure.
Cook on high pressure for 50 minutes. Release the pressure naturally.

Nutrition: Calories: 866.9; Fats: 26.5g; Carbs: 87.1g; Fiber: 20.1g; Sugars: 27.5g; Protein: 71.4g

146.   Bacon Potato Salad

Preparation Time: 20 minutes   **Cooking Time: 70 minutes**
Servings: 5-6

Ingredients:

- 6 slices smoked bacon, chopped
- 2 red onions, sliced
- 6 red potatoes, peeled and quartered
- ½ cup of water
- teaspoon flat-leaf parsley, chopped
- teaspoons mustard
- ½ cup apple cider vinegar
- tablespoons honey
- teaspoon salt
- 3 teaspoon black pepper

Directions: Preheat the griller for 3-5 minutes.
In the pot, add the bacon and cook until crispy on both sides for 3-4 minutes. Set aside.
In a mixing bowl (medium-large size), combine honey, salt, mustard, vinegar, water, and black pepper.

In the pot, combine the potatoes, chopped bacon, honey mixture, and onions; stir the mixture.
Close the top by placing the pressing lid. Do not forget to set the temperature valve in a locked or sealed position. Adjust cooking time to 6 minutes.
After cooking time is over, allow the build-up pressure to get released for around 10 minutes in a natural manner. Divide into serving plates or bowls; serve warm with some parsley on top.

Nutrition: Calories: 412.8; Fats: 16.8g; Carbs: 46.8g; Fiber: 3.9g; Protein: 13.2g

147.   Filet Mignon with Pineapple Salsa

Preparation Time: 15 minutes   **Cooking Time: 8 minutes**
Servings: 4

Ingredients:

- 4 (6- to 8-ounce) filet mignon steaks
- 1 tablespoon canola oil, divided
- Sea salt
- Freshly ground black pepper
- ½ medium pineapple, cored and diced
- 1 medium red onion, diced
- 1 jalapeño pepper, seeded, stemmed, and diced
- 1 tablespoon freshly squeezed lime juice
- ¼ cup chopped fresh cilantro leaves
- Chili powder
- Ground coriander

Directions: Rub each filet on all sides with ½ tablespoon of the oil, then season with the salt and pepper.
Insert and close the hood with the Grill Grate. For 8 minutes, pre-heat the griller.
Attach the filets to the Grill Grate when the device beeps to signal that it has preheated. To maximize grill marks, gently push the filets down, then close the cover.
After 4 minutes, open the hood and flip the filets. Close the hood and continue cooking for an additional 4 minutes, or until the filets' internal temperature reads 125°F on a food thermometer. Remove the filets from the grill; they will continue to cook (called carry-over cooking) to a food-safe temperature even after removing them from the grill.
Let the filets rest for 10 minutes; this allows the natural juices to redistribute into the steak.

Nutrition: Calories: 570.8; Fats: 24.8g; Carbs: 19.8g; Fiber: 2.8g; Protein: 65.2g

148.   Glazed Lamb Chops

Preparation Time: 10 minutes   **Cooking Time: 15 minutes**
Servings: 4

Ingredients:

- 1 tablespoon Dijon mustard
- ½ tablespoon fresh lime juice
- 1 teaspoon honey
- ½ teaspoon olive oil
- Salt and ground black pepper, as required
- 4 (4-ounce) lamb loin chops

Direction: In a large black pepper bowl, mix the mustard, lemon juice, oil, honey, salt, and black pepper.
Add the chops and coat with the mixture generously.
Place the chops onto the greased "Sheet Pan".
Press your griller's "Power Button" and turn the dial to select the "Air Bake" mode.
Press the Time button and again turn the dial to set the cooking time to 15 minutes.
Now push the Temp button and rotate the dial to set the temperature at 390 degrees F.
Press the "Start /Pause" button to start. Open the lid when the unit beeps to show that it is preheated.
Insert the "Sheet Pan" in the oven.
Flip the chops once halfway through. Serve hot.

Nutrition: Calories: 223.8; Fats: 8.9g; Carbs: 1.5g; Fiber: 0.1g; Sugar: 1.3g; Protein: 32.1g

149.   Herbed Lamb Chops

Preparation Time: 5-10 minutes   **Cooking Time: 13 minutes**
Servings: 6

Ingredients:

- 3 pounds lamb chops
- 3 tablespoons olive oil
- 3 basil leaves, crushed
- 2 teaspoons dried oregano, crushed
- Salt and ground black pepper to taste
- 1 clove garlic, minced
- 1 bay leaf
- 1 fresh rosemary spring
- 1 cup chicken broth

Directions: In a mixing bowl, mix the oregano, salt, and black pepper. Rub the lamb chops with the herb mixture. Arrange it over a cooking platform and open the top lid.

In the pot, add the butter and sauté. Grill and for after about 4-5 minutes, the butter will melt.

Add the basil, rosemary, garlic, and bay leaf and cook for about 1 minute. Attach the lamb chops and cook on each side for approximately 4 minutes.

Seal the multi-cooker by locking it with the pressure lid; ensure to keep the pressure release valve locked /sealed. Set the pressure level of the griller to high. Then, set the timer to 5 minutes; it will start the cooking process by building up inside pressure.

Rapid release pressure when the timer goes off, by adjusting the pressure valve to the VENT. After pressure gets released, open the pressure lid. Serve warm.

Nutrition: Calories: 482.8; Fats: 24.1g; Carbs: 1.9g; Fiber: 0.4g; Protein: 11.2g

150.   Braised Leg of Lamb

Preparation Time: 15 minutes
Servings: 10

Cooking Time: 37 minutes

Ingredients:

- 1 (4-pound) bone-in leg of lamb
- Salt and ground black pepper, as required
- 1 tablespoon olive oil
- 1 large yellow onion, sliced thinly
- 1½ cups chicken broth, divided
- 2 tablespoons fresh lemon juice
- 6 garlic cloves, crushed
- 6 fresh thyme sprigs
- 3 fresh rosemary sprigs

Directions: Season the leg of lamb with salt and black pepper generously

Select the "Sauté/Sear" setting of Ninja Foodi and place the butter into the pot.

Press "Start/Stop" to begin cooking and heat for about 2-3 minutes.

Add the leg of lamb and sear for about 4 minutes per side. Transfer the leg of the lamb onto a large plate.

Add the onion and a little salt in the pot and cook for about 3 minutes.

Add a little broth and cook for about 2 minutes, scraping the brown bits from the bottom.

Press "Start/Stop" to stop cooking and stir in the cooked leg of lamb and remaining ingredients.

Close the Ninja Foodi with the pressure lid and place the pressure valve in the "Seal" position.

Select "Pressure" and set it to "High" for 75 minutes.

Press "Start/Stop" to begin cooking. Do a "Natural" release.

Open the lid and with tongs, transfer the leg of lamb onto a cutting board for about 10 minutes.

Strain the pan liquid into a bowl. Cut the leg of lamb into desired sized slices.

Pour strained liquid over the sliced leg of lamb and serve.

Nutrition: Calories: 625.8; Fats: 42.1; Carbs: 2.4g; Fiber: 0.5g; Protein: 54.6g

151.   Crazy Greek Lamb Gyros

Preparation Time: 10 minutes
Servings: 8

Cooking Time: 25 minutes

Ingredients:

- 8 garlic cloves
- 1 and ½ teaspoon salt
- 2 teaspoons dried oregano
- 1 and ½ cups of water
- 2 pounds lamb meat, ground
- 2 teaspoons rosemary
- ½ teaspoon pepper
- 1 small onion, chopped
- 2 teaspoons ground marjoram

Directions: Add onions, garlic, marjoram, rosemary, salt, and pepper to a food processor.

Process until combined well, add round lamb meat, and process again.

Press the meat mixture gently into a loaf pan. Transfer the pan to your Ninja Foodi pot.

Lock the lid and select "Bake/Roast" mode. Bake for 25 minutes at 375 degrees F.

Nutrition: Calories: 241.8; Fats: 14.8g; Carbs: 2.1g ; Protein: 21.3g

152.   Ground Lamb Kebabs

Preparation Time: 1 hour   **Cooking Time: 45 minutes**
Servings: 2-4

The Meat:
- Ground Lamb – 1-1/2 lb.

The Mixture:
- Minced onions – 1/3 cup.
- Minced garlic – ½ cloves.
- Cilantro – 3 tbsp.
- Minced fresh mint – 1 tbsp.
- Ground cumin 1 tsp.
- Paprika – 1 tsp.
- Salt – 1 tsp.
- Ground coriander – ½ tsp.
- Cinnamon – ¼ tsp.
- Pita bread - to serve.

The Fire:
- Wood pellet smoker, cherry wood pellets.

Directions: Take a large mixing bowl and put in all ingredients except pita bread. Now start making meatballs out of the mixture. The meatballs should be about 2 inches in diameter.
Take a bamboo skewer for each of the meatballs. Wet your hands to easily mold the skewered meal. Mold them each into a cigar shape.
Leave it in the refrigerator for 30 minutes at least or preferably overnight. Set your wood pellet smoker on the smoke option and open the fire with the lid. It takes about 4-5 minutes.
Prepare the temperature to 350F and preheat it for about 10-15 minutes. During preheating, keep the lid closed. Put the kebabs on the grill. After 30 minutes turn them over.
Also, if the internal temperature reads 160F, it is time to turn them over. Warm the bread before serving it with kebobs.

153.   Lamb Rack Wrapped In Apple Wood Walnut

Preparation Time: 25 minutes   **Cooking Time: 60 to 90 minutes**
Servings: 4

Ingredients:
- 3 tablespoons of Dijon mustard
- 2 pieces of garlic, chopped or 2 cups of crushed garlic
- ½ teaspoon of garlic
- ½ teaspoon kosher salt
- ½ teaspoon black pepper
- ½ teaspoon rosemary
- 1 (1½ pound) ram rack, French
- 1 cup crushed walnut

Directions: Place mustard, garlic powder, garlic, pepper, salt and rosemary in a small bowl.
Spread the seasoning mix evenly on all sides of the lamb and sprinkle with crushed walnuts. Lightly press the walnuts by hand to attach the nuts to the meat.
Wrap the walnut-coated lamb rack loosely in plastic wrap and refrigerate overnight to allow the seasoning to penetrate the meat.
Remove the walnut-covered lamb rack from the refrigerator and let it rest for 30 minutes to reach room temperature.
Prepare the wood pellet r grill for indirect cooking and preheat to 225 ° F using apple pellets.
Lay the grill directly on the rack with the lamb bone down.
Smoke at 225 ° F until the thickest part of the ram rack reaches the desired internal temperature. This is measured with an instantaneous digital thermometer near the time listed on the chart.
Put the mutton under a loose foil tent for 5 minutes before eating

Nutrition: Calories: 164.8; Carbs: 0g; Fats: 7.9g; Protein: 20.3g

154.   Greek Leg of Lamb

Preparation Time: 15 minutes   **Cooking Time: 25 minutes**
Servings: 6

Ingredients:
- 2 tablespoons finely chopped fresh rosemary
- 1 tablespoon ground thyme
- 5 garlic cloves, minced
- 2 tablespoons sea salt
- 1 tablespoon freshly ground black pepper
- Butcher's string
- 1 whole boneless (6- to 8-pound) leg of lamb
- ¼ cup extra-virgin olive oil
- 1 cup red wine vinegar

73

- *½ cup canola oil*

Directions: Take a container, mix the rosemary, garlic, salt, thyme, and pepper; set aside.

Using butcher's string, tie the leg of lamb into the shape of a roast. Your butcher should also be happy to truss the leg for you.

Rub the lamb with olive oil and season with the spice mixture. Put it to a plate, cover with plastic wrap, and refrigerate for 4 hours.

Remove the lamb from the refrigerator but do not rinse.

Supply your smoker with wood pellets and follow the manufacturer's specific start-up procedure. Preheat, with the lid closed, to 325°F. Take a small bowl, combine the red wine vinegar and canola oil for basting.

Put the lamb directly on the grill, close the lid, and smoke for 20 to 25 minutes per pound (depending on desired doneness), basting with the oil and vinegar mixture every 30 minutes. Lamb is generally served medium-rare to medium, so it will be done when a meat thermometer where inserted in the thickest part reads 140°F to 145°F. Let the lamb meat rest for about 15 minutes before slicing to serve.

Nutrition: Calories: 129.8; Carbs: 1.9g; Fats: 4.9g; Protein: 19.2g

155.   Lamb Chops

Preparation Time: 15 minutes   **Cooking Time: 20 minutes**
Servings: 4

Ingredients:

For The Marinade
- *½ cup rice wine vinegar*
- *1 teaspoon liquid smoke*
- *2 tablespoons extra-virgin olive oil*
- *2 tablespoons dried minced onion*
- *1 tablespoon chopped fresh mint*

For The Lamb Chops
- *8 (4-ounce) lamb chops*
- *½ cup hot pepper jelly*
- *1 tablespoon Sriracha*
- *1 teaspoon salt*
- *1 teaspoon freshly ground black pepper*

Directions: Take a small container, whisk together the rice wine vinegar, olive oil, liquid smoke, minced onion, and mint.

Put the lamb chops in an aluminum roasting pan. Pour the marinade over the meat, turning to coat thoroughly. Cover it with a plastic wrapper and marinate in the refrigerator for 2 hours.

Supply your smoker with wood pellets and follow the manufacturer's specific start-up procedure. With the lid closed, prepare to 165°F, or the "Smoke" setting.

Put your saucepan top of the stove then low heat, mix the hot pepper jelly and Sriracha and keep warm.

Remove them from the marinade and pat dry. Discard the marinade.

Season all the chops with a salt and pepper, then place them directly on the grill grate, close the lid, and smoke for 5 minutes to "breathe" some smoke into them.

Remove the chops from the grill. Increase the pellet cooker temperature to 450°F, or the "High" setting. Once your griller is up to temperature, place the chops on the grill and sear, cooking for 2 minutes per side to achieve medium-rare chops. A meat thermometer that usually inserted in the thickest part of the meat should read 145°F. Continue grilling, if necessary, to your desired doneness.

Serve the chops with the warm Sriracha pepper jelly on the side.

Nutrition: Calories: 276.8; Carbs: 0g; Fats: 25.8g; Protein: 18.2g

156.   Grilled Lamb

Preparation Time: 10 minutes   **Cooking Time: 1 hour**
Servings: 6

Ingredients:
- *2 racks of lamb, fat trimmed*
- *2 tablespoons Dijon mustard*
- *Steak seasoning*
- *1 teaspoon fresh rosemary, chopped*
- *1 tablespoon fresh parsley, chopped*

Directions: Coat the lamb with the mustard.

Sprinkle all sides with the seasoning, rosemary and parsley.

Prepare the wood pellet grill to 400 degrees F. Sear the meat side of the lamb for 6 minutes. Reduce temperature to 300 degrees F. Grill it for about 20 minutes, turning once or twice. Let rest for 10 minutes before slicing and serving.

Nutrition: Calories: 240.9; Carbs: 0g; Fats: 16.8g; Protein: 21.3g

157. Hickory Rack of Lamb

Preparation Time: 10 minutes **Cooking Time: 2 hours**
Servings: 3

Ingredients:
- 1 (3 pounds) rack of lamb (drenched)

Marinade Ingredients:
- 1 lemon (juiced)
- 1 teaspoon ground black pepper
- 1 teaspoon thyme
- ¼ cup balsamic vinegar
- 1 teaspoon dried basil
- 2 tablespoons Dijon mustard
- 2 cloves garlic (crushed)

Rub Ingredients:
- ½ teaspoon cayenne pepper
- ½ teaspoon ground black pepper
- ¼ teaspoon Italian seasoning
- 1 teaspoon oregano
- 1 teaspoon dried mint
- 1 teaspoon paprika
- 1 teaspoon garlic powder
- 1 teaspoon onion powder
- 1 teaspoon dried parsley
- 1 teaspoon dried basil
- 1 teaspoon dried rosemary
- 4 tablespoons olive oil

Directions: Place the marinade ingredients in an empty container. Pour the marinade into a gallon zip-lock bag. Add the rack of lamb and massage the marinade into the rack. Seal the bag and place it in a refrigerator. Refrigerate for 8 hour or overnight.
Remove the rack of lamb from the marinade and let it sit for about 2 hour or until it is at room temperature.
Mix the rub ingredients except the olive oil in a mixing bowl.
Rub the rub mixture over the rack of lamb generously. Drizzle rack with the olive oil.
Start the grill on smoke with the lid opened until fire starts. Cover and preheat grill to 225°F using hickory wood pellets. Put the rack of your lamb on the grill grate, bone side down. Smoke it for about two hours or until the internal temperature of the meat reaches 140-145°F.
Take off the rack of lamb from the grill and let it rest for about 10 minutes to cool.

Nutrition: Calories: 799.8; Fats: 40.9g; Carbs: 6.5g; Protein 94.1g

158. Smoked Lamb chops

Preparation Time: 10 minutes **Cooking Time: 50 minutes**
Servings: 4

Ingredients:
- 1 rack of lamb, fat trimmed
- 2 tablespoons rosemary, fresh
- 2 tablespoons sage, fresh
- 1 tablespoon garlic cloves, roughly chopped
- 1/2 tablespoon salt
- 1/2 tablespoon pepper, coarsely ground
- 1/4 cup olive oil
- 1 tablespoon honey

Directions: Prepare the wood pellet smoker to 225°F using a fruitwood.
Place your ingredients except the lamb in a food processor. Liberally apply the mixture on the lamb.
Put the lamb on the smoker for 45 minutes or until the internal temperature reaches 120°F.
Sear the lamb on the grill for 2 minutes per side. Let rest for 5 minutes before serving. Slice and enjoy.

Nutrition: Calories: 703.8; Fats: 55.8g; Carbs: 23.9g; Protein: 27.2g

159. Smoked Pulled Lamb Sliders

Preparation Time: 10 minutes **Cooking Time: 7 hours**
Servings: 7

Ingredients:

For the Lamb's shoulder:
- 5 pound lamb shoulder, boneless
- 1/2 cup olive oil
- 1/4 cup dry rub
- 10 ounces spritz
- The Dry Rub
- 1/3 cup kosher salt
- 1/3 cup pepper, ground
- 1-1/3 cup garlic, granulated
- The Spritz
- 4 ounces Worcestershire sauce
- 6 ounces apple cider vinegar

Directions: Prepare the wood pellet smoker with a water bath to 2500 F.
Trim any fat from the lamb then rub with oil and dry rub.
Put the lamb on the smoker for 90 minutes then spritz with a spray bottle every 30 minutes until the internal temperature reaches 1650 F.
Transfer the lamb shoulder to a foil pan with the remaining spritz liquid and cover tightly with foil.
Put back in the smoker and smoke until the internal temperature reaches 2000 F.
Remove from the smoker and let rest for 30 minutes before pulling the lamb and serving with slaw, bun, or aioli.

Nutrition: Calories: 338.7; Fats: 21.9; Carbs: 15.8g; Protein: 18.2g

160. Crown Rack of Lamb

Preparation Time: 10 minutes
Servings: 6
Cooking Time: 30 minutes

Ingredients:
- 2 racks of lamb, drenched
- 1 tablespoon garlic, crushed
- 1 tablespoon rosemary, finely chopped
- 1/4 cup olive oil
- 2 feet twine

Directions: Rinse the racks with cold water then pat them dry with a paper towel.
Lay the racks on a flat board then score between each bone, about ¼ inch down.
Take a mixing bowl, mix garlic, rosemary, and oil then generously brush on the lamb.
Take each lamb rack and bend it into a semicircle forming a crown-like shape.
Use the twine to wrap the racks about four times, starting from the base to the top. Make sure you tie the twine tightly to keep the racks together.
Prepare the wood pellet to 400-4500 F then put the lamb racks on a baking dish. Place the baing dish on the pellet grill. Cook for 10 minutes then reduce temperature to 3000 F. cook for 20 more minutes or until the internal temperature reaches 1300 F. Remove the lamb rack from the wood pellet and let rest for 15 minutes.
Serve when hot with veggies and potatoes.

Nutrition: Calories: 389.8; Fats: 34.9g; Carbs: 0g; Protein: 17.2g

161. Wood Pellet Grilled Aussie Leg of Lamb Roast

Preparation Time: 30 minutes
Servings: 8
Cooking Time: 2 hours

Ingredients:
- 5 pounds Aussie leg of lamb, boneless
- Smoked Paprika Rub
- 1 tablespoon raw sugar
- 1 tablespoon kosher salt
- 1 tablespoon black pepper
- 1 tablespoon smoked paprika
- 1 tablespoon garlic powder
- 1 tablespoon rosemary, dried
- 1 tablespoon onion powder
- 1 tablespoon cumin
- 1/2 tablespoon cayenne pepper
- Roasted Carrots
- 1 bunch rainbow carrots
- Olive oil
- Salt
- Pepper

Directions: Preheat the wood pellet grill to 3750 F. Trim any excess fat from the lamb.
Place all rub ingredients and rub all over the lamb. Put the lamb on the grill and smoke for 2 hours.
Toss the carrots in oil, pepper and salt, then add to the grill after the lamb has cooked for 1 ½ hour.
Cook until the roast internal temperature reaches 1350 F. remove the lamb from the grill and cover with foil. Let rest for 30 minutes. Remove the carrots from the grill once soft and serve with the lamb.

Nutrition: Calories: 256.8; Fats: 7.9g; Carbs: 5.8g; Protein: 37.2g

162. Grilled Lamb with Brown Sugar Glaze

Preparation Time: 15 minutes
Servings: 4

Cooking Time: 10 minutes

Ingredients:

- 1/4 cup brown sugar
- 2 tablespoons ginger, ground
- 2 tablespoons tarragon, dried
- 1 teaspoon cinnamon, ground
- 1 tablespoons black pepper, ground
- 1 tablespoons garlic powder
- 1/2 tablespoons salt
- 4 lamb chops

Directions: Take a mixing bowl, mix sugar, dried tarragon, ginger, garlic, cinnamon, black pepper, and salt.
Rub the lamb chops with the seasoning and put it on a plate. Refrigerate for an hour to marinate.
Prepare the grill to high heat then brush the grill grate with oil.
Arrange the lamb chops on the grill grate in a single layer and cook for 5 minutes on each side. Serve and enjoy.

Nutrition: Calories: 240.9; Fats: 12.9g; Carbs: 15.6g; Protein: 14.8g

163. Grilled Lamb Loin Chops

Preparation Time: 10 minutes
Servings: 6

Cooking Time: 10 minutes

Ingredients:

- 2 tablespoons herbs de Provence
- 1-1/2 tablespoons olive oil
- 2 garlic cloves, minced
- 2 tablespoons lemon juice
- 5 ounces lamb loin chops
- Salt and black pepper to taste

Directions: Take a small mixing bowl, mix herbs de Provence, oil, garlic, and juice. Rub the mixture on the lamb chops then refrigerate for an hour.
Prepare the wood pellet grill to medium-high then lightly oil the grill grate.
Seasoned the lamb chops using salt and black pepper.
Place the lamb chops on the griller and cook for 4 minutes on each side.
Take off the chops from the grill and place them on an aluminum covered plate. Let rest for 5 minutes before serving.

Nutrition: Calories: 578.7; Fats: 43.5g; Carbs: 0.5g; Protein: 42.8g

164. Wood pellet grill Lamb

Preparation Time: 15 minutes
Servings: 8

Cooking Time: 50 minutes

Ingredients:

- 2/3 cup lemon juice
- 1/2 cup brown sugar
- 1/4 cup Dijon mustard
- 1/4 cup soy sauce
- 1/4 cup olive oil
- 2 garlic cloves, minced
- 1 piece ginger root, freshly sliced
- 1 tablespoon salt
- 1/2 tablespoon black pepper, ground
- 5 pounds leg of lamb, butterflied

Directions: Take a mixing bowl, mix lemon juice, sugar, oil, Dijon mustard, salt, sauce, garlic cloves, ginger root, and pepper.
Place the lamb in a container and pour the seasoning mixture over it. Cover the dish and put in a fridge to marinate for 8 hours.
Prepare a wood pellet grill to medium heat. Drain the marinade from the dish and bring it to boil in a small saucepan.
Reduce heat and let simmer while whisking occasionally.
Oil the grill grate and place the lamb on it. Cook for 50 minutes or until the internal temperature reaches 1450 F while turning occasionally. Slice the lamb and cover with the marinade. Serve and enjoy.

Nutrition: Calories: 450.9; Fats: 27.1g; Carbs: 17.5g; Protein: 32.6g

165.   Grilled Lamb Chops

Preparation Time: 1 hour   **Cooking Time: 8 minutes**
Servings: 3

Ingredients:
- 2 garlic cloves, crushed
- 1 tablespoons rosemary leaves, fresh chopped
- 2 tablespoons olive oil
- 1 tablespoon lemon juice, fresh
- 1 tablespoon thyme leaves, fresh
- 1 tablespoon salt
- 9 lamb loin chops

Directions: Put the garlic, oil, rosemary, juice, salt, and thyme in a food processor. Pulse until smooth.
Rub the marinade on the lamb chops both sides and let marinate for 1 hour in a fridge. Take it from the fridge and let sit at room temperature for 20 minutes before cooking.
Prepare the wood pellet smoker to high heat. Smoke the lamb chops for 5 minutes on each side.
Sear the lamb chops for 3 minutes on each side. Remove from the grill and serve with a green salad.

Nutrition: Calories: 1139.8; Fats: 98.8g; Carbs: 0.9g; Protein: 55.2g

Chicken Recipes

166.   Cinnamon Apricot Smoked Chicken Thighs

Preparation Time: 15 minutes   **Cooking Time: 1 hour 35 minutes**
Servings: 10

Ingredients:
- Chicken thighs (3-lb., 1.4-kg.)

The Rub:
- 2 teaspoons Ground cinnamon
- 1 tablespoon Smoked paprika
- ¾ tablespoon Cumin
- ¾ teaspoon Ginger
- ¾ teaspoon Salt
- 1 ½ teaspoon Pepper
- 2 tablespoons Brown sugar
- a pinch Ground clove
- ¼ teaspoon Cayenne

The Glaze:
- 1 cup Apricot marmalade
- 2 tablespoons Soy sauce
- 1 tablespoon Apricot syrup
- 1 tablespoon Cider vinegar
- ½ teaspoon Ground mustard

Directions: Mix the rub ingredients, cinnamon, cumin, smoked paprika, brown sugar, salt, ginger, pepper, ground clove, and cayenne then stir until combined.
Rub the spices mixture over your chicken thighs, then let it rest for a few minutes.
Plug the wood pellet smoker then fill the hopper with the wood pellet. Turn the switch on.
Prepare the wood pellet smoker for indirect heat then adjust the temperature to 275°F (135°C).
Arrange the seasoned chicken thighs in the wood pellet smoker and smoke for an hour and 30 minutes.
Put apricot marmalade to a bowl then stir in soy sauce, apricot syrup, cider vinegar, and ground mustard to the bowl. Mix until incorporated and set aside.
Wait until the internal temperature of the smoked chicken thighs has reached 170°F (77°C) and coat the smoked chicken thighs with the apricot mixture.
Let the glazed smoked chicken thighs sit in the wood pellet smoker for 5 minutes then take them out.
Arrange the smoked chicken thighs on a serving dish then serve.

Nutrition: Calories: 269.9; Carbs: 23.8g; Fats: 12.8g; Protein: 15.2g

167.   Sweet Smoked Chicken Breast with Celery Seeds

Preparation Time: 10 minutes   **Cooking Time: 1 hour 10 minutes**
Servings: 6

Ingredients:
- Boneless chicken breast (4-lbs., 1.8-kg.)

The Rub
- Olive oil – 3 tablespoons
- Brown sugar – ¼ cup
- Celery seeds – ¾ teaspoon
- Smoked paprika – 3 tablespoons
- Salt – 1 teaspoon
- Black pepper – ½ teaspoon
- Cayenne pepper – 1 ½ teaspoon
- Garlic powder – 1 tablespoon
- Onion powder – 1 tablespoon

Directions: Mix brown sugar with celery seeds, smoked paprika, salt, black pepper, cayenne pepper, garlic powder, and onion powder and set aside.
Rub the chicken breast with olive oil then sprinkle the dry spice mixture over the chicken breast. Let it rest for approximately 30 minutes.
Next, plug the wood pellet smoker then fill the hopper with the wood pellet. Turn the switch on.
Prepare the wood pellet smoker for indirect heat then adjust the temperature to 350°F (177°C)
Put the seasoned chicken breast in the wood pellet smoker and smoke for an hour.
Check the internal temperature of the chicken breast; once it reaches 170°F (77°C), remove it from the wood pellet smoker.
Transfer the smoked chicken breast to a serving dish then cut into thick slices. Serve and enjoy.

Nutrition: Calories: 179.8; Carbs: 0g; Fats: 9.9g; Protein: 22.3g

168.   Wood Pellet Smoked Chicken Breasts

Preparation Time: 15 minutes
Servings: 4

Cooking Time: 45 minutes

Ingredients:

- 4 boneless and skinless chicken breasts.
- 1 tablespoon of olive oil.
- 2 tablespoons of brown sugar.
- 2 tablespoons of turbinate sugar.
- 1 teaspoon of celery seeds.
- 2 tablespoons of paprika.
- 2 tablespoons of kosher salt to taste.
- 1 teaspoon of black pepper to taste.
- 1 teaspoon of cayenne pepper.
- 2 tablespoons of garlic powder.
- 2 tablespoons of onion powder.

Directions: Take a large mixing bowl, put in the celery seeds, paprika, sugars, cayenne pepper, salt, garlic powder, onion powder and pepper to taste then mix properly to combine. Use paper towels to pat the chicken dry then rub all sides with the oil. Add some sprinkles of the mixed rub all over the chicken breast, wrap the chicken in a plastic bag then set aside in the fridge to rest for about fifteen to thirty minutes.

Prepare a Wood Pellet smoker and Grill (the smoker precisely) to smoke for about five minutes then turn the heat to 350 degrees and preheat for about fifteen minutes with the lid closed. Put the spiced/coated chicken on the grill then cook for about twelve to thirteen minutes.

Flip the chicken side to side, over and cook for another eight to ten minutes until it attains an internal temperature of 165 degrees F. once cooked, warp the chicken in aluminum foil and let rest for about three to five minutes. Slice and serve.

Nutrition: Calories: 326.8; Fats : 8.8g; Carbs: 22.8g; Protein: 40.2g

169.   Wood Pellet Grilled Chicken Satay

Preparation Time: 15 minutes
Servings: 4

Cooking Time: 35 minutes

Ingredients:

Marinade:

- 1 1/2 pounds of a boneless and skinless chicken breasts or thighs.
- 3/4 cup of coconut milk.
- 2 tablespoons of fish sauce.
- 2 tablespoons of soy sauce.
- 2 tablespoons of lime juice.
- 1/2 teaspoon of kosher salt to taste.
- 1/2 teaspoon of black pepper to taste.
- 1/2 teaspoon of garlic powder.
- 1/4 teaspoon of cayenne pepper.

Dipping sauce:

- 1/2 cup of coconut milk.
- 1/3 cup of peanut butter.
- 2 minced cloves of garlic.
- 1 tablespoon of soy sauce.
- 1 teaspoon of fish sauce.
- 1 tablespoon of lime juice.
- 1/2 tablespoon of swerve sweetener.
- 1 tablespoon of sriracha hot sauce.
- 1 cup of chopped cilantro.

Directions: Properly slice the chicken as desired, preferably lengthwise then add to a Ziploc bag, set aside. Using a large mixing bowl, add in the milk, fish sauce, soy sauce, cayenne pepper, lime juice, garlic powder, salt, and pepper to taste then mix properly to combine. Pour the marinade into the resealable bag then shake properly to coat, refrigerate for about thirty minutes to three hours.

For the dipping sauce: put all its ingredients in a mixing bowl, mix properly to combine, and set aside. Prepare a Wood Pellet Smoker and Grill to 350 degrees F, thread the chicken onto skewers then place the skewers on the preheated grill.

Cook the chicken satay for about ten to fifteen minutes until it reads 165o F. make sure you flip the chicken occasionally as you cook. Serve with the prepared dipping sauce and enjoy.

Nutrition: Calories: 487.8; Fats: 31.8g; Carbs: 9.9g; Protein: 41.2g

170.   Smoked Whole Chicken with Dry Rub

Preparation Time: 10 minutes   **Cooking Time: 1 hour 25 minutes**
Servings: 4

Ingredients:

- 1 whole chicken.
- 1 can of beer or soda.
- 3 tablespoons of dry chicken rub.
- 2 tablespoons of olive oil.
- Lemon wedges for serving

Directions: Prepare the Wood Pellet Smoker and Grill to 350 degrees F. Use paper towels to pat the chicken dry then rub oil on the entire surface of the chicken. Coat the chicken with the dry rub then set aside.
Discard about half of the bear (you can choose to drink it up), add a few tablespoons of the dry rub into the rest of the bear in the can then gently place the can into the chicken's cavity a way that the chicken stands upright.
Put the chicken on a baking sheet pan then place the pan on the grill gates. Cook the chicken for about one hour to one and a half hours until an inserted thermometer reads 165 degrees F. Once cooked, let the chicken cool for about fifteen minutes, slice, and serve with lemon wedges.

Nutrition: Calories: 336.8; Fats: 17.9g ; Carbs: 1.2g; Protein: 36.2g

171.   Yan's Grilled Quarters

Preparation Time: 20 minutes   **Cooking Time: 1 to 1.5 hours**
Servings: 4

Ingredients:

- 4 fresh or thawed frozen chicken quarters
- 4-6 glasses of extra virgin olive oil
- 4 tablespoons of Yang's original dry lab

Directions: Cut off excess skin and fat chicken. Carefully peel the chicken skin and rub olive oil above and below each chicken skin.
In Jean's original dry lab, apply seasonings to the top and bottom of the skin and the back of the chicken house.
Wrap the seasoned chicken in plastic wrap and store refrigerated for 2-4 hours to absorb flavor.
Prepare a wood pellet smoker grill for indirect cooking and use the pellets to preheat to 325 ° F.
Put chicken on grill and cook at 325 ° F for 1 hour.
After one hour, raise the pit temperature to 400 ° F to finish the chicken and crisp the skin.
When the inside temperature of the thickest part of the thighs and feet reaches 180 ° F and the juice becomes clear, pull the crispy chicken out of the grill.
Let the crispy grilled chicken rest under a loose foil tent for 15 minutes before eating.

Nutrition: Calories: 249.9; Carbs: 0g; Fats: 11.8g; Protein: 21.3g

172.   Teriyaki Smoked Drumstick

Preparation Time: 15 minutes   **Cooking Time: 1.5 hours to 2 hours**
Servings: 4

Ingredients:

- 3 cup teriyaki marinade and cooking sauce like Yoshida's original gourmet
- Poultry seasoning 3 teaspoons
- 1 teaspoon garlic powder
- 10 chicken drumsticks

Directions: Mix the marinade and cooking sauce with the chicken seasoning and garlic powder in a medium bowl. Peel off the skin of the drumstick to promote marinade penetration.
Place the drumstick in a marinade pan or 1 gallon plastic sealable bag and pour the marinade mixture into the drumstick. Refrigerate overnight. Rotate the chicken leg in the morning.
Prepare a wood pellet smoking grill for indirect cooking.
Put the skin on the drumstick and, while the grill is preheating, hang the drumstick on a poultry leg and wing rack to drain the cooking sheet on the counter. If you do not have a poultry leg and feather rack, you can dry the drumstick by tapping it with a paper towel. Prepare wood pellet smoker grill to 180 ° F using hickory or maple pellets. Make marinated chicken leg for 1 hour.
After 1 hour, raise the whole temperature to 350 ° F and cook the drumstick for another 30-45 minutes until the thickest part of the stick reaches an internal temperature of 180 ° F.

Put the chicken drumstick under the loose foil tent for 15 minutes before serving.

Nutrition: Calories: 279.9; Carbs: 0g; Fats: 12.8g; Protein: 35.2g

173. Hickory Smoke Patchcock Chicken

Preparation Time: 20 minutes
Servings: 6

Cooking Time: 3-4 hours

Ingredients:

- 1 fresh or thawed frozen young chicken
- ¼ Extra virgin olive oil with cup roasted garlic flavor
- 6 poultry seasonings or original dry lab in January

Directions: Use poultry scissors or a big butcher knife to carefully remove the chicken spine along both sides.
Press down on the sternum to flatten the patch-cocked chicken.
Remove excess fat and skin from the breast.
Slowly separate the skin of your chicken from the breast and leave the skin alone. Apply olive oil intrathoracic ally, under the skin and on the skin.
Sprinkle seasoning or dry rub with seasoning on the chest cavity, under the skin and on skin.
Prepare a wood pellet smoking grill for indirect cooking and preheat to 225 ° F using hickory pellets.
Put the chicken skin down on a non-stick grill mat made of Teflon-coated fiberglass.
Suck the chicken at 225 ° F for 2 hours. After 2 hours, raise the pit temperature to 350 ° F.
Roast chicken until the thickest part of the chest reaches an internal temperature of 170 ° F and the juice is clear.
Put the Hickory smoked roast chicken under a loose foil tent for 20 minutes before engraving.

Nutrition: Calories: 179.8; Carbs: 0.9g; Fats: 15.8g; Protein: 7.2g

174. Lemon Cornish Chicken Stuffed With Crab

Preparation Time: 30 minutes
Servings: 4

Cooking Time: 1 hour 30 minutes

Ingredients:

- 2 Cornish chickens (about 1¾ pound each)
- Half lemon, half
- 4 tablespoons western rub or poultry rub
- 2 cups stuffed with crab meat

Directions: Rinse chicken thoroughly inside and outside, tap lightly and let it dry.
Carefully loosen the skin on the chest and legs. Rub the lemon under and over the skin and into the cavity. Rub the western lab under and over the skin on the chest and legs. Carefully return the skin to its original position.
Wrap the Cornish hen in plastic wrap and refrigerate for 2-3 hours until the flavor is absorbed.
Prepare crab meat stuffing according to the instructions. Make sure it is completely cooled before packing the chicken. Loosely fill the cavities of each hen with crab filling.
Tie the Cornish chicken legs with a butcher's leash to put the filling.
Prepare the wood pellet smoker grill for indirect cooking and preheat to 375 ° F with pellets.
Put the stuffed animal on the rack in the baking dish. If you do not have a small enough rack to fit, you can also put the chicken directly on the baking dish.
Roast the chicken at 375 ° F until the inside temperature of the thickest part of the chicken breast reaches 170 ° F, the thigh reaches 180 ° F, and the juice is clear.
Test the crab meat stuffing to see if the temperature has reached 165 ° F.
Put the roasted chicken under a loose foil tent for 15 minutes before serving.

Nutrition: Calories: 274.8; Carbs: 0g; Fats: 2.9g; Protein: 32.1g

175. Smoked Chicken Patties

Preparation Time: 15 minutes
Servings: 6

Cooking Time: 55 minutes

Ingredients:

- 2 pounds ground chicken breast
- 2/3 cup minced onion
- 1 Tablespoon cilantro (chopped)
- 2 Tablespoons fresh parsley, finely chopped

- 2 Tablespoons olive oil
- 1/8 teaspoon crushed red pepper powdered for the taste
- 1/2 teaspoon ground cumin
- 2 Tablespoons fresh lemon juice
- 3/4teaspoonkosher salt
- 2 teaspoons paprika
- Hamburger buns for serving

Directions: Take a bowl and mix all ingredients from the list.
Using your hands, mix well. Form mixture into 6 patties. Refrigerate until ready to grill (about 30 minutes).
Prepare the pellet grill on SMOKE with the lid open until the fire is established). Set the temperature to 350°F and preheat and cover for 10 to 15 minutes.
Arrange chicken patties on the grill rack and cook for 35 to 40 minutes, turning once.
Serve hot with hamburger buns and your favorite condiments.

Nutrition: Calories: 257.9; Carbs: 2.4g; Fats: 9.1g; Protein: 39.2g

176.   Smoked Chicken Breasts in Lemon Marinade

Preparation Time: 10 minutes   **Cooking Time: 1 hour**
Servings: 6

Ingredients:
- 4 pounds boneless chicken breast
- 6 lemons sliced, without seeds
- 2 tablespoons olive oil
- 1 tablespoon of garlic minced
- 2 tablespoons of onion finely chopped
- 1 teaspoon of allspice
- Salt and powdered black pepper for taste
- 1/2 cup water

Directions: Take a large bowl, and put chicken pieces and lemon rings.
In a separate bowl, mix all remaining ingredients.
Pour the spice mixture over the chicken and mix thoroughly. Refrigerate for 4 hours.
Prepare the pellet grill on SMOKE with the lid open until the fire is established). Put the temperature to 250°F and allow to preheat, cover for 10 to 15 minutes. Put the marinated chicken into the smoker, and cook for 35 to 45 minutes. Your chicken is ready when the internal temperature reaches 165 °F.
Allow to rest for 15 minutes, slice and serve.

Nutrition: Calories: 617.9; Carbs: 12.5g; Fats: 72.8g; Protein: 11.8g

177.   Smoked Chicken Burgers with Feta Cheese

Preparation Time: 10 minutes   **Cooking Time: 1 hour**
Servings: 6

Ingredients:
- 2 pounds of minced chicken meat
- Zest of 1 lemon
- 1 tablespoon olive oil
- 2 teaspoons oregano, fresh chopped
- 1/2 teaspoons of fresh thyme and marjoram finely chopped
- 1 teaspoon fresh parsley finely chopped
- Salt and ground pepper to taste
- 1 cup Feta cheese crumbled
- Olive oil for brushing

Directions: mix minced meat, olive oil, lemon zest, oregano, thyme and salt and pepper to taste.
Wet your heads and knead the meat mixture.
Cut Feta into small cubes and start making the meatballs.
Take about half a tablespoon of minced meat, roll in the shape of a circle, press in the middle with our thumb, place a piece of cheese there, "close" and gently roll into balls.
Prepare the pellet grill on SMOKE (hickory or apple pellets) with the lid open until the fire is established. Set the temperature to 380°F and preheat, lid closed, for 10 to 15 minutes.
Put burgers into the smoker and cook for 35 to 40 minutes.
Your chicken burgers are ready when the internal temperature reaches 165 °F. Serve hot.

Nutrition: Calories: 455.1; Carbs: 9.8g; Fats: 24.1g; Protein: 27.4g

178.   Grilled Chicken Salad

Preparation Time: 20 minutes
Servings: 6

Cooking Time: 1 hour and 15 minutes

Ingredients:

- 1 whole chicken
- 3 tablespoons poultry rub
- For the Salad:
- 4 green onions, chopped
- 1 cup red grapes, halved

- 4 celery stalks, chopped
- 1 cup green grapes, halved
- ¾ teaspoon salt
- ½ teaspoon ground black pepper

- 2 tablespoons brown sugar
- ½ cup sour cream
- ½ cup mayonnaise
- 1 lemon, juiced

Directions: Open the hopper of the smoker, add dry pallets, make sure the ash-can is in place, then open the ash damper, power on the smoker and close the ash damper.
Prepare the smoker's temperature to 250 degrees F, let preheat for 30 minutes or until the green light on the dial blinks that indicates smoker has reached to set temperature.
Break the whole chicken into thighs, legs, breasts, and wings and then season with poultry rub until well coated. Put chicken pieces on the smoker grill, shut with lid and smoke for 35 to 45 minutes.
Transfer chicken pieces to a cutting board, let it rest for 5 minutes, then separate bones from the meats, discard bones and skin, and shred chicken with two forks.
Prepare the salad and place onion, grapes and celery in a large salad bowl, drizzle with lemon juice and sprinkle with black pepper, salt, and sugar.
Whisk together sour cream and mayonnaise, add into the salad bowl along with chicken pieces and stir the salad gently until mixed. Serve immediately.

Nutrition: Calories: 351.2; Fats: 9.8g; Protein: 43.9g; Carbs: 20.3g; Fiber: 4.2g; Sugar: 6.9g

179.   Parmesan Chicken Wings

Preparation Time: 1 hour and 10 minutes
Servings: 6

Cooking Time: 45 minutes

Ingredients:

- 2 pounds chicken wings, trimmed

- 2 tablespoons butter, unsalted, melted

- ¼ cup grated parmesan cheese

For the Marinade:

- 1 ½ tablespoon minced garlic
- 2 tablespoons chicken seasoning

- 2 tablespoons parsley, chopped
- 2 tablespoons Dijon mustard

- 1 lemon, juiced
- ¼ cup olive oil

Directions: Put the ingredients for the marinade in a small bowl and then stir until combined.
Put chicken wings in a large plastic bag, pour in prepared marinade, then seal the bag, turn it upside down to coat the chicken wings with the marinade and let marinate in the refrigerator for 1 hour.
Open the hopper of the smoker, add dry pallets, make sure the ash-can is in place, then open the ash damper, power on the smoker and close the ash damper.
Prepare the smoker's temperature to 350 degrees F, let preheat for 30 minutes or until the green light on the dial blinks indicates the smoker has reached to set temperature.
Remove chicken wings from the marinade, place them on the smoker grill, shut with a lid and smoke for 15 minutes or until the internal temperature reaches 165 degrees F, flipping the chicken wings halfway through.
Transfer the chicken wings to a large bowl, add butter and cheese and toss until well coated.
Serve straight away.

Nutrition: Calories: 509.8; Fats: 39.8g; Protein: 35.2g; Carbs: 2.9g

180.   Balsamic Vinegar Chicken Breasts

Preparation Time: 1 hour
Servings: 4

Cooking Time: 3 hours

Ingredients:

- 6 tablespoons of olive oil
- 1 cup balsamic vinegar
- 3 cloves of garlic cloves, minced

- 1 teaspoon of basil, fresh
- 1 teaspoon of chili powder
- Salt and black pepper, to taste

- 2 pounds of chicken breast, boneless and skinless

Directions: Take a zip lock bag, put oil, basil leaves, balsamic vinegar, garlic cloves, chili powder, salt, and black pepper. Put the chicken in the zip lock bag and mix well. Marinate the chicken in the sauce for 3 hours in the refrigerator. Prepare the grill for 20 minutes at 225 degrees F.
Put the chicken onto the grill, and smoke for 3 hours.
Once the internal temperature reaches 150 degrees, remove it from the grill, and then let it cool for 10 minutes before serving.

181.   Herbed Smoked Hen

Preparation Time: 40 minutes   **Cooking Time: 50 minutes**
Servings: 5

Ingredients:

- 12 cups of filtered water
- 3 cups of beer nonalcoholic
- Sea Salt, to taste
- ⅓ Cup brown sugar
- 2 tablespoons of rosemary
- ½ teaspoon of sage
- 2.5 pounds of a whole chicken, trimmed and giblets removed
- 6 tablespoons of butter
- 2 tablespoons of Olive oil, for basting
- 1/3 cup Italian seasoning
- 1 tablespoon garlic powder
- 1 tablespoon of lemon zest

Directions: Take a large cooking pot, pour water and then add sugar and salt to the water.
Boil the water until the sugar and salt dissolve. Now to the boiling water, add rosemary and sage.
Boil it until the aroma comes. Now pour the beer into the water and then submerge the chicken into the boiling water. Turn off the heat and refrigerate the chicken for a few hours.
After a few hours, remove it from the brine, and then pat dry with the paper towel.
Let the chicken sit for a few minutes at room temperature.
Now rub the chicken with the butter and massage it completely for fine coating.
Season the chicken with garlic powder, lemon zest, and Italian seasoning.
Prepare the Electrical smoker at 270 degrees Fahrenheit until the smoke starts to build.
Baste the chicken with olive oil and put it on the grill grate.
Cook the chicken with the lid closed, for 30 to 40 minutes, or until the internal temperature reaches 165 degrees F. Serve and enjoy.

182.   Maple Glazed Whole Chicken

Preparation Time: 40 minutes   **Cooking Time: 3 Hours**
Servings: 4

Ingredients for The Rub:

- Black pepper and salt, to taste
- 3 garlic cloves, minced
- 3 teaspoons of onion powder
- 1.5 teaspoons of ginger, minced
- ½ teaspoon of five-spice powder

Basic Ingredients:

- 2.5 pounds whole chicken
- 4 tablespoons of melted butter
- 1 cup of grapefruit juice
- 2.5 cups chicken stock

Ingredients for The Glaze:

- 6 teaspoons of coconut milk
- 3 tablespoons of sesame oil
- 3 tablespoons of maple syrup
- 1 tablespoon of lemon juice
- 4 tablespoons of melted butter

Directions: Take a small cooking pot, pour the coconut milk and add sesame oil, melted butter, maple syrup, and lemon juice. Cook the mixture for a few minutes until the glaze is ready for all the ingredients are combined well. Reserve some of the mixture for further use.
Add chicken stock, butter, and grapefruit juice in a separate cooking pot.
Simmer the mixture for a few minutes, and then add the chicken to this liquid.
Submerge the chicken completely in the brain and let it sit for a few hours for marinating.
Take a separate bowl, mix all the rub ingredients.
After a few hours pass, take out the chicken from the liquid and pat dry with a paper towel.
Cover the chicken with the rub mixture. Prepare the smoker grill for 20 minutes at 225 degrees Fahrenheit.
Cherry or apple wood chip can be used to create the smoke.
Put chicken onto the smoker grill grate and cook for 3 hours by closing the lid.
After every 30 minutes, baste the chicken with the maple glaze.
Once the internal temperature of the chicken reaches 165 degrees Fahrenheit the chicken is ready to be served.

Remove the chicken from the grill grate and baste it with the glaze and additional butter on top.
Let the chicken sit at the room temperature for 10 minutes before cutting and serving.

183.   Rosemary Chicken

Preparation Time: 4 hours and 10 minutes   **Cooking Time: 1 hour and 5 minutes**
Servings: 6

Ingredients:

- 4 pounds chicken thighs, boneless
- 2 teaspoons garlic powder
- 2 teaspoons salt
- 1/2 cup brown sugar
- 1 teaspoon ground black pepper
- 4 teaspoons fresh rosemary, chopped
- 1/4 cup soy sauce
- 1/2 cup apple cider vinegar
- 1/2 cup Worcestershire sauce
- 1/2 cup olive oil
- 1/2 of a lemon, juiced
- 1/4 cup Dijon mustard

Directions: Put the ingredients in a small bowl, except for chicken, and stir well until combined.
Put chicken thighs in a large plastic bag, pour in the prepared mixture, seal the bag, turn it upside down to coat the chicken pieces and let marinate in the refrigerator for a minimum for 4 hours.
Open the hopper of the smoker, add dry pallets, make sure the ash-can is in place, then open the ash damper, power on the smoker and close the ash damper.
Prepare the temperature of the smoker to 350 degrees F, let preheat for 30 minutes.
Remove chicken thighs from the marinade, place them on the smoker grill, shut with a lid and smoke for 35 minutes or until thoroughly cooked and the internal temperature of the chicken reaches to 165 degrees F.
Transfer chicken to a dish and serve straight away.

Nutrition: Calories: 108.9; Fats: 5.2g; Protein: 13.9g; Carbs: 0.5g; Fiber: 0.2g

184.   Orange Chicken Wings

Preparation Time: 1 hour and 10 minutes   **Cooking Time: 1 hour and 15 minutes**
Servings: 4

For the Sauce:

- 1 orange, zested
- 1 tablespoon corn starch
- 1 teaspoon ground ginger
- ½ teaspoon salt
- 1/4 teaspoon ground white pepper
- 1/3 cups brown sugar
- 1 tablespoon chili garlic paste
- 2 tablespoons soy sauce
- 1 cup orange juice, fresh
- 1/4 cup chicken stock

For the Wings:

- 2 pounds chicken wings
- 2 tablespoons salt

Directions: Spread the chicken wings on a wire rack put on a sheet pan and lined with paper towels, then pat dry the chicken wings, sprinkle them with salt and place them in the refrigerator for 1 hour.
Open the hopper of the smoker, add dry pallets, put the ash-can is in place, then open the ash damper, power on the smoker and close the ash damper.
Prepare the smoker to 350 degrees F, and let preheat for 30 minutes.
Put chicken wings on the smoker grill, shut with a lid and smoke for 45 minutes or until their skin is golden brown and the internal temperature of chicken wings reaches to 170 degrees F.
Prepare the orange sauce and for this, pour the chicken stock into a bowl, add corn starch, stir well and set aside until required.
Put the remaining ingredients for the sauce in a saucepan, whisk well until combined, then place it over medium heat and bring the sauce to simmer.
Then whisk in corn starch-chicken stock mixture until mixed and continue simmering the sauce for 10 minutes or until the sauce has thickened; remove the pan from heat and set aside until required.
When chicken wings are done, transfer them in a large bowl, pour in prepared orange sauce and toss until the chicken wings are well covered. Serve straight away.

Nutrition: Calories: 219.8; Fats: 7.9g; Protein: 12.3g; Carbs: 24.8g; Fiber: 0.9g; Sugar: 11.9g

Turkey Recipes

185. Turkey Breast

Preparation Time: 12 hours
Servings: 6

Cooking Time: 8 hours

Ingredients:

For the Brine:
- 2 pounds turkey breast, deboned
- 2 tablespoons ground black pepper
- ¼ cup salt
- 1 cup brown sugar
- 4 cups cold water

For the BBQ Rub:
- 2 tablespoons dried onions
- 2 tablespoons garlic powder
- ¼ cup paprika
- 2 tablespoons ground black pepper
- 1 tablespoon salt
- 2 tablespoons brown sugar
- 2 tablespoons red chili powder
- 1 tablespoon cayenne pepper
- 2 tablespoons sugar
- 2 tablespoons ground cumin

Directions: For the brine: in a large bowl, put black pepper, sugar and salt in it, pour in water, and stir until sugar has dissolved.
Put turkey breast in it, submerge it completely and let it soak for a minimum of 12 hours in the refrigerator.
For the BBQ rub: in a small bowl, put all of its ingredients in it and mix well, set aside until required.
Then remove turkey breast from the brine and season well with the prepared BBQ rub.
Prepare the Traeger grill, fill the grill hopper with apple-flavored wood pellets, power the grill on and select 'smoke' on the temperature dial, or set the temperature to 180 degrees F and let it preheat for a minimum of 15 minutes.
Put turkey breast on the grill grate, shut the grill, change the smoking temperature to 225 degrees F, and smoke for 8 hours until the internal temperature reaches 160 degrees F.
Transfer turkey to a cutting board, let it rest for 10 minutes, then cut it into slices and serve.

Nutrition: Calories: 249.9; Fats: 4.8g; Carbs: 30.9g; Protein: 18.2g

186. Savory-Sweet Turkey Legs

Preparation Time: 10 minutes
Servings: 4

Cooking Time: 5 hours

Ingredients:
- 1 gallon hot water
- 1 cup curing salt (such as Morton Tender Quick)
- ¼ cup packed light brown sugar
- 1 teaspoon freshly ground black pepper
- 1 teaspoon ground cloves
- 1 bay leaf
- 2 teaspoons liquid smoke
- 4 turkey legs
- Mandarin Glaze, for serving

Directions: Take a huge container with a lid, mix the water, brown sugar, curing salt, pepper, bay leaf, cloves, and liquid smoke until the salt and sugar are dissolved; let come to room temperature.
Submerge the turkey legs in the seasoned brine, cover, and refrigerate overnight.
Remove the turkey legs from the brine and rinse them; discard the brine.
Supply the smoker with wood pellets and follow the manufacturer's specific start-up procedure. Prepare, with the lid closed, to 225°F.
Arrange the turkey legs on the grill, close the lid, and smoke for 4 to 5 hours, or until dark brown and a meat thermometer inserted in the thickest part of the meat reads 165°F.
Serve with Mandarin Glaze on the side or drizzled over the turkey legs.

Nutrition: Calories: 189.8; Carbs: 0.9g; Fats: 8.8g; Protein: 24.3g

187. Maple Bourbon Turkey

Preparation Time: 15 minutes

Cooking Time: 3 hours

Servings: 8

Ingredients:

- 1 (12 pounds) turkey
- 8 cup chicken broth
- 1 stick butter (softened)
- 1 teaspoon thyme
- 2 garlic clove (minced)

- 1 teaspoon dried basil
- 1 teaspoon pepper
- 1 teaspoon salt
- 1 tablespoon minced rosemary
- 1 teaspoon paprika

- 1 lemon (wedged)
- 1 onion
- 1 orange (wedged)
- 1 apple (wedged)

Maple Bourbon Glaze:

- ¾ cup bourbon
- 1/2 cup maple syrup

- 1 stick butter (melted)
- 1 tablespoon lime

Directions: Wash the turkey meat inside and out under cold running water.

Insert the onion, orange, lemon and apple into the turkey cavity.

Mix the butter, thyme, paprika, basil, garlic, pepper, salt, basil and rosemary.

Brush the turkey generously with the herb butter mixture.

Set a rack into a roasting pan and place the turkey on the rack. Put 5 cups of chicken broth into the bottom of the roasting pan. Prepare the grill to 350°F with the lid closed for 15 minutes, using maple wood pellets.

Put the roasting pan in the grill and cook for 1 hour.

Mix well all the maple bourbon glaze ingredients in a mixing bowl.

Baste the turkey with a glaze mixture. Continue cooking, basting turkey every 30 minutes and adding more broth as needed for 2 hours.

Take off the turkey from the grill and let it rest for a few minutes. Cut into slices and serve.

Nutrition: Calories: 1535.8; Fats: 58.2g; Carbs: 23.9g; Protein: 20.5g

188. Spatchcock Smoked Turkey

Preparation Time: 15 minutes

Cooking Time: 4 hours 3 minutes

Servings: 6

Ingredients:

- 1 (18 pounds) turkey
- 2 tablespoons finely chopped fresh parsley
- 1 tablespoon finely chopped fresh rosemary

- 2 tablespoons finely chopped fresh thyme
- ½ cup melted butter
- 1 teaspoon garlic powder
- 1 teaspoon onion powder
- 1 teaspoon ground black pepper

- 2 teaspoons salt or to taste
- 2 tablespoons finely chopped scallions

Directions: Remove the turkey giblets and rinse the turkey, in and out, under cold running water.

Put the turkey on a working surface, breast side down. Use a poultry shear to cut the turkey along both sides of the backbone to remove the turkey backbone.

Flip the turkey over, backside down, and then press it down to flatten it.

Mix the parsley, scallions, rosemary, butter, thyme, salt, pepper, garlic, and onion powder in a mixing bowl.

Rub butter mixture over all sides of the turkey.

Prepare the grill to HIGH (450°F) with lid closed for 15 minutes.

Place the turkey directly on the grill grate and cook for 30 minutes. Reduce the heat to 300°F and cook for an additional 4 hours, or until the internal temperature of the thickest part of the thigh reaches 165°F.

Take out the turkey meat from the grill and let it rest for a few minutes. Cut into sizes and serve.

Nutrition: Calories: 779.8; Fats: 18.7g; Carbs: 29.5g; Protein: 116.6g

189. Turkey Jerky

Preparation Time: 15 minutes

Cooking Time: 4 hours

Servings: 6

Ingredients:

Marinade:

- 1 cup pineapple juice
- ½ cup brown sugar
- 2 tablespoons sriracha
- 2 teaspoons onion powder
- 2 tablespoons minced garlic
- 2 tablespoons rice wine vinegar
- 2 tablespoons hoisin
- 1 tablespoon red pepper flakes
- 1 tablespoon coarsely ground black pepper flakes
- 2 cups coconut amino
- 2 jalapenos (thinly sliced)

Meat:

- 3 pounds turkey boneless skinless breasts (sliced to ¼ inch thick)

Directions: Pour the marinade mixture ingredients in a container and mix well.
Place the turkey slices in a gallon sized zip lock bag and pour the marinade into the bag. Massage the marinade into the turkey. Seal the bag and refrigerate for 8 hours. Remove the turkey slices from the marinade.
Activate the pellet grill for smoking and leave lip opened for 5 minutes until fire starts.
Cover and prepare the pellet grill to 180°F, using a hickory pellet.
Remove the turkey slices from the marinade and pat them dry with a paper towel.
Arrange the turkey slices on the grill in a single layer. Cook the turkey for about 3 to 4 hours, often turning after the first 2 hours of smoking. The jerky should be dark and dry when it is done.
Remove the jerky from the grill and let it sit for about 1 hour to cool. Serve immediately or store in the refrigerator.

Nutrition: Calories: 108.7; Carbs: 11.9g; Fats: 0.9g; Protein: 14.2g

190.   Smoked Whole Turkey

Preparation Time: 20 minutes   **Cooking Time: 8 hours**
Servings: 6

Ingredients:

- 1 Whole Turkey of about 12 to 16 lb
- 1 Cup of your Favorite Rub
- 1 Cup of Sugar
- 1 Tablespoon of minced garlic
- ½ Cup of Worcestershire sauce
- 2 Tablespoons of Canola Oil

Directions: Thaw the Turkey and remove the giblets. Pour in 3 gallons of water in a non-metal bucket of about 5 gallons. Put the BBQ rub and mix very well.
Put the sugar, the garlic and the Worcestershire sauce then, submerge the turkey into the bucket.
Refrigerate the turkey in the bucket for an overnight.
Place the Grill on a High Smoke and cook the Turkey for about 3 hours.
Switch the grilling temp to about 350 degrees F; then push a metal meat thermometer into the thickest part of the turkey breast.
Cook for about 4 hours; then take off the wood pellet grill and let rest for about 15 minutes
Slice the turkey, then serve and enjoy your dish!

Nutrition: Calories: 164.8; Fats: 13.9g; Carbs: 0.4g; Protein: 15.3g

191.   Whole Turkey

Preparation Time: 10 minutes   **Cooking Time: 7 hours and 30 minutes**
Servings: 10

Ingredients:

- 1 frozen whole turkey, giblets removed, thawed
- 2 tablespoons orange zest
- 2 tablespoons chopped fresh parsley
- 1 teaspoon salt
- 2 tablespoons chopped fresh rosemary
- 1 teaspoon ground black pepper
- 2 tablespoons chopped fresh sage
- 1 cup butter, unsalted, softened, divided
- 2 tablespoons chopped fresh thyme
- ½ cup water
- 14.5-ounce chicken broth

Directions: Open the hopper of the smoker, put dry pallets, make sure the ash-can is in place, then open the ash damper, power on the smoker and close the ash damper. Preheat the smoker to 180 degrees F.
For the turkey: tuck its wings under it by using kitchen twine.

Put ½ cup butter in a bowl, add thyme, parsley, orange zest, sage, orange zest, and rosemary, mix well and then brush this mixture generously on the inside and outside of the turkey and season the external of turkey with salt and black pepper.
Put the turkey on a roasting pan, breast side up, pour in broth and water, add the remaining butter in the pan, then place the pan on the smoker grill and shut with lid.
Cook the turkey for 3 hours, then increase the temperature to 350 degrees F and continue smoking the turkey for 4 hours, basting the turkey with the dripping every 30 minutes, but not in the last hour.
Take off the roasting pan from the smoker and let the turkey rest for 20 minutes.
Carve turkey into pieces and serve.

Nutrition: Calories: 145.8; Fats: 7.9g; Protein: 18.2g; Carbs: 0.9g

192. Jalapeno Injection Turkey

Preparation Time: 15 minutes
Servings: 4

Cooking Time: 4 hours and 10 minutes

Ingredients:

- 15 pounds whole turkey, giblet removed
- ½ of medium red onion, peeled and minced
- 8 jalapeño peppers
- 2 tablespoons minced garlic
- 4 tablespoons garlic powder
- 6 tablespoons Italian seasoning
- 1 cup butter, softened, unsalted
- ¼ cup olive oil
- 1 cup chicken broth

Directions: Open the hopper of the smoker, add dry pallets, put ash-can in place, then open the ash damper, power on the smoker and close the ash damper.
Preheat the smoker up to 200 degrees F.
Put a large saucepan over medium-high heat, add oil and butter and when the butter melts, add garlic, onion, and peppers and cook for 3 to 5 minutes or until nicely golden brown.
Pour in broth, mix well, let the mixture boil for 5 minutes, then remove pan from the heat and strain the mixture to get just liquid.
Inject turkey generously with prepared liquid, then spray the outside of turkey with butter spray and season well with garlic and Italian seasoning.
Put the turkey on the smoker grill, shut with lid, and smoke for 30 minutes, then increase the temperature to 325 degrees F and continue smoking the turkey for 3 hours.
Transfer turkey to a cutting board, let rest for 5 minutes, then carve into slices and serve.

Nutrition: Calories: 130.9; Fats: 6.9g; Protein: 13.2g; Carbs: 2.8g

193. Buttery Smoked Turkey Beer

Preparation Time: 15 minutes
Servings: 6

Cooking Time: 4 hours

Ingredients:

- Whole turkey (4-lbs., 1.8-kg.)

The Brine

- Beer – 2 cans
- Salt – 1 tablespoon
- White sugar – 2 tablespoons
- Soy sauce – ¼ cup
- Cold water – 1 quart

The Rub

- Unsalted butter – 3 tablespoons
- Smoked paprika – 1 teaspoon
- Garlic powder – 1 ½ teaspoon
- Pepper – 1 teaspoon
- Cayenne pepper – ¼ teaspoon

Directions: Pour beer into a container, then add white sugar, salt, and soy sauce then stir well.
Put the turkey into the brine mixture cold water over the turkey. Make sure that the turkey is completely soaked.
Soak the turkey in the brine for at least 6 hours or overnight and store in the fridge to keep it fresh.
On the next day, remove the turkey from the fridge and take it out of the brine mixture.
Wash and rinse the turkey then pat it dry.
Plug the wood pellet smoker then fill the hopper with the wood pellet. Turn the switch on.
Prepare the wood pellet smoker for indirect heat then adjust the temperature to 275°F (135°C).
Open the beer can then push it in the turkey cavity.

Put the seasoned turkey in the wood pellet smoker and make a tripod using the beer can and the two turkey legs. Cook the turkey for 4 hours.

Once it is done, remove the smoked turkey from the wood pellet smoker and transfer it to a serving dish.

Nutrition: Calories: 228.8; Carbs: 33.8g; Fats: 7.9g; Protein: 3.2g

194.   Hot Sauce Smoked Turkey Tabasco

Preparation Time: 20 minutes   **Cooking Time: 4 hours 15 minutes**
Servings: 8

Ingredients:
- Whole turkey (4-lbs., 1.8-kg.)

The Rub
- Brown sugar – ¼ cup
- Smoked paprika – 2 teaspoons
- Salt – 1 teaspoon
- Onion powder – 1 ½ teaspoon
- Oregano – 2 teaspoons
- Garlic powder – 2 teaspoons
- Dried thyme – ½ teaspoon
- White pepper – ½ teaspoon
- Cayenne pepper – ½ teaspoon

The Glaze
- Ketchup – ½ cup
- Hot sauce – ½ cup
- Cider vinegar – 1 tablespoon
- Tabasco – 2 teaspoons
- Cajun spices – ½ teaspoon
- Unsalted butter – 3 tablespoons

Directions: Rub the turkey with two tablespoons of brown sugar, salt, smoked paprika, dried thyme, onion powder, white pepper, garlic powder, and cayenne pepper. Let the turkey rest for an hour.

Plug the wood pellet smoker then fill the hopper with the wood pellet. Turn the switch on.

Prepare the wood pellet smoker for indirect heat then adjust the temperature to 275°F (135°C).

Put the seasoned turkey in the wood pellet smoker and smoke for 4 hours.

Put ketchup, hot sauce, cider vinegar, Tabasco, and Cajun spices in a saucepan then bring to a simmer.

Remove the sauce from heat and quickly add unsalted butter to the saucepan. Stir until melted.

After 4 hours of smoking, baste the Tabasco sauce over the turkey then continue smoking for 15 minutes.

Once the internal temperature of the smoked turkey has reached 170°F (77°C), remove from the wood pellet smoker and place it on a serving dish.

Nutrition: Calories: 159.8; Carbs: 1.9g; Fats: 13.8g; Protein: 7.2g

195.   Cured Turkey Drumstick

Preparation Time: 20 minutes   **Cooking Time: 2.5 hours to 3 hours**
Servings: 3

Ingredients:
- 3 fresh or thawed frozen turkey drumsticks
- 3 tablespoons extra virgin olive oil
- Brine component
- 4 cups of filtered water
- ¼Cup kosher salt
- ¼ cup brown sugar
- 1 teaspoon garlic powder
- Poultry seasoning 1 teaspoon
- 1/2 teaspoon red pepper flakes
- 1 teaspoon pink hardened salt

Directions: Put the salt water ingredients in a 1 gallon sealable bag and, add the turkey drumstick to the salt water and refrigerate for 12 hours.

After 12 hours, remove the drumstick from the saline, rinse with cold water, and pat dry with a paper towel.

Air dry the drumstick in the refrigerator without a cover for 2 hours.

Remove the drumsticks from the refrigerator and rub a tablespoon of extra virgin olive oil under and over each drumstick.

Prepare the wood pellet or grill for indirect cooking and preheat to 250 degrees Fahrenheit using hickory or maple pellets. Put the drumstick on the grill and smoke at 250 ° F for 2 hours.

After 2 hours, increase grill temperature to 325 ° F.

Cook the turkey drumstick at 325 ° F until the internal temperature of the thickest part of each drumstick is 180 ° F with an instant reading digital thermometer.

Put a smoked turkey drumstick under a loose foil tent for 15 minutes before eating.

Nutrition: Calories: 277.8; Carbs: 0g; Fats: 12.8g; Protein: 37.2g

196.   Roast Turkey Orange

Preparation Time: 30 minutes
Servings: 4

Cooking Time: 2 hours 30 minutes

Ingredients:

- 1 Frozen Long Island turkey
- 3 tablespoons west

- 1 large orange, cut into wedges
- Three celery stems chopped into large chunks

- Half a small red onion, a quarter

Orange sauce:

- 2 orange cups
- 2 tablespoons soy sauce

- 2 tablespoons orange marmalade
- 2 tablespoons honey

- 3 teaspoons grated raw

Directions: Remove the jibble from the turkey's cavity and neck and retain or discard it for another use. Wash the duck and pat some dry paper towels.

Remove excess fat from tail, neck and cavity. Use a sharp scalpel knife tip to pierce the turkey's skin entirely, so that it does not penetrate the duck's meat, to help dissolve the fat layer beneath the skin.

Put the seasoning inside the cavity with one cup of rub or seasoning.

Season the outside of the turkey with the remaining friction or seasoning.

Fill the cavity with orange wedges, celery and onion. Duck legs are tied with butcher twine to make filling easier.

Put the turkey's breast up on a small rack of shallow roast bread.

For the sauce: mix the ingredients in the saucepan over low heat and cook until the sauce is thick and syrupy. Set aside and let cool.

Prepare the wood pellet smoker grill for indirect cooking and use the pellets to preheat to 350 ° F and, roast the turkey at 350 ° F for 2 hours.

After 2 hours, brush the turkey freely with orange sauce.

Roast the orange glass turkey for another 30 minutes, making sure that the inside temperature of the thickest part of the leg reaches 165 ° F.

Put turkey under a loose foil tent for 20 minutes before serving.

Discard the orange wedge, celery and onion. Serve with a quarter of turkey with poultry scissors.

Nutrition: Calories: 215.8; Carbs: 1.9g; Fats: 10.8g; Protein: 34.1g

Fish and Seafood Recipes

197. Mahi-Mahi

Preparation Time: 10 minutes
Servings: 4

Cooking Time: 10 minutes

Ingredients:

- 4 (6-ounce) mahi-mahi fillets
- 2 tablespoons olive oil
- Salt and ground black pepper, as required

Directions: Prepare the griller set to 350 degrees F.
Coat fish fillets with vegetable oil and season with salt and black pepper evenly.
Put the fish fillets onto the grill and cook for about 5 minutes per side.
Remove the fish fillets from the grill and serve hot.

Nutrition: Calories: 194.8; Protein: 31.8g; Carbs: 0g; Fats: 6.8g

198. Lemony Lobster Tails

Preparation Time: 15 minutes
Servings: 4

Cooking Time: 25 minutes

Ingredients:

- ½ cup butter, melted
- 2 garlic cloves, minced
- 2 teaspoons fresh lemon juice
- Salt and ground black pepper, as required
- 4 (8-ounce) lobster tails

Directions: Prepare the "Wood Pellet Smoker and Grill" on the grill set to 450 degrees F.
Add all ingredients apart from lobster tails in a metal pan and blend well.
Put the pan onto the grill and cook for about 10 minutes.
Meanwhile, hamper the highest of the shell and expose lobster meat.
Remove the pan of the butter mixture from the grill.
Coat the lobster meat with a butter mixture.
Put the lobster tails onto the grill and cook for about a quarter-hour, coating with butter mixture once halfway through. Remove from the grill and serve hot.

Nutrition: Calories: 408.7; Protein: 43.2g; Carbs: 0.5g; Fats: 23.8g

199. Parsley Prawn Skewers

Preparation Time: 15 minutes
Servings: 5

Cooking Time: 8 minutes

Ingredients:

- ¼ cup fresh parsley leaves, minced
- 1 tablespoon garlic, crushed
- 2½ tablespoons olive oil
- 2 tablespoons Thai chili sauce
- 1 tablespoon fresh lime juice
- 1½ pounds prawns, peeled and deveined

Directions: Put all the ingredients to a bowl. Do not include the prawns, and mix well.
Take a resealable bag, add marinade and prawns. Seal the bag, shake it and coat it well.
Refrigerate for about 20-30 minutes.
Prepare the "Wood Pellet Smoker and Grill" on the grill set to 450 degrees F.
From the marinade, detach the prawns and thread them onto metal skewers.
Arrange the skewers onto the grill and cook for about 4 minutes per side.
Remove the grill from the skewers and serve sweet.

Nutrition: Calories: 233.8; Protein: 31.4g; Carbs: 4.6g; Fats: 8.7g

200.   Baked Steelhead

Preparation Time: 15 minutes   **Cooking Time: 20 minutes**
Servings: 4

Ingredients:

- 1 Lemon
- 2 Garlic cloves, minced
- ½ Shallot, minced
- 3 tbsp. Butter, unsalted
- Saskatchewan seasoning, blackened
- Italian Dressing
- 1 Steelhead (a fillet)

Directions: Prepare the grill to 350F with a closed lid.
Take an iron pan, and put the butter. Place the pan in the grill while preheating so that the butter melts. Coat the fillet with Italian dressing. Rub with Saskatchewan rub. Confirm the layer is thin.
Mince the garlic and shallot. Remove the pan from the grill and add the garlic and shallots.
Spread the mixture on the fillet. Slice the lemon into slices. Place the slice on the butter mix.
Put the fish on the grate. Cook for 20 – 30 minutes.
Remove from the grill and serve. Enjoy!

Nutrition: Calories: 229.8; Protein: 28.3g; Carbs: 1.9g; Fats: 13.8g

201.   Sesame Seeds Flounder

Preparation Time: 15 minutes   **Cooking Time: 2½ hours**
Servings: 4

Ingredients:

- ½ cup sesame seeds, toasted
- ½ teaspoon kosher salt flakes
- 1 tablespoon canola oil
- 1 teaspoon sesame oil
- 4 (6-ounce) flounder fillets

Directions: Prepare the "Wood Pellet Smoker and Grill" on a grill set to 225 degrees F.
With a mortar and pestle, crush sesame seeds with kosher salt slightly.
Take a small bowl, mix both oils.
Coat fish fillets with oil mixture generously, then, rub with sesame seeds mixture.
Put fish fillets onto the lower rack of the grill and cook for about 2-2½ hours.
Remove the fish fillets from the grill and serve hot.

Nutrition: Calories: 342.8; Protein: 44.5g; Carbs: 4.1g; Fats: 15.8g

202.   Spicy Filet Mignon with Sweet Onion

Preparation Time: 20 minutes   **Cooking Time: 10 minutes**
Serving: 4

Ingredients:

- Cooking spray
- 2 cups Vidalia
- 1/7 tsp. of salt
- 1 tsp. garlic powder
- ½ tsp. ground cumin
- ½ tsp. dried oregano
- ¼ tsp. salt
- ¼ tsp. of ground red pepper
- ¼ tsp. black pepper
- 4 4-oz. filet mignon
- 2 small onions, sliced

Directions: Heat the grill pan over medium-high heat and apply some cooking spray to it. Then, add the onion slices to the pan and season with a pinch of salt and black pepper. Sauté the onions for eight minutes, stirring occasionally. Then, remove them from the pan and keep them warm.
Mix the garlic powder with the remaining five ingredients in a small bowl and rub it into both sides of the beef.
Then, proceed to grill the beef in the pan for 5 minutes. Serve with the onion mixture.

Nutrition: Fats: 3.5g; Carbs: 8.1g; Protein: 24.8g

203.   Italian Grilled Shrimp

Preparation Time: 5 minutes   **Cooking Time: 15 minutes**
Serving: 4

Ingredients:

- 2 tbsp. honey
- 3 tbsp. olive oil
- 1 ½ lb. of raw shrimp (with tails)
- Grapeseed oil
- 2 cups loosely packed arugula
- 1¼ cups chopped heirloom tomatoes
- ½ cup kalamata olives, halved
- ½ cup sliced red onion
- 1 tbsp. red wine vinegar
- ½ tsp. salt
- ½ tsp. black pepper
- 2 tbsp. fresh oregano leaves

Directions: Prepare the grill until it reaches a high temperature of 450°F to 550°F. Then, whisk together the honey and olive oil in a medium-sized bowl. Proceed to add the shrimp and toss it to coat.
Then, brush the grill grate with grapeseed oil. Grill the shrimp and cover with the grill lid until it is done, for about 1.5 minutes per side.
Then, toss together the tomatoes, olives, arugula, and onion pieces in the large bowl. Add some vinegar, olive oil, shrimp, salt, and pepper. Toss the contents, transfer the mixture to a platter, and sprinkle with oregano.
Serve it immediately.

Nutrition: Fats: 19.8g; Carbs: 18.7g; Protein: 25.3g

204.   White Bean Grilled Salmon and Arugula Salad

Preparation Time: 30 minutes   **Cooking Time: 20 minutes**
Serving: 4

Ingredients:

- 1 tbsp. chopped capers, rinsed and drained.
- ¼ tsp. grated lemon rind
- 3 tbsp. fresh lemon juice
- 2 tbsp. olive oil
- ¾ tsp. salt
- ½ tsp. fresh garlic, minced
- 1/8 tsp. ground red pepper
- 1 can of great northern beans, rinsed and drained
- Cooking spray
- 4 6-oz. salmon fillets
- ¼ tsp. black pepper
- 4 cups loosely packed arugula
- ½ cup sliced red onion

Directions: Take a bowl, and mix the capers, garlic, oil, salt, juice, rind, and red pepper together. Then, add the beans.
Put the grill pan over a medium-high flame. Then, apply some oil spray to the pan and the salmon. Season it with salt and pepper before placing the salmon on the pan, skin-side down. Cook the fish for about 6 minutes before flipping it over. Sauté the other side for 1 minute or until you're finished.
Add the arugula and onions to the bean dish. Add any leftover capers and divide the salad and fillets between four plates. Serve immediately.

Nutrition: Fats: 15.1g; Carbs: 20.8g; Protein: 40.2g

205.   Grilled Flounder with Banana Leaves

Preparation Time: 5 minutes   **Cooking Time: 10 minutes**
Serving: 4

Ingredients:

- 1/4 cup finely chopped cilantro
- 1/4 cup olive oil
- 3 tbsp. minced shallot
- 2 tbsp. fresh lime juice
- 1 small chili from Fresno, seeded and finely chopped (about 2 tbsp.)
- 1 tbsp. finely chopped lemongrass (from 1 stalk)
- 1½ tsp. light brown sugar
- 1 tsp. grated peeled fresh ginger.
- 3/4 tsp. fish sauce
- 4 6-oz. skinless flounder fillets
- ¾ tsp. salt
- 2 (12-inch square or round) banana leaves or pieces of heavy-duty aluminum foil
- 4 banana leaves for serving (optional)

Directions: Prepare the grill to around 450°F (medium-high heat). In a medium-sized bowl, combine the first 6 ingredients.
Sprinkle the fillets with some salt. Then, place the banana leaves on the grill grates and place two flounder fillets onto each leaf. Then, spoon 1/4 cup of the shallot mixture onto the fillets. Grill the fish for 5 minutes.
Using two spatulas, carefully remove the leaves and fish from the grill. Place each fillet onto unused banana leaves. Serve immediately.

Nutrition: Fats: 16.8g; Carbs: 5.9g; Protein: 22.3g

206.   Grilled Salmon with Lemon-Pepper

Preparation Time: 5 minutes   **Cooking Time: 10 minutes**
Serving: 4

Ingredients:
- 4 6-oz. salmon fillets (skin-on)
- 2 tbsp. unsalted butter
- 1 tsp. lemon pepper
- ½ tsp. salt
- 8 thin slices of lemon
- 4 sprigs of flat-leaf parsley

Directions: Prepare the grill to medium-high heat.
Position 4 (12") aluminum foil square pieces in a row and apply some cooking spray to each layer. Place 1 piece of salmon on each sheet, skin-side down.
Cover each filet with half a teaspoon of butter, one-eighth of a teaspoon of lemon pepper, a pinch of salt, 2 slices of lemon, and 1 sprig of parsley.
Fold the sides of every foil pack together to secure them. Place these packets on the grill and cook them for 10 to 12 minutes until they are fully cooked.

Nutrition: Fats: 11.8g; Carbs: 1.2g; Protein: 34.2g

207.   Shrimp Kebabs

Preparation Time: 10 minutes   **Cooking Time: 10 minutes**
Serving: 6

Ingredients:
- ¼ cup unsalted butter
- 3 cloves of garlic, minced
- 1 tbsp. Cajun seasoning
- 1 tbsp. chopped thyme
- 1 lb. of Dutch yellow potatoes
- 3 ears of corn
- 1 lb. of deveined medium-sized shrimp
- 1 12.8-oz. smoked and packaged sausage
- 2 cut lemons
- 2 tbsp. chopped parsley leaves

Directions: Take a small bowl, mix some butter, Cajun seasoning, garlic, and thyme. Set aside.
Put a pot of water on the stove and allow it to boil. Add salt and cook all the potatoes for 10 to 13 minutes. Mix in the corn 5 minutes before the cooking time and then drain.
Thread the shrimp, corn, potatoes, and sausage onto the skewers.
Prepare the grill until it reaches medium-high heat. Place aluminum foil on the grill.
Then, place the kebabs on the grill and brush them with the butter mixture. Flip the skewers halfway until the shrimp becomes opaque and the corn softens.
Serve the kebabs with lemon wedges and parsley, if needed.

Nutrition: Fats: 14.5g; Carbs: 30.2g; Protein: 28.3g

Vegetarian Recipes

208.   Stuffed Tomatoes

Preparation Time: 15 minutes   **Cooking Time: 14 minutes**
Servings: 2

Ingredients:

- 2 large tomatoes
- ½ cup broccoli, chopped finely
- ½ cup cheddar cheese, shredded
- 1 tablespoon unsalted butter, melted
- ½ teaspoon dried thyme, crushed

Directions: Carefully cut the top of each tomato and scoop out pulp and seeds.
Take a bowl, place the chopped broccoli and cheese and mix.
Stuff each tomato with broccoli mixture evenly. Arrange the "Crisper Basket" in the pot of Griller.
Cover the Griller and select "Air Crisp". Set the temperature to 355 degrees F to preheat.
Press "Start/Stop" to begin preheating.
When the display shows "Add Food" opens the lid and places the tomatoes into the "Crisper Basket".
Drizzle the tomatoes with the butter. Close the Griller with lid and set the time for 15 minutes.
Press "Start/Stop" to begin cooking.
When the cooking time is completed, press "Start/Stop" to stop cooking and open the lid.
Serve with the garnishing of thyme.

Nutrition: Calories: 205.8; Fats: 15.3g; Carbs: 8.7g; Fiber: 2.7g; Protein: 9.6g

209.   Potato Gratin

Preparation Time: 15 minutes   **Cooking Time: 20 minutes**
Servings: 4

Ingredients:

- 2 large potatoes, sliced thinly
- 5½ tablespoons cream
- 2 eggs
- 1 tablespoon plain flour
- ½ cup cheddar cheese, grated

Directions: Arrange the "Crisper Basket" in the pot of Griller.
Close the Griller with the lid and select "Air Crisp". Set the temperature to 355 degrees F to preheat.
Press "Start/Stop" to begin preheating.
When the display shows "Add Food" opens the lid and place the potato slices into the "Crisper Basket".
Cover the Griller with a lid and set the time for 10 minutes. Press "Start/Stop" to begin cooking.
Meanwhile, in a bowl, add cream, eggs and flour and mix until a thick sauce form.
When the cooking time is completed, press "Start/Stop" to stop cooking and open the lid.
Remove the potato slices from the "Crisper Basket".
Divide the potato slices in 4 ramekins evenly and top with the egg mixture evenly, followed by the cheese.
Arrange the ramekins into the "Crisper Basket". Close the Griller with lid and select "Air Crisp".
Set the temperature to 390 degrees F for 10 minutes. Press "Start/Stop" to begin cooking.
When the cooking time is completed, press "Start/Stop" to stop cooking and open the lid. Serve warm.

Nutrition: Calories: 232.9; Fats: 7.9g; Carbs: 31.2g; Fiber: 4.3g; Protein: 9.9g

210.   Tofu with Orange Sauce

Preparation Time: 15 minutes   **Cooking Time: 20 minutes**
Servings: 4

Ingredients:

For Tofu:

- 1 pound extra-firm tofu, pressed and cubed
- 1 tablespoon cornstarch
- 1 tablespoon tamari

For Sauce:

- ½ cup water
- 1/3 cup fresh orange juice
- 1 tablespoon honey
- 1 teaspoon orange zest, grated
- 1 teaspoon garlic, minced
- 1 teaspoon fresh ginger, minced
- 2 teaspoons cornstarch
- ¼ teaspoon red pepper flakes, crushed

Directions: Take a bowl, put the cornstarch, tofu, and tamari and toss to coat well.
Set the tofu aside to marinate for at least 15 minutes. Arrange the greased "Crisper Basket" in the pot of Griller.
Close the Griller with the lid and select "Air Crisp". Set the temperature to 390 degrees F to preheat.
Press "Start/Stop" to begin preheating.
When the display shows "Add Food" opens the lid and place the tofu cubes into the "Crisper Basket".
Close the Griller with a lid and set the time for 10 minutes.
Press "Start/Stop" to begin cooking.
For the sauce: take a small pan, add all the ingredients over medium-high heat and bring to a boil, stirring continuously.
When the cooking time is completed, press "Start/Stop" to stop cooking and open the lid.
Transfer the tofu to a serving bowl. Put the sauce and gently mix. Serve immediately.

Nutrition: Calories: 146.8; Fats: 6.5g; Carbs: 12.5g; Fiber: 0.6g; Protein: 12.3g

211. Grilled Eggplant and Pepper Goat Cheese Sandwiches

Preparation Time: 10 minutes
Servings: 4

Cooking Time: 35 minutes

Ingredients:

- One red bell pepper
- One eggplant, sliced lengthwise into quarter-inch slices
- Three tbsp. low-fat bottled Italian
- You may also use balsamic vinaigrette
- Eight slices of whole-grain bread
- You may go for a French baguette cut lengthwise
- Two ounces soft goat cheese
- Quarter cup tapenade

Directions: Preheat the grill medium-high.
Cut off the bell pepper's top; discard the rind and seeds. Get the pepper sliced into pieces. Eggplant slices and bell pepper pieces are coated with low-fat bottled balsamic vinaigrette.
Put the bell pepper pieces and eggplant slices on a grill covered with canola cooking spray. Grill till tender plus slightly browned (8-10 minutes), about 6 inches from the fire, turning after 4-5 minutes.
Spread four bottom bread slices with goat cheese, then with tapenade. Cover with the slices of eggplant and a strip of red pepper the tapenade, then top with the remaining slices of bread.
Cut each sandwich (if using whole-grain bread) into 2 or 4 triangles and eat.

Nutrition: Calories: 316.8

212. Grilled Fava Beans with Mint, Lemon Zest and Sumac

Preparation Time: 5 minutes
Servings: 4

Cooking Time: 25 minutes

Ingredients:

- Twenty to thirty fresh Fava beans
- Olive oil for coating
- One pinch salt
- Three tbsp. olive oil
- One finely minced garlic clove
- One tbsp. finely chopped shallot
- One medium lemon zest
- Half teaspoon salt
- One tsp. sumac
- Quarter cup chopped fresh mint
- Quarter cup Italian Parsley
- Half teaspoon Aleppo chili
- One lemon juice

Directions: Toss a little drizzle of olive oil with fava beans, just enough even to coat, and sprinkle with salt generously.
Grill each side until the grill marks become prominent (4-5 minutes, each side). Try out a tester to ensure that the inner bean is tender.
Spread on a plate, spoon dressing over the top. Sprinkle with parsley, Aleppo chili flakes and fresh mint. You may taste one for salt.
You may put lemon juice if you want more lemon taste.

Nutrition: Calories: 228.9

213.   Grilled Romaine Salad with Maitake Mushrooms

Preparation Time: 5 minutes   **Cooking Time: 20 minutes**
Servings: 2

Ingredients

- One large Maitake Mushroom (Should be the size of a large orange)
- Two tbsp. olive oil or butter or use both in combination
- One smashed garlic clove
- Use salt and pepper as per taste

- One large head of romaine lettuce
- Garnish with capers, chives
- Use furikake seasoning for sprinkling
- Quarter cup mayo
- One tbsp. rice wine vinegar
- Two tsp. anchovy paste

- Half teaspoon finely minced or grated fresh ginger
- One finely minced or grated fat garlic clove
- Quarter teaspoon salt
- Use pepper as per taste
- Half teaspoon furikake seasoning

Directions: Heat grill to medium-high.

Cut the Maitake mushroom halfway to the end of the stem. Slice each half into thick slices of one-third of an inch. There are 6-8 slices you can have. Over medium melt heat, the oil or butter in a skillet. Season the oil thoroughly with salt and pepper and apply the crushed clove of garlic, stirring until fragrant for around 2 minutes. Get the garlic removed. Pan sear until golden, soft and slightly crispy on either side of the mushroom. Each side for about 4-5 minutes. Just put aside.

For the dressing: Mash them with garlic and ginger with a mortar and pestil when using whole anchovies. In a small bowl, combine with the remaining ingredients.

If Anchovy paste is used, whisk-mayo, vinegar, and anchovy paste until they are smooth. Ginger, garlic, salt and a few twists of cracked pepper are added. Stir in optional seasoning for furikake and set aside.

Cut the romaine lettuce in half when the grill is hot. Brush with the olive oil the cut side of the romaine. On the grill, put the cut side down and sear, leaving the lid open. Just sear before grill marks surface, about 2 minutes. In Romaine, you want to leave the crispness, but don't overdo it or let it collapse. Take it off the grill and put it on two plates.

Divide the mushrooms of the pan-seared Maitake and put on top of each half of the grilled Romaine. Over the Romaine and mushrooms, spoon the dressing. Sprinkle with the furikake seasoning and a few capers. Scatter with some fresh chives. Serve quickly with a knife and fork and devour.

Nutrition: Calories: 383.9

214.   Grilled Zucchini with Zaatar

Preparation Time: 5 minutes   **Cooking Time: 25 minutes**
Servings: 5

Ingredients:

- Three finely minced cloves of garlic
- Relish with flat-leaf parsley, labneh or yogurt, Aleppo Chili

- pepper (or chili flakes), lemon, olive oil, baby tomatoes
- Two pounds zucchini (or summer squash)

- One tbsp. Olive oil
- Two tbsp. Zaatar spice
- One tsp. salt

Directions: Preheat grill to medium-high heat.

Cut the zucchini into half-inch thick diagonal slices and put it into a big bowl. Sprinkle with olive oil, brush with zaatar and salt and complement with the garlic. Use your hands to mix the ingredients.

Place the zucchini on the sizzling grill. Switch the heat down to moderate and leave the lid closed, then cook for 5 minutes. After you grill, turn off. Turn heat to medium, cover & grill till cooked for another 5 minutes or so. Cook them on little heat or put them in a saucepan & cover them with foil, making them steam.

When cooked, put zucchini on a dish. On the side of the pan, or in a small bowl, spoon on the Smoked Yogurt, with a garnish of cherry tomatoes, squash of lemon, Italian parsley & if you want, a small sprinkle of olive oil. Scatter Aleppo pepper on the yogurt. It goes well with Chicken Shawarma.

Nutrition: Calories: 337.9

215.   Grilled Salmon Salad with Avocado Cucumber Salsa

Preparation Time: 3 minutes   **Cooking Time: 22 minutes**
Servings: 4

Ingredients:

- Two tsp. cumin
- Two tsp. chili powder
- One avocado (slightly firm) diced
- One cup diced cucumber
- Half jalapeno
- Quarter cup chopped cilantro
- One lime- juice and zest
- Twenty-four ounces salmon filet
- One tsp. salt
- Half teaspoon pepper
- Two tsp. Olive oil
- Half teaspoon salt
- Half tsp. salt
- Half tsp. pepper
- Four heads little gems lettuce
- Half cup plain Greek yogurt
- lime juice from one small lime
- One garlic clove minced
- One tbsp. olive oil
- One-eighth cup chopped cilantro

Directions: Heat grill to medium-high heat.

Insert pepper, salt, cumin and chili powder in a small bowl to prepare the rub. All sides of salmon are to be rubbed with the spice rub.

Then prepare the dressing by whisking the ingredients in a small bowl.

Next, prepare the salsa by mixing all of the ingredients, with the exception of avocado, in a medium bowl. The avocado has to be gently folded in the end to remain intact. Remember not to over mix.

Slice the lettuce into four pieces vertically. Then set aside.

Then salmon is to be grilled at medium-high heat on a greased grill. Grill each side for a couple of minutes until you achieve the desired doneness.

Then lettuce has to be tossed gently, covering it with a little dressing. Place on a plate. Make a bed of salmon. Then spoon avocado salsa over the top.

Enjoy by serving with cilantro sprigs and lime wedges.

Nutrition: Calories: 333.9

216.   Grilled Artichokes

Preparation Time: 5 minutes
Servings: 4

Cooking Time: 1 hour 20 minutes

Ingredients:

- Three to four lemon slices
- One eighth cup lemon juice
- Half cup mayo or Vegenaise
- Add salt and pepper to taste
- A few sage leaves (or bay leaves)
- One cup Italian parsley
- Quarter cup Basil leaves
- One garlic clove
- Four medium-sized artichokes- trimmed
- Two garlic cloves smashed
- One tbsp. capers
- One third cup olive oil

Directions: Put a large pot on the stove with enough water to only hit the inside of a steamer basket. Add the lemon slices, garlic cloves and sage to the water (or bay leaves). Just bring it to a boil.

Prepare the artichokes: Trim off the stems and tips with a very sharp knife and remove small tough exterior leaves. Place them in a steamer basket, bring water to a boil, cover and, depending on the size, simmer on low heat for 20-45 minutes. Then steam, until just tender. Let it cool. (You may refrigerate for up to 3 days before grilling at this point.) Make the Herb Oil and optional Aioli in the meantime.

Put the herbs and garlic in a food processor and pulse 5 times until neatly chopped. Add the capers, lemon juice, olive oil, and a generous pinch of salt and pepper.

Repeat, then scratch down the sides and pulse a few more times.

Set aside the herb oil. Before you grill, you will use this to brush on the artichokes, and for the aioli, the rest will be used. (Alternatively, you should only use the Herb Oil and ignore the aioli, since just the Herb Oil would spice the artichokes)

Apply one-third to the remaining Herb Oil- that is still in the food processor; the more you add, the less brazen it would be. Pulse several times until it's all combined. Don't over-mix. Add more salt, or even, if you like, chili flakes or Aleppo. This is your flavorful dipping sauce, Herbed Aoili.

Heat your grill to medium. If used, get wood chips to smoke. Cut the artichokes into half or quarters and use a spoon to scoop out the fibrous inside, right next to the heart.

Brush or spoon a little herb drizzle on the open side of the artichokes. Place the artichokes on the hot grill, with the open side facing down. Brush the tops with a little oil from the herbs. Move the grill to medium, cover for 5-7 minutes, and do not touch it. It could be 3-4 minutes if you use small artichokes, giving them good grill marks. Flip and cook for an extra 2 minutes.

Platter them up with the leftover herb oil or the Aioli once you see a little char.

Nutrition: Calories: 245.9

217.   Nicoise Salad with Grilled Fish

Preparation Time: 10 minutes   **Cooking Time: 40 minutes**
Servings: 6

Ingredients:
- One teaspoon kosher salt
- One ground pepper
- zest of one lemon
- Quarter cup olive oil
- Four finely minced cloves garlic
- Four to six boneless fish, without skin-filets – (4 or 6 ounces individually, thicker slices) use grillable fish: black
- cod, salmon, rockfish, halibut, bass, Mahi, or tuna
- One tbsp. mustard (whole grain)

Salad ingredients
- Half cup sliced roasted red bell pepper
- Greens, spinach or arugula for 4-6 people, approx. 1 lb.
- Eight ounces cherry tomatoes
- Half pound green beans trimmed and blanched
- Quarter cup kalamata or niçoise olives sliced
- Fifteen ounces canned cannellini beans washed & drained (or one
- and a half cup boiled) or sub three eggs (boiled), sliced in half
- Ten baby potatoes halved & blanched
- Two tablespoons' capers, drained.

Dressing Ingredients of Nicoise
- One tablespoon fresh thyme leaves or oregano
- Half cup chopped Italian parsley
- Quarter cup lemon juice (fresh) & zest of 1 lemon (Meyer Lemon is fine)
- One tbsp of vinegar (red wine)
- Three fourth teaspoon Kosher Salt
- fresh ground black pepper
- Half cup of olive oil (extra-virgin)
- Half cup of finely diced red onion
- Two tsp. wholegrain mustard

Directions: Mix all fish marinade ingredients in a middle-sized bowl & coat on the fish, marinating for minimum of half an hour or, ideally, overnight.
Boil green beans and white potatoes. When cooled, put it aside.
Preheat the grill to a medium temperature.
Prepare Nicoise dressing. In a medium-sized bowl, combine the ingredients. Add roasted peppers, cannellini beans, capers and olives to the dressing, and let marinate.
Grill the fish in a medium-high grill & flip thoroughly after every 5 minutes with a metal spatula, and if possible, lower heat or transfer to a chiller spot-or put on foil. You can also put on a layer of the lemon slices till cooked appropriately. Put aside and lightly cover with foil.
Prepare the salad. Place a hearty bed of the greens on an enormous dish. To coat the greens, scoop a small part of Nicoise dressing from cup & half of the marinated vegetables over the greens.
Arrange the green beans and potatoes and top them with the charred fish. Then garnish it with the sliced cherry tomatoes & remaining spoon dressing (depending on the size of the dressing- you might not require all) and finish with white beans or peppers over the top.
Give the fish a little lemon squeeze and crack some pepper for taste.

Nutrition: Calories: 537.9

218.   Sprouted Lentil Burgers

Preparation Time: 24 hours   **Cooking Time: 20 minutes**
Servings: 4

Ingredients:
- One tbsp. miso paste
- One tbsp. olive oil
- Two tsp. wholegrain mustard
- Two tsp. granulated garlic (or onion)
- One tsp. cumin
- One tbsp. sugar or any alternative sweetener
- Half teaspoon salt
- Optional add-ons- finely sliced shallots or red onions, cumin, whole coriander, or the fennel seeds
- Half teaspoon coriander
- One and a half cup sprouted green, brown or black lentils
- One cup cooked rice, brown
- One cup lightly toasted walnuts
- Half teaspoon salt
- Half teaspoon pepper
- Two to four tbsp. tablespoons fresh herbs- scallions, cilantro parsley, basil, etc.
- Two to three tbsp. toasted sesame seeds
- One raw beet, size of the tennis ball or smaller, peeled & grated
- Half cup of vinegar (red wine)
- Half cup water

Directions: Put one cup of whole lentils and 3-4 cups of water in a big mason jar in the morning and soak on the counter all day (8 hours).

Drain well in the evening. Turn the jar on its side, let the lentils dry out a little, and let the lentils continue to sit overnight on the counter. They are ready once you spot the tiny tip of the white sprout starting to appear. Usually, it takes 24-30 hours.

Put in the food processor one and a half cup of raw sprouted lentils (drained properly), miso, cooked rice, toasted walnuts, oil, salt, mustard, garlic, spices and pepper and repeatedly pulse until well mixed and becomes a sturdy dough. Do not over process. You want it to be rough, not smooth. Otherwise, it could get pasty!

Check one for salt. If it tastes bland, make sure the miso has been correctly mixed in (give a few stirs with a spoon, look for miso clump and pulse again).

Put a piece of parchment on a small sheet pan or large plate. Sprinkle the sesame seeds on the parchment.

Divide the dough into four balls with wet hands and shape four burgers, around 1 inch thick. Put on the parchment and coat all sides with sesame seeds.

Place in the refrigerator uncovered while the grill is being heated (15 minutes- to firm up) (15 minutes- to firm up) (15 minutes- to firm up) (15 minutes- to firm up)

They can also be pan-seared and done in a warm oven.

Preheat the grill to medium-high heat grill and the oven to 400-degree F. Grease the grill. Sear the lentil burgers until generous grill marks emerge, around 4-5 minutes on either side, then put in the oven for ten more minutes to finish warming all the way (or move to a cooler part of the grill)

Make your burgers at this stage, or wrap and freeze for later.

To make pickled beets, take sugar, liquids, salt and spices and bring them to a simmer in a small pot. Add the onion and grated beets. Stir and cook for a couple of minutes before transferring to the fridge for chilling.

Nutrition: Calories: 225.8

Vegan Recipes

219. Toasted-Baked Tofu cubes

Preparation Time: 5 minutes
Serving: 2

Cooking Time: 30 minutes

Ingredients:

- 1/2 block of tofu, cubed
- 1 tbsp. olive oil
- 1 tbsp. nutritional yeast
- 1 tbsp. flour
- 1/4 tsp. black pepper
- 1 tsp. sea salt
- 1/2 tsp. garlic powder

Directions: Mix all the ingredients with tofu.
Prepare the Grill at 2300C or 4000F.
Cook tofu on a lined baking tray for 15-30 minutes, and turn it around every 10 minutes.

Nutrition: Calories: 99.8; Carbs: 4.9g; Protein: 8.2g; Fats: 5.9g

220. Sriracha Roasted Potatoes

Preparation Time: 5 minutes
Servings: 3

Cooking Time: 30 minutes

Ingredients:

- 3 potatoes, diced
- 2-3 tsp. sriracha
- 1/4 garlic powder
- Salt & pepper
- Olive oil
- Chopped fresh parsley

Directions: Mix the potatoes with the remaining ingredients.
Prepare the Grill at 2300C or 4500F.
Line the pan with olive oil and spread the coated potatoes.
Sprinkle parsley. Cook for 30 minutes.

Nutrition: Calories 146.8; Carbs: 24.1; Protein: 3.2g; Fats: 4.5g

221. Pumpkin Quesadillas

Preparation Time: 5 minutes
Serving: 3

Cooking Time: 10 minutes

Ingredients:

- 1/2 canned pumpkin (pure)
- 2 gluten-free tortillas
- 1/2 cup refried beans
- 1-2 tbsp. nutritional yeast
- 1 tsp. onion powder
- 1 tsp. garlic powder
- Pinch of cayenne
- Salt & pepper

Directions: Combine the pumpkin with nutritional yeast, , salt, cayenne, onion powder, garlic powder, and pepper. Spread the pumpkin paste mixture in one tortilla and the refried beans in another.
Sandwich them together and toast in the Grill for 5 minutes.

Nutrition: Calories: 281.9; Carbs: 36.8g; Protein: 13.2g; Fats: 9.8g

222. Stuffed Mushroom

Preparation Time: 5 minutes
Serving: 2

Cooking Time: 35 minutes

Ingredients:

- 2 large portobello mushrooms
- Breadcrumbs
- Nutritional yeast (gives a cheesy, savory flavor)
- 1 cup tofu ricotta
- 1/2 cup canned marinara sauce
- 1 cup spinach
- 1/2 tsp. garlic powder
- 1 tsp. dry basil & 1 tsp. dry thyme
- Salt & pepper

Directions: Make ricotta with tofu, nutritional yeast, lemon juice, salt, and pepper. Combine the tofu ricotta, thyme, spinach, basil, marinara sauce, and seasoning. Brush marinara sauce on each mushroom and stuff the filling. Top it with breadcrumbs, nutritional yeast, and some olive oil. Cook for 15 minutes at 2300C or 4500F in Grill.

Nutrition: Calories: 274.8; Carbs: 10.2g; Protein: 23.1g; Fats: 19.2g

223. Stuffed Squash

Preparation Time: 10 minutes   **Cooking Time: 80 minutes**
Serving: 4

Ingredients:

- Acorn squash, halved and deseeded
- 2 cups cooked quinoa
- 1/2 edamame (shelled)
- 1/2 corn kernels
- 1/4 cranberries
- Some scallions, basil, and mint (thinly sliced)
- 2 tbsp. Olive oil
- Salt and pepper
- Lemon juice

Directions: Brush squash pieces with olive oil, salt, and pepper. Cook it at 1760C or 3500F for 35 minutes in the Grill. Prepare the filling by mixing all the remaining ingredients. Stuff baked squash with filling and bake for another 15 minutes.

Nutrition: Calories: 271.8; Carbs: 44.8g; Protein: 7.2g; Fats: 8.8g

Grilled Side Dishes Recipes

224. <u>Tomato Green Bean Soup</u>

Preparation Time: 10 minutes **Cooking Time: 6 hours**
Serving: 8

Ingredients:

- *1 cup carrots, chopped*
- *3 cups fresh tomatoes, diced*
- *1 garlic clove, minced*
- *6 cups vegetable broth*
- *1 lb. fresh green beans – should be cut in 1 inch pieces*
- *1/4 tsp. black pepper*
- *1 cup onions, chopped*
- *1 tsp. basil, dried*
- *1/2 tsp. salt*

Directions: Put the inner pot in the Griller combo base.
To the inner dish, add all the ingredients and stir well.
Cover it with a glass lid.
Select slow cook mode, press the temperature button, and set the time for 6 hours. Press start.
When the timer reaches 0, then press the cancel button.
Serve and enjoy.

Nutrition: Calories 70.8; Fats: 1.2g; Carbs: 10.1g; Sugar 4.2g; Protein: 5.8g

225. <u>Stuffed Pepper</u>

Preparation Time: 10 minutes **Cooking Time: 25 minutes**
Serving: 4

Ingredients:

- *4 eggs*
- *1/4 cup baby broccoli florets*
- *1/4 cup cherry tomatoes*
- *1 tsp. dried sage*
- *2.5oz cheddar cheese, grated*
- *7 oz. almond milk*
- *2 bell peppers, remove seeds, cut in half*
- *Pepper*
- *Salt*

Directions: Take a bowl, and whisk together milk, eggs, sage, broccoli, cherry tomatoes, pepper, and salt.
Pour the egg mixture into the bell pepper halves. Sprinkle cheese on top of bell pepper.
Put the inner pot in the Griller combo base. Put stuffed peppers into the inner pot.
Cover the inner pot with an air frying lid.
Select bake mode then set the temperature to 390 F and time for 25 minutes. Press start.
When the timer reaches 0, then press the cancel button. Serve and enjoy.

Nutrition: Calories: 284.9; Fats: 24.9g; Carbs: 5.6g; Sugar 3.1g; Protein: 11.7g

226. <u>Baked Tomato</u>

Preparation Time: 10 minutes **Cooking Time: 30 minutes**
Serving: 2

Ingredients:

- *2 eggs*
- *2 large fresh tomatoes*
- *1 tsp. fresh parsley*
- *Pepper*
- *Salt*

Directions: Cut off the top of a tomato and spoon out the tomato innards.
Break the egg in each tomato.
Put the inner pot in the Griller combo base.
Put tomato into the inner pot. Cover the inner pot with an air frying lid.
Select bake mode then set the temperature to 350 F and time for 15 minutes. Press start.
When the timer reaches 0, then press the cancel button.
Season tomato with parsley, pepper, and salt. Serve and enjoy.

Nutrition: Calories: 95.8; Fats: 4.5g; Carbs: 7.3g; Sugar: 4.8g; Protein: 7.4g

227.   Baked Beans

Preparation Time: 10 minutes   **Cooking Time: 10 minutes**
Serving: 2

Ingredients:

- 2 tbsp. BBQ sauce
- 1 1/2 tbsp. maple syrup
- 1 1/2 tsp. lemon juice
- 16 oz. can white beans- should be rinsed and drained
- 1 tbsp. prepared yellow mustard

Directions: Put the inner pot in the Griller combo base. Put the ingredients into the inner pot and stir well. Cover the pot with a lid.
Select simmer mode, press the temperature button, and set the time for 10 minutes. Press start.
When the timer reaches 0, then press the cancel button. Stir well and serve.

Nutrition: Calories: 277.9; Fats: 0.3g; Carbs: 52.6g; Sugar 14.5g; Protein: 14.5g

228.   Baked Eggplant & Zucchini

Preparation Time: 10 minutes   **Cooking Time: 35 minutes**
Serving: 6

Ingredients:

- 1 medium eggplant, sliced
- 3 medium zucchinis, sliced
- 3 oz. Parmesan cheese, grated
- 4 tbsp. parsley, chopped
- 4 tbsp. basil, chopped
- 1 tbsp. olive oil
- 4 garlic cloves, minced
- 1 cup cherry tomatoes, halved
- 1/4 tsp. pepper
- 1/4 tsp. salt

Directions: Take a mixing bowl, add cherry tomatoes, zucchini, eggplant, garlic, olive oil, basil, cheese, pepper, and salt toss well until combined. Transfer the eggplant mixture into the greased baking dish.
Put the inner pot in the Griller combo base. Put baking dish into the inner pot. Cover the pot with a lid.
Select bake mode then set the temperature to 350 F and time for 35 minutes. Press start.
When the timer reaches 0, then press the cancel button. Garnish with chopped parsley and serve.

Nutrition: Calories: 109.8; Fats: 5.6g; Carbs: 10.2g; Sugar 4.6g; Protein: 7.2g

229.   Broccoli Casserole

Preparation Time: 10 minutes   **Cooking Time: 30 minutes**
Serving: 6

Ingredients:

- 15 oz. broccoli florets
- 10 oz. can cream of mushroom soup
- 1 cup mozzarella cheese, shredded
- 1/3 cup milk
- 1/2 tsp. onion powder

For topping:

- 1 tbsp. butter, melted
- 1/2 cup crushed crackers

Directions: Put the inner pot in the Griller combo base. Put all ingredients except topping ingredients into the inner pot. Take a small bowl, mix cracker crumbs and melted butter and sprinkle over the inner pot mixture. Cover the inner pot with an air frying lid.
Select bake mode then set the temperature to 350 F and time for 30 minutes. Press start.
When the timer reaches 0, then press the cancel button. Serve and enjoy.

Nutrition: Calories: 178.7; Fats: 10.4g; Carbs: 11.6g; Sugar 3.5g; Protein: 7.2g

230.   Slow Cooked Vegetables

Preparation Time: 10 minutes   **Cooking Time: 5 hours**
Serving: 6

Ingredients:

- 1 lb. eggplant, peeled and cut 1-inch cubes
- 1 zucchini, chopped
- 3 fresh tomatoes, diced
- 1/2 onion, diced
- 1 red bell pepper, chopped
- 1 tbsp. olive oil
- 3 oz. feta cheese, crumbled
- 2 tsp. dried basil
- 1 tbsp. garlic, minced
- Pepper
- Salt

Directions: Put the inner pot in the Griller combo base.
Put all ingredients except feta cheese into the inner pot and stir well.
Cover the pot with a lid.
Select slow cook mode, press the temperature button, and set the time for 5 hours. Press start.
When the timer reaches 0, then press the cancel button.
Top with crumbled cheese and serve.

Nutrition: Calories: 104.8; Fats: 5.6g; Carbs: 11.2g; Sugar: 6.3g; Protein: 4.3g

231. Mushroom Barley Soup

Preparation Time: 10 minutes
Serving: 8

Cooking Time: 8 hours

Ingredients:
- 2/3 cup pearl barley
- 16 oz. button mushrooms, sliced
- 1 large onion, diced
- 6 cups vegetable broth
- 1 garlic clove, minced
- 1/4 tsp. pepper
- 1/2 tsp. salt

Directions: Put the inner pot in the Griller combo base. Put all ingredients into the inner pot and mix well.
Cover the pot with a lid.
Select slow cook mode, press the temperature button, and set the time for 8 hours. Press start.
When the timer reaches 0, then press the cancel button. Serve and enjoy.

Nutrition: Calories: 107.9; Fats: 1.2g; Carbs: 17.2g; Sugar: 2.3g; Protein: 7.5g

232. Mac & Cheese

Preparation Time: 10 minutes
Serving: 10

Cooking Time: 20 minutes

Ingredients:
- 1 lb. cooked macaroni
- 1/2 cup breadcrumbs
- 12 oz. cheddar cheese, shredded
- 4 1/2 cups milk
- 1/2 cup flour
- 1/2 cup butter
- Pepper
- Salt

Directions: Put the inner pot in the Griller combo base.
Put all ingredients except breadcrumbs into the inner pot and mix well. Sprinkle breadcrumbs on top.
Cover the inner pot with an air frying lid.
Select bake mode then set the temperature to 350 F and time for 20 minutes. Press start.
When the timer reaches 0, then press the cancel button. Serve and enjoy.

Nutrition: Calories: 485.7; Fats: 23.5g; Carbs: 48.1g; Sugar: 6.5g; Protein: 19.7g

233. Red Beans Rice

Preparation Time: 10 minutes
Serving: 8

Cooking Time: 8 hours

Ingredients:
- 1 cup dried red beans, soaked overnight
- 1 1/2 cups rice, rinsed
- 1/2 tsp. thyme
- 1 lime juice
- 2 cups of coconut milk
- 3 cups vegetable stock
- 2 garlic cloves, minced
- 1/4 tsp. allspice
- 1 tsp. red pepper flakes
- 1/2 tsp. ground ginger
- 1/2 tsp. salt

Directions: Drain beans and place them into the large pot. Add fresh water and bring to boil for 10-15 minutes.
Put the inner pot in the Griller combo base. Drain beans and add them into the inner pot.

Put remaining ingredients and stir well. Cover the pot with a lid.
Select slow cook mode, press the temperature button, and set the time for 8 hours. Press start.
When the timer reaches 0, then press the cancel button. Serve and enjoy.

Nutrition: Calories: 347.9; Fats: 14.7g; Carbs: 46.3g; Sugar: 2.7g; Protein: 9.5g

Appetizers and Sides Recipes

234. Mushrooms Stuffed With Crab Meat

Preparation Time: 20 minutes   **Cooking Time: 30 to 45 minutes**
Servings: 4 to 6

Ingredients:

- 6 medium-sized Portobello mushrooms
- Extra virgin olive oil
- ⅓ Grated parmesan cheese cup

Club Beat Staffing:

- 8 ounces fresh crab meat or canned or imitation crab meat
- 2 tablespoons extra virgin olive oil
- ⅓ Chopped celery
- Chopped red peppers
- ½ cup chopped green onion
- ½ cup Italian bread crumbs
- ½ Cup mayonnaise
- 8 ounces cream cheese at room temperature
- ½ teaspoon of garlic
- 1 tablespoon dried parsley
- Grated parmesan cheese cup
- 1 teaspoon of Old Bay seasoning
- ¼ teaspoon of kosher salt
- ¼ teaspoon black pepper

Directions: Clean up the mushroom cap with a damp paper towel, cut off the stem, and save it.
Remove the brown gills from the bottom of the mushroom cap with a spoon and discard.
Prepare crab meat stuffing. If you are a fan of using canned crab meat, rinse, drain, and remove shellfish.
Heat the pan with olive oil first over medium high heat. Put celery, green onions, peppers and green onions and fry for 5 minutes. Set aside for cooling.
Gently pour the chilled sautéed vegetables and the remaining ingredients into a large bowl.
Cover and refrigerate crab meat stuffing until ready to use.
Place the crab mixture in each mushroom cap and make a mound in the center.
Sprinkle extra virgin olive oil and sprinkle parmesan cheese on each stuffed mushroom cap. Place the mushrooms in a 10 x 15 inch baking dish.
Use the pellets to set the wood pellet smoker and grill to indirect heating and preheat to 375 ° F.
Cook for 30-45 minutes.

Nutrition: Calories: 159.8; Carbs: 13.8g; Fats: 7.9g; Protein: 10.2g

235. Brisket Baked Beans

Preparation Time: 20 minutes   **Cooking Time: 1 to 2 hours**
Servings: 10

Ingredients:

- 2 tablespoons extra virgin olive oil
- 1 large diced onion
- 1 diced green pepper
- 1 red pepper diced
- 2 to 6 jalapeno peppers diced
- Texas style brisket flat chopped 3 pieces
- 1 baked beans, like Bush's country style baked beans
- 1 pork and beans
- 1 red kidney beans, rinse, drain
- 1 cup barbecue sauce like Sweet Baby Ray's barbecue sauce
- ½ cup stuffed brown sugar
- 3 garlics, chopped
- 2 teaspoons of mustard
- ½ teaspoon kosher salt
- ½ teaspoon black pepper

Directions: Heat the skillet with olive oil over medium heat and add the diced onion, jalapeno and peppers. Sauté the food for about 8-10 minutes.
In a 4 quart casserole dish, mix chopped brisket, baked beans, kidney beans, pork beans, cooked onions, barbecue sauce, peppers, garlic, brown sugar, mustard, black pepper and salt.
Using the selected pellets, configure a wood pellet smoking grill for indirect cooking and preheat to 325 ° F. Cook the beans baked in the brisket for 2 hours. Rest for 15 minutes before eating.

Nutrition: Calories: 198.7; Carbs: 34.9g; Fats: 1.9g; Protein: 9.2g

236. Apple Wood Smoked Cheese

Preparation Time: 1 hour 15 minutes   **Cooking Time: 2 hours**
Servings: 6

Ingredients:

- Gouda
- Sharp cheddar
- Very sharp 3 year cheddar
- Monterey Jack
- Pepper jack
- Swiss

Directions: According to the shape of the cheese block, cut the cheese block into an easy-to-handle size (approximately 4 x 4 inch block) to promote smoke penetration.

Leave the cheese on the counter for one hour to form a very thin skin or crust, which acts as a heat barrier, but allows smoke to penetrate.

Prepare the wood pellet smoking grill for indirect heating and install a cold smoke box to prepare for cold smoke. Make sure that the louvers on the smoking box are fully open to allow moisture to escape from the box.

Prepare the wood pellet smoker and grill to 180 ° F or use apple pellets and smoke settings, if any, to get a milder smoke flavor.

Put the cheese on a Teflon-coated fiberglass non-stick grill mat and let cool for 2 hours.

Remove the smoked cheese and cool for 1 hour on the counter using a cooling rack.

After labeling the smoked cheese with a vacuum seal, refrigerate for two weeks or more, then smoke will permeate and the cheese flavor will become milder.

Nutrition: Calories: 101.9; Carbs: 0g; Fats: 8.8g; Protein: 6.2g

237. Garlic Parmesan Wedge

Preparation Time: 15 minutes
Servings: 4

Cooking Time: 30 to 35 minutes

Ingredients:

- 3 large russet potatoes
- ¼ cup of extra virgin olive oil
- 1 teaspoon salt
- ¾ teaspoon black hu pepper
- 2 teaspoon garlic powder
- ¾ cup grated parmesan cheese
- 3 tablespoons of fresh coriander or flat leaf parsley (optional)
- ½ cup blue cheese or ranch dressing per serving, for soaking (optional)

Directions: Gently rub the potatoes with cold water using a vegetable brush to dry the potatoes.

Cut the potatoes in half vertically and cut them in half.

Wipe off any water released when cutting potatoes with a paper towel. Moisture prevents wedges from becoming crunchy.

Place the potato wedge, salt, olive oil, pepper and garlic powder in a large bowl and shake lightly by hand to distribute the oil and spices evenly.

Put the wedges on a single layer of non-stick grill tray / pan / basket (about 15 x 12 inches).

Set the wood pellet r grill for indirect cooking and use all types of wood pellets to preheat to 425 degrees F.

Place the grill tray in the preheated smoker and grill, roast the potato wedge for 15 minutes, and turn. Roast the potato wedge for an additional 20 minutes until the potatoes are soft inside and crispy golden on the outside.

Sprinkle potato wedge with parmesan cheese and add coriander or parsley as needed. If necessary, add blue cheese or ranch dressing for the dip.

Nutrition: Calories: 111.8; Carbs: 16.8g; Fats: 2.9g; Protein: 3.2g

238. Buffalo Turds

Preparation Time: 30 to 45 minutes
Servings: 6

Cooking Time: 1.5 hours to 2 hours

Ingredients:

- 10 Medium Jalapeno Pepper
- 8 ounces regular cream cheese at room temperature
- ¾ Cup Monterey Jack and Cheddar Cheese Blend Shred (optional)
- 1 teaspoon smoked paprika
- 1 teaspoon garlic powder
- ½ teaspoon cayenne pepper
- Teaspoon red pepper flakes (optional)
- 20 smoky sausages
- 10 sliced bacon, cut in half

Directions: Wear food service gloves when using. Jalapeno peppers are washed vertically and sliced. Carefully remove seeds and veins using a spoon or paring knife and discard. Put Jalapeno on a grilled vegetable tray and set aside.

In a small bowl, mix cream cheese, paprika, shredded cheese, garlic powder, cayenne pepper if used, and red pepper flakes if used, until thoroughly mixed.
Mix cream cheese with half of the jalapeno pepper.
Put the Little Smokiness sausage on half of the filled jalapeno pepper.
Wrap half of the thin bacon around half of each jalapeno pepper.
Fix the bacon to the sausage with a toothpick so that the pepper does not pierce. Put the ABT on the grill tray or pan.
Prepare the wood pellet smoker and grill for indirect cooking and preheat to 250 degrees Fahrenheit using hickory pellets or blends.
Suck jalapeno peppers at 250 ° F for about 1.5 to 2 hours until the bacon is cooked and crisp.
Remove the ABT from the grill and let it rest for 5 minutes before hors d'oeuvres.

Nutrition: Calories: 130.9; Carbs: 0.9g; Fats: 11.8g; Protein: 5.2g

239.   Grilled Corn

Preparation Time: 15 minutes   **Cooking Time: 25 minutes**
Servings: 6

Ingredients:

- 6 fresh ears corn
- Salt
- Black pepper
- Olive oil
- Vegetable seasoning
- Butter for serving

Directions: Preheat the grill to high with closed lid.
Peel the husks. Remove the corn's silk. Rub with black pepper, salt, vegetable seasoning, and oil.
Close the husks and grill for 25 minutes. Turn them occasionally. Serve topped with butter and enjoy.

Nutrition: Calories: 69.8; Protein: 3.2g; Carbs: 17.9g; Fats: 1.9g

240.   Grilled Broccoli

Preparation Time: 15 minutes   **Cooking Time: 10 minutes**
Servings: 4 to 6

Ingredients:

- 4 bunches of Broccoli
- 4 tablespoons Olive oil
- Black pepper and salt to taste
- ½ Lemon, the juice
- ½ Lemon cut into wedges

Directions: Prepare the grill to High with a closed lid.
Take a bowl, add the broccoli and drizzle with oil. Coat well. Season with salt.
Grill for 5 minutes and then flip. Cook for 3 minutes more.
Once done transfer on a plate. Squeeze lemon on top and serve with lemon wedges.

Nutrition: Calories: 34.8; Protein: 2.7g; Carbs: 4.9g; Fats: 0.9g

241.   Potato Roast

Preparation Time: 15 minutes   **Cooking Time: 35 minutes**
Servings: 6

Ingredients:

- 4 Potatoes, large (scrubbed)
- 1 ½ cups gravy (beef or chicken)
- Rib seasoning to taste
- 1 ½ cups Cheddar cheese
- Black pepper and salt to taste
- 2 tablespoons sliced Scallions

Directions: Prepare the grill to high with a closed lid.
Slice each potato into wedges or fries. Transfer into a bowl and drizzle with oil. Season with Rib seasoning.
Spread the wedges/fries on a baking sheet (rimmed). Roast for about 20 minutes. Turn the wedges/fries and cook for 15 minutes more.
Take a saucepan and warm the chicken/beef gravy. Cut the cheese into small cubes.
Once done cooking, place the potatoes on a plate or into a bowl. Distribute the cut cheese and pour hot gravy on top. Serve garnished with scallion. Season with pepper.

Nutrition: Calories: 219.8; Protein: 3.2g; Carbs: 37.9g; Fats: 14.8g

242.   Nut Mix on the Grill

Preparation Time: 10 minutes
Servings: 8

Cooking Time: 20 minutes

Ingredients:

- 3 cups Mixed Nuts, salted
- 1 teaspoon Thyme, dried
- 1 ½ tablespoon brown sugar, packed
- 1 tablespoon Olive oil
- ¼ teaspoon of Mustard powder
- ¼ teaspoon Cayenne pepper

Directions: Prepare the grill to 250F with a closed lid.
Take a bowl, mix the ingredients, and place the nuts on a baking tray lined with parchment paper. Put the try on the grill. Cook 20 minutes. Serve and enjoy.

Nutrition: Calories: 64.8; Protein: 23.4g; Carbs: 3.8g; Fats: 51.8g

243.   Grilled French Dip

Preparation Time: 15 minutes
Servings: 8

Cooking Time: 35 minutes

Ingredients:

- 3 lbs. onions, thinly sliced (yellow)
- 2 tablespoons oil
- 2 tablespoons of Butter
- Salt to taste
- Black pepper to taste
- 1 teaspoon Thyme, chopped
- 2 teaspoon of Lemon juice
- 1 cup Mayo
- 1 cup of Sour cream

Directions: Prepare the grill to high with a closed lid.
Take a pan and mix the oil and butter. Put on the grill to melt. Add 2 teaspoons salt and add the onions.
Mix it well and close the lid of the grill. Cook 30 minutes stirring often.
Add the thyme. Cook for an additional 3 minutes. Set aside and add black pepper.
Once cooled add lemon juice, mayo, and sour cream. Stir to combine. Taste and add more black pepper and salt if needed. Serve with veggies or chips.

Nutrition: Calories: 59.8; Protein: 4.2g; Carbs: 4.8g; Fats: 5.9g

244.   Smoked Jerky

Preparation Time: 20 minutes
Servings: 6

Cooking Time: 6 hours

Ingredients:

- 1 Flank Steak (3lb.)
- ½ cup of Brown Sugar
- 1 cup of Bourbon
- ¼ cup Jerky rub
- 2 tablespoons of Worcestershire sauce
- 1 can of Chioplete
- ½ cup Cider Vinegar

Directions: Slice the steak into ¼ inch slices. Mix the remaining ingredients in a bowl. Stir well.
Put the steak in an empty bag and add the marinade sauce. Marinade in the fridge overnight.
Prepare the grill to 180F with a closed lid. Remove the flank from the marinade. Put directly on a rack and on the grill. Smoke for 6 hours. Cover them lightly for 1 hour before serving. Store leftovers in the fridge.

Nutrition: Calories: 104.8; Protein: 14.2g; Carbs: 3.9g; Fats: 2.8g

245.   Smoked Guacamole

Preparation Time: 15 minutes
Servings: 8

Cooking Time: 30 minutes

Ingredients:

- ¼ cup chopped Cilantro
- 7 Avocados, peeled and seeded
- ¼ cup chopped Onion, red
- ¼ cup chopped tomato
- 3 ears corn
- 1 teaspoon of Chile Powder
- 1 teaspoon of Cumin
- 2 tablespoons of Lime juice
- 1 tablespoon minced Garlic

- *1 Chile, poblano*
- *Black pepper and salt to taste*

Directions: Prepare the grill to 180F with a closed lid.
Smoke the avocado for 10 min.
Set the avocados aside and increase the temperature of the girl to high.
Once heated grill the corn and chili. Roast for 20 minutes.
Cut the corn. Set aside. Put the chili in a bowl. Cover it with a wrapper and let it sit for about 10 minutes. Peel the chili and dice. Add it to the kernels.
Take a bowl and mash the avocados, leave few chunks. Put the remaining ingredients and mix.
Serve right away because it is best eaten fresh.

Nutrition: Calories: 50.8; Protein: 1.2g; Carbs: 2.8g; Fats: 4.2g

246.   Shrimp Cocktail

Preparation Time: 10 minutes   **Cooking Time: 15 minutes**
Servings: 4

Ingredients:
- *2 lbs. of Shrimp with tails, deveined*
- *Black pepper and salt*
- *1 teaspoon of Old Bay*
- *2 tablespoons Oil*
- *½ cup of Ketchup*
- *1 tablespoon of Lemon Juice*
- *2 tablespoons Horseradish, Prep Timeared*
- *1 tablespoon of Lemon juice*
- *For garnish: chopped parsley*
- *Optional: Hot sauce*

Directions: Prepare the grill to 350F with a closed lid.
Clean the shrimp. Pat dry using paper towels.
Take a bowl and put the shrimp, Old Bay, and oil. Toss to coat. Spread on a baking tray. Put the tray on the grill and let it cook for 7 minutes.
In the meantime, make the sauce: mix the lemon juice, ketchup and horseradish. Season with black pepper and sauce and if you like add hot sauce. Stir.
Serve the shrimp with the sauce and enjoy.

Nutrition: Calories: 79.9; Protein: 8.2g; Carbs: 4.9g; Fats: 0.9g

247.   Smoked Russet Potatoes

Preparation Time: 15 minutes   **Cooking Time: 2 hours**
Servings: 6

Ingredients:
- *8 large Russet potatoes*
- *1/2 cup of garlic-infused olive oil*
- *Kosher salt and black pepper to taste*

Directions: Prepare the pellet grill on SMOKE with the lid open until the fire is established. Set the temperature to 225 °F and preheat, lid closed, for 10 to 15 minutes. Rinse and dry your potatoes; pierce with a fork on all sides.
Drizzle with garlic-infused olive oil and rub all your potatoes generously with salt and pepper.
Put the potatoes on the pellet smoker and close the lid.
Cook potatoes for about 2 hours. Serve hot with your favorite dressing.

Nutrition: Calories: 383.8; Carbs: 47.9g; Fats: 18.1g; Fiber: 3.5g; Protein: 6.2g

248.   Smoked Asparagus with Parsley and Garlic

Preparation Time: 10 minutes   **Cooking Time: 1 hour**
Servings: 3

Ingredients:
- *1 bunch of fresh asparagus, cleaned*
- *1 Tbs of finely chopped parsley*
- *1 Tbs of minced garlic*
- *1/2 cup of olive oil*
- *Salt and ground black pepper to taste*

Directions: Prepare the pellet grill on SMOKE with the lid open until the fire is established. Set the temperature to 225 °F and preheat, lid closed, for 10 to 15 minutes. Rinse and cut the ends off of the asparagus.
Mix olive oil, minced garlic, chopped parsley, and salt and pepper in a bowl.
Season your asparagus with olive oil mixture. Put the asparagus on a heavy-duty foil and fold the sides.
Cook for 55 to 60 minutes or until soft (turn every 15 minutes). Serve hot.

Nutrition: Calories: 351.8; Carbs: 6.5g; Fats: 35.9g; Fiber: 2.8g; Protein: 3.6g

249. Smoked Sweet Pie Pumpkins

Preparation Time: 15 minutes   **Cooking Time: 2 hours**
Servings: 6

Ingredients:
- *4 small pie pumpkins*
- *avocado oil to taste*

Directions: Prepare the pellet grill on SMOKE with the lid open until the fire is established. Set the temperature to 250 °F and preheat, lid closed, for 10 to 15 minutes.
Cut pumpkins in half, top to bottom, and drizzle with avocado oil.
Put pumpkin halves on the smoker away from the fire.
Smoke pumpkins from 1 1/2 to 2 hours. Remove pumpkins from smoked and allow to cool. Serve to taste.

Nutrition: Calories: 166.9; Carbs: 9.8g; Fats: 13.9g; Fiber: 0.9g; Protein: 1.9g

Rubs, Sauces, Marinades, Glazes

250. North Carolina Barbecue Sauce

Ingredients:

- 1 qt cider vinegar
- 12 oz ketchup
- 2/3 C packed brown sugar
- 2 Tbsp. salt
- ¼ C lemon juice

- 1 Tbsp. red pepper flakes
- 1 Tbsp. smoked paprika
- 1 Tbsp. onion powder
- 1 tsp each: black pepper, dry mustard

Directions: Bring the ingredients to a boil, and then simmer for 30-45 minutes, stirring frequently. Allow to cool and serve or bottle.

251. Texas Brisket Sauce

Ingredients:

- ½ C brisket drippings (defatted)
- ½ C vinegar
- 1 Tbsp. Worcestershire sauce
- ½ C ketchup

- ½ tsp hot pepper sauce (Franks)
- 1 lg onion, diced
- 2 cloves of garlic, pressed
- 1 Tbsp. salt

- ½ tsp chili powder
- Juice of one lemon

Directions: Mix all ingredients. Simmer, occasionally stirring, for 15 minutes and then, allow to cool and refrigerate 24-48 hours before using.

252. Spicy Thai Peanut Sauce

Ingredients:

- 3 C creamy peanut butter
- 3/4 C coconut milk
- 1/3 C fresh lime juice

- 1/3 C soy sauce
- 1 Tbsp. fish sauce
- 1 Tbsp. hot sauce

- 1 Tbsp. minced fresh ginger root
- 5 cloves garlic. minced

Directions: Mix the peanut butter, lime juice, ginger, coconut milk, fish sauce, soy sauce, hot sauce, and garlic. Simmer for 10 minutes, cool and serve.

253. Gorgonzola Dipping Sauce

Ingredients:

- 1 C crumbled blue cheese
- 2/3 C sour cream
- ½ C mayonnaise

- 1 clove garlic, minced
- 1 oz white wine
- 2 tsp Worcestershire sauce

- 1 tsp salt
- 1 tsp fresh ground black pepper

Directions: Take a glass or plastic bowl, mix the ingredients, using the salt and pepper to finalize the taste and the white wine to set the consistency.

254. Brisket Rub

Ingredients:

- (For 4 full briskets 7-8lbs. each)
- 1 C fine sea salt

- 1 C coarse pepper
- 1 C granulated garlic

- 1/4 C smoked paprika

Directions: Rub briskets and refrigerate for 12-24 hours. Allow briskets to come to room temp before smoking. Smoke brisket(s) with a combination of oak and pecan wood pellets, at a temp between 225-25
The difference between good brisket and amazing brisket is patience.
Double wrap the finishing brisket in foil, wrap that in a towel, and let the whole thing rest in a closed cooler for 1-2 hours. Then, once you've unwrapped it, allow it to sit and cool slightly for 15-20 minutes for slicing or pulling.

255.   Hawaiian Mojo

Ingredients:

- 1 C orange juice
- 1 C pineapple juice
- ½ C mesquite liquid smoke
- 1 Tbsp. oregano
- 1 Tbsp. minced garlic
- 1 tsp cumin
- 3 tsp salt
- 4 oz. of water

Directions: Combine all the ingredients and let it sit for a minimum of one hour.
For marinade/injection, add the above recipe to 1 ½ gallons of water, and 13 oz. of table salt.
Blend the ingredients and let it sit for a minimum of one hour, strain and inject, or place meat in a cooler and pour marinade to cover. Allow marinating overnight.
After injecting/soaking the pig or shoulder, pat dry with paper towels and apply a salt rub all over the meat, use Kosher salt or coarse sea salt.

256.   Queen Spice Rub

Preparation Time: 10 minutes
Servings: 4

Cooking Time: 60 minutes

Ingredients:

- 1 tablespoon salt
- 6 teaspoons ground cayenne pepper
- 6 teaspoons ground white pepper
- 2 teaspoons ground black pepper
- 4 teaspoons paprika
- 5 teaspoons onion powder
- 2 teaspoons garlic powder

Directions: Prepare the smoker grill at 220 degrees Fahrenheit by closing the lid.
You can use an apple wood chip to create the smoke.
The internal temperature should be 100 degrees Fahrenheit, to smoke the spices. Take a bowl and mix the listed ingredients.
Transfer all the spices into an aluminum pipe and place it on the grate.
Cover the smoker and let it smoke for 1 hour.
Afterward, remove the foil tin from the grill and store in a tight jar for further use.

Nutrition: Calories: 23.8; Carbs: 4.9g; Fat: 0.9g; Protein: 1.2g

257.   Three Pepper Rub

Preparation Time: 10 minutes
Servings: 3

Cooking Time: 3 hours

Ingredients:

- 2 tablespoons of black pepper
- 2 tablespoons of white pepper
- 2 tablespoons of red pepper
- 1 tablespoon of onion powder
- 2 teaspoons of garlic powder
- 2 tablespoons of dried thyme
- 4 tablespoons of paprika
- 2 tablespoons of dried oregano

Directions: Combine the spices in the bowl and transfer them to an aluminum foil tin.
Prepare the smoker grill at 220 degrees F for 20 minutes.
Put the aluminum foil tin onto the grill grate and smoke for 3 hours by closing the lid.
Once done, store it in the tight jar for further use.

Nutrition: Calories: 66.9; Carbs: 15.9g; Fat: 1.9g; Protein: 2.2g

258.   (Not Just For Pork) Rub

Preparation Time: 5 minutes

Servings: 4

Ingredients:

- ½ teaspoon ground thyme
- ½ teaspoon paprika
- ½ teaspoon coarse kosher salt
- ½ teaspoon garlic powder
- ½ teaspoon onion powder
- ½ teaspoon chili powder
- ¼ teaspoon dried oregano leaves
- ¼ teaspoon freshly ground black pepper
- ¼ teaspoon ground chipotle chili pepper
- ¼ teaspoon celery seed

Directions: Using an airtight bag, mix the thyme, salt, paprika, onion powder, garlic powder, chipotle pepper, chili powder, oregano, black pepper, and celery seed. Close the container and shake to mix. Unused rub will keep in an airtight container for months.

Nutrition: Calories: 63.9; Carbs: 9.9g; Fat: 0.8g; Protein: 1.2g

259. Dill Seafood Rub

Preparation Time: 5 minutes   Servings: 2

Ingredients:
- *2 tablespoons coarse kosher salt*
- *2 tablespoons dried dill weed*
- *1 tablespoon garlic powder*
- *1½ teaspoons lemon pepper*

Directions: Combine the salt, garlic powder, dill, and lemon pepper using an airtight bag. Close the container and shake to mix. The unused rub will keep in an airtight container for months.

Nutrition: Calories: 14.9; Carbs: 2.9g; Fat: 0g; Protein: 0g

260. Espresso Brisket Rub

Preparation Time: 5 minutes   Servings: 2

Ingredients:
- *3 tablespoons coarse kosher salt*
- *2 tablespoons ground espresso coffee*
- *2 tablespoons freshly ground black pepper*
- *1 tablespoon garlic powder*
- *1 tablespoon light brown sugar*
- *1½ teaspoons dried minced onion*
- *1 teaspoon ground cumin*

Directions: Take a small airtight container or zip-top bag, and mix the salt, black pepper, espresso, minced onion, garlic powder, brown sugar, and cumin. Cover the container and shake to mix. Unused rub will keep in an airtight container for months.

Nutrition: Calories: 55.9; Carbs: 12.9g; Fat: 0.9g; Protein: 2.1g

261. Sweet and Spicy Cinnamon Rub

Preparation Time: 10 minutes   Servings: 3

Ingredients:
- *2 tablespoons light brown sugar*
- *1 teaspoon coarse kosher salt*
- *1 teaspoon garlic powder*
- *1 teaspoon onion powder*
- *1 teaspoon sweet paprika*
- *½ teaspoon freshly ground black pepper*
- *½ teaspoon cayenne pepper*
- *½ teaspoon dried oregano leaves*
- *½ teaspoon ground ginger*
- *½ teaspoon ground cumin*
- *¼ teaspoon smoked paprika*
- *¼ teaspoon ground cinnamon*
- *¼ teaspoon ground coriander*
- *¼ teaspoon chili powder*

Directions: Using an airtight bag, combine the brown sugar, salt, onion powder, garlic powder, sweet paprika, black pepper, ginger, cayenne, oregano, and cumin, cinnamon, smoked paprika, coriander, and chili powder. Close the container and shake to mix. The unused rub will keep in an airtight container for months.

Nutrition: Calories: 24.9; Carbs: 5.9g; Fat: 0g; Protein: 1.2g

262. Turkey Brine

Preparation Time: 5 minutes   Servings: 4

Ingredients:
- *2 gallons water*
- *2 cups coarse kosher salt*
- *2 cups packed light brown sugar*

Directions: In a clean 5-gallon bucket, mix the water, brown sugar and salt until the salt and sugar dissolve completely.

263. Chimichurri Sauce

Preparation Time: 5 minutes

Servings: 2

Ingredients:
- ½ cup extra-virgin olive oil
- 1 bunch fresh parsley, stems removed
- 1 bunch fresh cilantro, stems removed
- 1 small red onion, chopped
- 3 tablespoons dried oregano
- 1 tablespoon minced garlic
- Juice of 1 lemon
- 2 tablespoons red wine vinegar
- 1 teaspoon salt
- 1 teaspoon freshly ground black pepper
- 1 teaspoon cayenne pepper

Directions: Using a blender or processor, mix all of the ingredients and pulse several times until finely chopped. The chimichurri sauce will keep in an airtight container in the refrigerator for up to 5 days.

Nutrition: Calories: 50.8; Carbs: 0.9g; Fat: 4.8g; Protein: 1.2g

264. Cilantro-Balsamic Drizzle

Preparation Time: 5 minutes

Servings: 2

Ingredients:
- ½ cup balsamic vinegar
- ½ cup dry white wine
- ¼ cup extra-virgin olive oil
- ½ cup chopped fresh cilantro
- 2 teaspoons garlic powder
- 1 teaspoon salt
- 1 teaspoon freshly ground black pepper
- 1 teaspoon red pepper flakes
- Splash of Sriracha

Directions: Take a medium container, and whisk together the balsamic vinegar, olive oil, wine, garlic powder, cilantro, pepper, salt, and red pepper flakes until well combined.
Add a dash of Sriracha and stir.
The best storage is an airtight container put in the refrigerator for up to 2 weeks.

Nutrition: Calories: 20.8; Carbs: 5.9g; Fat: 0g; Protein: 2.1g

265. Mandarin Glaze

Preparation Time: 5 minutes
Servings: 2

Cooking Time: 25 minutes

Ingredients:
- 1 (11-ounce) can mandarin oranges, with their juices
- ½ cup ketchup
- 3 tablespoons brown sugar
- 1 tablespoon apple cider vinegar
- 1 tablespoon yellow mustard
- 1 teaspoon ground cloves
- 1 teaspoon ground cinnamon
- 1 teaspoon garlic powder
- 1 teaspoon onion powder
- 1 teaspoon salt
- 1 teaspoon freshly ground black pepper

Directions: Take a blender, mix the mandarin oranges and juice, the ketchup, brown sugar, apple cider vinegar, mustard, onion powder, salt, cloves, garlic powder, cinnamon, and pepper, and pulse until the oranges are in tiny pieces. Transfer all the mixture to a small saucepan on the stovetop and bring to a boil over medium heat, stirring occasionally. Lower the heat to low and simmer for 15 minutes.
Remove from the heat and strain out the orange pieces if desired. Serve the glaze hot.
Keep the glaze in an airtight container in the refrigerator for up to 5 days.

Nutrition: Calories: 34.8; Carbs: 8.9g; Fat: 0g; Protein: 0g

266. Dry Rub

Preparation Time: 10 minutes

Servings: 2

Ingredients:
- ¼ cup paprika
- ¼ cup turbinate sugar
- 3 tablespoons Cajun seasoning
- 1 tablespoon packed brown sugar

- *1½ teaspoons chili powder*
- *1½ teaspoons cayenne pepper*
- *1½ teaspoons ground cumin*

Directions: Take a small bowl, and combine the paprika, brown sugar, turbinate sugar, chili powder, Cajun seasoning, cayenne pepper, and cumin.
Store the rub in an airtight container at room temperature for up to a month.

Nutrition: Calories: 62.8; Carbs: 0g; Fat: 0g; Protein: 0g

267. Sweet and Spicy Jalapeño Relish

Preparation Time: 10 minutes   Servings: 2

Ingredients:
- *6 jalapeño peppers, stemmed, seeded, and cut into pieces*
- *1 Serrano chili, stemmed, seeded, and cut into pieces*
- *1 red bell pepper, stemmed, seeded, and cut into pieces*
- *1 cucumber, coarsely chopped*
- *1 onion, coarsely chopped*
- *½ cup rice wine vinegar*
- *¼ cup apple cider vinegar*
- *2 tablespoons sugar*
- *3 teaspoons minced garlic*
- *1 teaspoon salt*

Directions: Take a food processor or blender, mix the jalapeños, bell pepper, Serrano chili, cucumber, and onion, and pulse until coarsely chopped.
Mix the rice wine vinegar, minced garlic, apple cider vinegar, sugar, and salt, and pulse until minced but not puréed.
The relish will keep in an airtight container in the refrigerator for up to 1 week.

Nutrition: Calories: 29.8; Carbs: 6.8g; Fat: 0g; Protein: 0g

268. Spicy Sausage & Cheese Balls

Preparation Time: 20 minutes minutes   Cooking Time: 40
Servings: 4

Ingredients:
- *1lb Hot Breakfast Sausage*
- *2 cups Bisquick Baking Mix*
- *8 ounces Cream Cheese*
- *8 ounces Extra Sharp Cheddar Cheese*
- *1/4 cup Fresno Peppers*
- *1 tablespoon Dried Parsley*
- *1 teaspoon Killer Hogs AP Rub*
- *1/2 teaspoon Onion Powder*

Directions: Get ready smoker or flame broil for roundabout cooking at 400⁰.
Blend Sausage, destroyed cheddar, Baking Mix, cream cheddar, and remaining fixings in a huge bowl until all-around fused.
Utilize a little scoop to blend into chomp to estimate balls and roll tenderly fit as a fiddle.
Spot wiener and cheddar balls on a cast-iron container and cook for 15mins.

Nutrition: Calories: 94.8; Carbs: 3.9g; Fat: 6.8g; Protein: 5.2g

269. Cheesy Jalapeño Skillet Dip

Preparation Time: 10 minutes minutes   Cooking Time: 15
Serving: 8

Ingredients:
- *8 ounces cream cheese*
- *16 ounces shredded cheese*
- *1/3 cup mayonnaise*
- *4 ounces diced green chilies*
- *3 fresh jalapeños*
- *2 teaspoons Killer Hogs AP Rub*
- *2 teaspoons Mexican Style Seasoning*

For the topping:
- *¼ cup Mexican Blend Shredded Cheese*
- *Sliced jalapeños*
- *Mexican Style Seasoning*
- *3 tablespoons Killer Hogs AP Rub*

- 2 tablespoons Chili Powder
- 2 tablespoons Paprika
- 2 teaspoons Cumin
- ½ teaspoon Granulated Onion
- ¼ teaspoon Cayenne Pepper
- ¼ teaspoon Chipotle Chili Pepper ground
- ¼ teaspoon Oregano

Directions: Prepare smoker or flame broil for roundabout cooking at 350°
Join fixings in a big bowl and spot in a cast to press skillet
Top with Mexican Blend destroyed cheddar and cuts of jalapeno's
Spot iron skillet on flame broil mesh and cook until cheddar hot and bubbly and the top has seared
Marginally about 25mins.
Serve warm with enormous corn chips (scoops), tortilla chips, or your preferred vegetables for plunging.

Nutrition: Calories: 149.9; Carbs: 21.8g; Fat: 5.8g; Protein: 3.2g

270.   Juicy Loosey Cheeseburger

Preparation Time: 10 minutes minutes   **Cooking Time: 10**
Servings: 6

Ingredients:
- 2 lbs. ground beef
- 1 egg beaten
- 1 Cup dry bread crumbs
- 3 tablespoons evaporated milk
- 2 tablespoons Worcestershire sauce
- 1 tablespoon Grilla Grills All Purpose Rub
- 4 slices of cheddar cheese
- 4 buns

Directions: Start by consolidating the hamburger, egg, dissipated milk, and Worcestershire and focus on a bowl. Utilize your hands to blend well. Partition of this blend into 4 equivalent parts. At that point, take every one of the four sections and partition them into equal parts. Take every one of these little parts and smooth them. The objective is to have 8 equivalent level patties that you will then join into four burgers.
When you have your patties smoothed, put your cheddar in the center and, afterward, place the other patty over this and firmly squeeze the sides to seal. You may even need to push the meat back towards the inside piece to shape a marginally thicker patty. The patties ought to be marginally bigger than a standard burger bun as they will recoil a bit during cooking.
Prepare your Kong to 300°.
Keep in mind during flame broiling that you fundamentally have two meager patties, one on each side, so the cooking time ought not to have a place. You will cook these for 5 to 8mins per side—closer to 5mins on the off chance that you favor an uncommon burger or more towards 8mins in the event that you like a well to done burger.
At the point when you flip the burgers, take a toothpick and penetrate the focal point of the burger to permit steam to get away. This will shield you from having a hit to out or having a visitor who gets a jaw consume from liquid cheddar as they take their first nibble.
Toss these on a pleasant roll and top with fixings that supplement whatever your burgers are loaded down with.

Nutrition: Calories: 299.8; Carbs: 32.8g; Fat: 11.9g; Protein: 15.2g

271.   Juicy Loosey Smokey Burger

Preparation Time: 30 minutes minutes   **Cooking Time: 30**
Servings: 2

Ingredients:
- 1 pound Beef
- 1/3 pound per burger
- Cheddar cheese
- Grilla AP Rub
- Salt
- Freshly Ground Black Pepper
- Hamburger Bun
- BBQ Sauce

Directions: Split every 1/3 pound of meat, which is 2.66 ounces per half.
Level out one half to roughly six inches plate. Place wrecked of American cheddar, leaving 1/2 inch clear.
Place another portion of the meat on top, and seal the edges. Rehash for all burgers.
Sprinkle with Grilla AP rub, salt, and pepper flame broil seasonings.
Smoke at 250 for 50mins. No compelling reason to turn.

Apply Smokey Dokey BBQ sauce, ideally a mustard-based sauce like Grilla Gold and Bold, or Sticky Fingers Carolina Classic. Cook for an extra 10 minutes or to favored doneness.

Nutrition: Calories: 263.8; Carbs: 56.8g; Fat: 1.8g; Protein: 4.2g

272.　　Grilled Cheese Sticks

Preparation Time: 2 hours　　　　　　　　　　　　　　**Cooking Time: 20 minutes**
Servings: 4

Ingredients:
- Bread, Medium 2 slices
- Butter 1 tbs
- Cheese, Medium 1/2 cup grated
- 1 slice sharp cheddar
- 1 slice of mild cheddar

Directions: Preheat the grill pan till hot and melt butter on it for a minute or two.
Take one slice of bread and apply butter on both sides. Then apply grated cheese thickly on the buttered side of the bread in a strip or a square shape, covering the width of the slice from edge to edge. Repeat this step with the second bread slice, placing the cheese in alternate strips or squares and creating an X pattern with both slices.
Put the prepared bread slice on the grill pan and let it fry till the base is crisp and golden.
Flip it over to the other side and let the other side cook till both sides are crispy, golden brown.
Once done, remove from heat and set aside to cool for a minute or two.
Take the other slice of bread and apply the same way as in step 2.
Put this bread slice on the grill pan and place the other slice of bread on top, buttered side first.
Cook until cheese melts well, turns golden brown, and is crispy from bottom to top.
Once done, remove from heat and let it cool for a minute or two before serving freshly prepared cheesy sticks.

Nutrition: Calories: 157.9; Carbs: 13.8g; Fat: 6.8g; Protein: 9.2g

273.　　Grilled Chicken Wingettes

Preparation Time: 10 minutes　　　　　　　　　　　　**Cooking Time: 35 minutes**
Servings: 4

Ingredients:
- Zest of 1 lemon
- 2 tsp. kosher salt
- 1 tsp. smoked paprika
- 1 tsp. garlic powder
- 6 lbs. chicken wings
- 6 sprigs fresh thyme
- 1/2 cup ghee or grass-fed butter (melted)

Directions: Trim chicken winglets of any excess fat. Remove the tips and discard or reserve for another use. Put winglets in a large bowl and add the juice of 1 lemon, 2 tsp. kosher salt, smoked paprika, and garlic powder. Toss to coat wings evenly. Allow marinating for at least an hour and up to overnight.
Rinse and pat dry chicken winglets. Preheat the grill to medium-high heat. Line a sheet pan with aluminum foil and lightly brush it with oil to prevent the wings from sticking.
Put the chicken winglets on the grill, being careful not to crowd them too close together or they will steam instead of getting nice and crispy. Cook for 10-12 minutes until crisp and starting to brown. Tossing halfway through cooking time if desired so both sides brown evenly.
Remove pan from the grill and allow to cool for a few minutes.
Put winglets on a prepared sheet pan. Brush each winglet with 1/2 cup ghee (melted) or melted grass-fed butter, and place under broiler until crisp (about 5 minutes).
Top the winglets with fresh thyme sprigs while warm.

Nutrition: Calories: 562.7; Carbs: 1.8g; Fat: 27.9g; Protein 35.2g

Desserts and Pies Recipes

274.   Grilled Banana Split

Preparation Time: 10 minutes   **Cooking Time: 10 minutes**
Servings: 4

Ingredients:

- 1 x 385g can sweeten condensed milk
- 1/2 cup cream whipping/heavy cream
- 1/2 cup brown sugar
- 1/2 cup butter, softened
- 2 x ripe bananas, peeled and sliced crosswise
- 1 x 397g can cherry pie filling (drain liquid)
- 1 x 397g can pineapple chunks (drained & undrained)
- 8 maraschino cherries with stems, chopped into small pieces

Directions: Mix the cream and sugar in a small bowl.
Take a separate bowl, whip butter until fluffy, then stir in condensed milk.
Fold in whipped cream mixture and combine well, set aside.
Spread condensed milk mixture into the prepared pan. Add banana slices on top and fill gaps with chunks of pineapple & cherries across the banana slices for even distribution throughout your dessert.
Spray a little cooking oil here and there on the top of the banana and pineapple to help with those grill marks.
Place under the grill for 5-7 minutes until golden brown and serve immediately.

Nutrition: Calories: 24.8; Carbs: 0.1g; Fat: 1.9g; Protein: 0.3g

275.   Grilled Cheese Crackers

Preparation Time: 15 minutes   **Cooking Time: 45 minutes**
Servings: 4

Ingredients:

- 10 round crackers
- 1/4 cup(s) grated cheddar cheese
- 1/2 teaspoon(s) margarine

For the filling:
- 3 tablespoon(s) grated cheddar cheese

Directions: Preheat the griller to 350 degrees F.(180 degrees C.)
Grease 2 baking sheets. Put crackers in a single layer on the prepared baking sheet.
Grill for 4 to 5 minutes until crisp. Remove from oven and sprinkle with 1/4 cup of cheese.

Nutrition: Calories: 119.8; Fat: 3.7g; Carbs: 1.8g; Protein 2.1g

276.   Grilled Pound Cake with Meyer Lemon Syrup

Preparation Time: 15 minutes   **Cooking Time: 60 minutes**
Servings: 8

Ingredients:

- 1 pound butter, room temperature
- 4 large eggs
- 1 cup granulated sugar
- 2 1/4 cups cake flour
- 1/2 teaspoon salt
- 1 teaspoon vanilla extract
- 1 cup Meyer lemon curd (recipe below)

Directions: Make a cake layer. Prepare grill to medium-low (about 350 degrees). Butter and flour 3 round cake pans. Line bottoms of pans with parchment paper. Take a large bowl, and using an electric mixer, cream butter until fluffy.
Add sugar and beat until light and fluffy, about 5 minutes, scraping down sides of bowl as needed. Add eggs one at a time, beating after each addition until incorporated. Beat in vanilla extract, then fold in flour and salt until just combined. Divide batter among prepared pans, smoothing tops.
Grill cakes until golden brown and crusty on the underside, about 10 minutes. Carefully flip cakes and continue grilling until golden brown and cooked through, about 10 minutes more. Cool completely in pans for 30 minutes, then turn out of pans onto wire racks.

Make the syrup while cake cools (can be made a day ahead). In a saucepan, stir Meyer lemon curd, sugar, and 1/4 cup water over medium heat until sugar dissolves. Cook until reduced to about 1 cup, frequently stirring to prevent scorching. Set aside and let cool completely.

Assemble cake. Spread 1/2 cup lemon syrup on each of 2 cake layers, then stack on a serving platter. Repeat with remaining layers and remaining syrup (you should have six layers. Chill cake in fridge until ready to serve.

Nutrition: Calories: 1436.8; Fat: 67.8g; Carbs: 176.8g; Fiber: 1.8g; Protein: 27.2g

277.   Grilled Strawberry Shortcake Kebabs

Preparation Time: 10 minutes   **Cooking Time: 20 minutes**
Servings: 10

Ingredients:

- 24 Strawberries, cleaned and de-stemmed
- 2 Tbsp. Brown Sugar
- 1/2 Cup Flour
- 1 Tbsp. Cornstarch
- 1/4 tsp. Salt
- 1/4 tsp. Cinnamon
- 3 tsp. Baking Powder
- 1 1/2 Cups Milk (I used 2%) + 1 Tbsp.

Directions: Prepare grill to 350 degrees. Mix flour, cornstarch, cinnamon and salt in a large bowl.

Cut butter into flour mixture using a pastry blender, until mixture resembles coarse crumbs with pea-sized pieces remaining. Stir in milk until the dough just holds together (you may not need all of the milk).

Roll dough into 10" circles about 1/8 thick on a lightly floured board.

Cut each circle into 4 wedges.

Brush one side of each wedge with water, and spread 1 tsp. of sugar on the other side of each wedge.

Put two strawberries on the wide end of each wedge - flat sides out, pointy ends in - and roll up the dough around the strawberries to form a "long john" shape.

Transfer all 6 kebabs to a baking sheet, place on grill and cook for about 15 minutes (turning every 4-5 minutes).

Remove from grill, dust with powdered sugar and serve warm with fresh whipped cream or vanilla ice cream.

Nutrition: Calories: 301.8; Protein: 4.1g; Fat: 11.8g; Carbs: 47g; Fiber: 2.6g

278.   Nutella Grilled Cheese

Preparation Time: 10 minutes   **Cooking Time: 15 minutes**
Serving: 2

Ingredients:

- 8 slices of white bread
- 1/4 cup Nutella
- 8 slices Cheddar cheese
- 2 Tbsp unsalted butter

Directions: Spread the Nutella on 4 of the bread slices.

Top with the remaining bread slices and cut in half to make sandwiches.

Grill the sandwiches. If you have a sandwich maker, use it to grill the sandwiches. Otherwise, butter a large frying pan and fry over medium heat until golden brown on both sides, about 5 minutes each side.

Nutrition: Calories: 206.8; Fat: 16.7g; Carbs: 11.3g; Sugar: 1.5g; Protein: 5.5g

279.   Grilled Maple-Glazed Acorn Squash

Preparation Time: 15 minutes   **Cooking Time: 30 minutes**
Serving: 8

Ingredients:

- Oil for grill gratings
- Unsalted butter with 1 stick (8 tablespoons)
- 1/2 cup of maple syrup in pure form
- 2 teaspoons vinegar for cider
- 1/2 teaspoon powder of dry mustard
- 1/2 teaspoon of red pepper crushed
- Kosher salt and black pepper, freshly ground
- 2 squashes of acorn (about 2 pounds each)
- 2 tablespoons toasted pepitas (roasted hulled pumpkin seeds)

- *1 tablespoon of powdered chili*
- *1 teaspoon of ground cilantro*
- *Cinnamon 1/2 teaspoon ground*

Directions: For cooking over medium heat, prepare a grill. Grease the grill grates gently.

Take a small saucepan, melt the butter and turn the heat off. Remove the melted butter from 1/4 cup and reserve. Take a saucepan and whisk together the maple syrup, cider vinegar, dry mustard, crushed red pepper, 3/4 teaspoon salt and a few chunks of pepper. To reduce slightly, bring to a simmer and cook for around 4 minutes. Remove the heat from the glaze and let it cool. Set aside 1/3 of a cup of glaze at the end to drizzle. Squashes are carefully halved from the stem to the bottom. Scoop with a spoon out the seeds and discard. Flat-side down, put the squash halves and slice crosswise into 1/2-inch scalloped half-moons. Place them in a very wide bowl with the slices.

Take a small cup, add the chili powder, coriander, cinnamon, 1/2 teaspoon salt and 1/4 teaspoon pepper together. Sprinkle over the squash slices with the spice mixture. Drizzle over the squash with the reserved 1/4 cup of melted butter. To make sure that the slices are uniformly covered, toss with your fingertips.

Put and cover the squash slices on the grill. Cook for about 10 minutes before dark grill marks emerge. Flip the squash slices; cover and cook for 7 to 8 more minutes until the squash is only soft enough to be pierced easily with a paring knife.

Brush the glaze with the squash slices and flip. Cook for 1 minute, glaze, flip, and cook for another minute on the other side. Remove from the grill and put on a large plate. Drizzle it with the glaze reserved. Sprinkle the pepitas with them. Serve at room temperature or hotter.

Nutrition: Calories: 121.9; Fat: 6.9g; Carbs: 16.1g; Sugar: 5.2g; Protein: 1.3g

280.   Bread Pudding

Preparation Time: 15 minutes minutes

Cooking Time: 45

Servings: 4

Ingredients:

- 8 stale donuts
- 3 eggs
- 1 cup milk
- 1 cup heavy cream
- ½ cup brown sugar
- 1 teaspoon vanilla

- 1 pinch salt
- Blueberry Compote
- 1 pint blueberries
- 2/3 cup granulated sugar
- ¼ cup water
- 1 lemon

- Oat Topping
- 1 cup quick oats
- ½ cup brown sugar
- 1 teaspoon flour
- 2 to 3 tablespoons room temperature butter

Directions: Prepare the Grill to 350°.

Cut your doughnuts into 6 pieces for every doughnut and put it in a safe spot. Blend your eggs, cream, milk, vanilla, darker sugar, and salt in a bowl until it's everything fused. Spot your doughnuts in a lubed 9 by 13 container at that point pour your custard blend over the doughnuts. Press down on the doughnuts to guarantee they get covered well and absorb the juices.

Take another bowl, consolidate your oats, dark colored sugar, flour and gradually join the spread with your hand until the blend begins to cluster up like sand. When that is prepared, sprinkle it over the highest point of the bread pudding and toss it on the barbecue around 40 to 45mins until it gets decent and brilliant dark-colored.

While the bread pudding is preparing, place your blueberries into a skillet over medium-high warmth and begin to cook them down so the juices begin to stream. When that occurs, include your sugar and water and blend well. Diminish the warmth to drug low and let it cook down until it begins to thicken up. When the blend begins to thicken, drizzle your lemon, add the get-up-and-go to the blueberry compote, and cut your lemon down the middle and squeeze it into the blend. What you're left with is a tasty, splendid compote that is ideal for the sweetness of the bread pudding.

Watch out for your bread pudding around the 40 to 50 mins mark. The blend will, in any case, shake a piece in the middle however will solidify as it stands once you pull it off. You can pull it early on the off chance that you like your bread pudding more sodden

Nutrition: Calories: 289.8; Carbs: 61.9g; Fat: 3.8g; Protein: 5.2g

281.   Bacon Sweet Potato Pie

Preparation Time: 15 minutes

Cooking Time: 50 minutes

Servings: 8

Ingredients:

- 1 pound 3 ounces sweet potatoes
- 1 ¼ cups plain yogurt
- ¾ cup packed, dark brown sugar
- ½ teaspoon of cinnamon
- ¼ teaspoon of nutmeg
- 5 egg yolks
- ¼ teaspoon of salt
- 1 (up to 9 inch) deep dish, frozen pie shell
- 1 cup chopped pecans, toasted
- 4 strips of bacon, cooked and diced
- 1 tablespoon maple syrup
- Optional: Whipped topping

Directions: In the first region, 3D shapes the potatoes right into a steamer crate and sees into a good-sized pot of stew water. Ensure the water is not any nearer than creeps from the base of the bushel. When steamed for 20mins, pound with a potato masher and installed a safe spot.

While your flame broil is preheating, location the sweet potatoes within the bowl of a stand blender and beat with the oar connection.

Include yogurt, cinnamon, dark colored sugar, yolks, nutmeg, and salt to flavor and beat until a whole lot joined. Take this hitter into the pie shell and see onto a sheet dish. Sprinkle walnuts and bacon on pinnacle and bathe with maple syrup.

Heat for 45 to 60mins or until the custard arrives at 165 to 180°. Take out from fish fry and funky. Keep refrigerated within the wake of cooling.

Nutrition: Calories: 269.8; Carbs: 38.7g; Fat: 11.8g; Protein: 4.2g

282. **Apple Pie on the Grill**

Preparation Time: 15 minutes
Servings: 6

Cooking Time: 30 minutes

Ingredients:

- ¼ cup of Sugar
- 4 Apples, sliced
- 1 tablespoon of Cornstarch
- 1 teaspoon Cinnamon, ground
- 1 Pie Crust, refrigerated, soften in according to the directions on the box
- ½ cup of Peach preserves

Directions: Prepare the grill to 375F with closed lid.
Take a bowl and mix the cornstarch, cinnamon, apples and sugar. Set aside.
Put the piecrust in a pie pan. Spread the preserves and then place the apples. Fold the crust slightly.
Put a pan on the grill (upside - down) so that you don't brill/bake the pie directly on the heat.
Cook 30 - 40 minutes. Once done, set aside to rest. Serve and enjoy

Nutrition: Calories: 159.8; Protein: 0.7g; Carbs: 34.8g; Fat: 1g

283. **Coconut Chocolate Brownies**

Preparation Time: 15 minutes
Servings: 6

Cooking Time: 25 minutes

Ingredients:

- 4 eggs
- 1 cup Cane Sugar
- ¾ cup of Coconut oil
- 4 ounces chocolate, chopped
- ½ teaspoon of Sea salt
- ¼ cup cocoa powder, unsweetened
- ½ cup flour
- 4 ounces Chocolate chips
- 1 teaspoon of Vanilla

Directions: Prepare the grill to 350F with a closed lid.
Take a baking pan (9x9), grease it and line a parchment paper.
In a bowl and mix the cocoa powder, salt and flour. Stir and set aside.
In the microwave or double boiler melt the coconut oil and chopped chocolate. Let it cool a bit.
Add the eggs, vanilla, sugar and mix to combine.
Add into the flour, and add chocolate chips. Pour the mixture into a pan.
Put the pan on the grate. Bake for 20 minutes. If you want dryer brownies to bake for 5 - 10 minutes more.
Let them cool before cutting. Cut the brownies into squares and serve.

Nutrition: Calories: 134.8; Protein: 2.1g; Carbs: 15.8g; Fat: 2.9g

284.   Bacon Chocolate Chip Cookies

Preparation Time: 30 minutes   **Cooking Time: 30 minutes**
Servings: 6

Ingredients:

- 8 slices cooked and crumbled bacon
- 2 ½ teaspoon apple cider vinegar
- 1 teaspoon vanilla
- 2 cup semisweet chocolate chips
- butter
- 2 room temp eggs
- 1 ½ teaspoon baking soda
- 1 cup granulated sugar
- ½ teaspoon salt
- 2 ¾ cup all-purpose flour
- 1 cup light brown sugar
- 1 ½ stick softened

Directions: Stir baking soda, salt and flour.
Cream the sugar and the butter together. Lower the speed. Add in the eggs, vinegar, and vanilla.
Place it on low fire, slowly add in the flour mixture, bacon pieces, and chocolate chips.
Add Preferred Wood Pellet pellets to your smoker and follow your cooker's startup procedure. Prepare the smoker, with your lid closed, until it reaches 375.
Put a parchment paper on a baking sheet you are using and drop a teaspoonful of cookie batter on the baking sheet. Let them cook on the grill, covered, for approximately 12 minutes or until they are browned.

Nutrition: Calories: 166.8; Carbs: 20.8g; Fat: 8.7g; Protein: 2.1g

285.   Apple Cobbler

Preparation Time: 30 minutes   **Cooking Time: 1 hour 50 minutes**
Servings: 8

Ingredients:

- 8 Granny Smith apples
- 1 cup sugar
- 1 stick melted butter
- 1 teaspoon cinnamon
- Pinch salt
- ½ cup brown sugar
- 2 eggs
- 2 teaspoons baking powder
- 2 cup plain flour
- 1 ½ cup sugar

Directions: Peel and quarter apples, and put into a bowl. Add in the cinnamon and one c. sugar. Stir well to coat and let it set for one hour.
Add Preferred Wood Pellet pellets to your smoker and follow your cooker's startup procedure. Prepare the smoker with your lid closed, until it reaches 350.
Add the eggs, salt, baking powder, sugar, brown sugar, and flour in a large bowl. Mix until it forms crumbles. Put apples into a Dutch oven. Add the crumble mixture on top and drizzle with melted butter.
Put on the grill and cook for 50 minutes.

Nutrition: Calories: 151.8; Carbs: 25.9g; Fat: 4.8g; Protein: 1.2g

286.   Exotic Apple Pie

Preparation Time: 20 minutes   **Cooking Time: 1 hour 30 minutes**
Servings: 4

Ingredients:

- 3 Apples (large, thinly sliced)
- 1/3 Cup of Sugar
- 1 Tablespoon of Flour
- 1/4 Teaspoon of Cinnamon (ground)
- 1 Tablespoon of Lemon juice
- Pinch of Nutmeg (ground)
- Pinch of salt
- Homemade pie or box of pie dough

Directions: Prepare the Grill. Stir apples, sugar and flour, cinnamon, salt, nutmeg, and lemon juice in a bowl thoroughly. Cut the dough into two.
Put one half of the dough into the 10" pie plate and press firmly with your hand.
Pour the apple mix into the dough and cover it with the other half.
Use your hand again to crimp the edges of the pie together.
Use knife cut the top of the dough. Pepping on the Pellet Smoker.
Set the Smoker grill to indirect cooking and preheat to 425°F.

Transfer to the smoker and bake, and then cover the edges of the pie with foil to avoid burn.
Bake the dough until it turns golden brown approximately 45 minutes
Remove and allow cooling for 1 hour. Slice, serve and enjoy.

Nutrition: Calories: 219.8; Carbs: 33.9g; Fat: 7.7g; Protein: 2.1g

287.   Blackberry Pie

Preparation Time: 15 minutes   **Cooking Time: 40 minutes**
Servings: 8

Ingredients:

- Butter, for greasing
- ½ cup all-purpose flour
- ½ cup milk

- 2 pints blackberries
- 2 cup sugar, divided
- 1 box refrigerated piecrusts

- 1 stick melted butter
- 1 stick of butter
- Vanilla ice cream

Directions: Put wood pellets to the smoker and follow the cooker's startup procedure. Prepare the smoker, with your lid closed, until it reaches 375. Butter a cast iron skillet.
Unroll a piecrust and lay it in the bottom and up the sides of the skillet. Use a fork to poke holes in the crust.
Lay the skillet on the grill and smoke for five mins.
Mix together 1 ½ c. of sugar, the flour, and the melted butter together. Add in the blackberries and toss everything together.
The berry mixture should be added to the skillet. The milk should be added on the top afterward. Sprinkle on half of the diced butter.
Unroll the second pie crust and lay it over the skillet. You can also slice it into strips and weave it on top to make it look like a lattice. Place the rest of the diced butter over the top. Sprinkle the rest of the sugar over the crust and place it skillet back on the grill.
Lower the lid and smoke for 15 to 20 minutes. You may want to cover with some foil to keep it from burning during the last few minutes of cooking. Serve the hot pie with some vanilla ice cream.

Nutrition: Calories: 392.8; Protein: 4.5g; Carbs: 53.3g; Fat: 18.5g

288.   Ice Cream Bread

Preparation Time: 10 minutes   **Cooking Time: 1 hour**
Servings: 6

Ingredients:

- 1 ½ quart full-fat butter pecan ice cream, softened
- 1 teaspoon salt

- 2 cups semisweet chocolate chips
- 1 cup sugar

- 1 stick melted butter
- Butter, for greasing
- 4 cups self-rising flour

Directions: Add wood pellets to your smoker and follow your cooker's startup procedure. Prepare the smoker, with your lid closed, until it reaches 350.
Stir together the sugar, flour, salt, and ice cream with an electric mixer set to medium for two minutes.
As the mixer is still running, add in the chocolate chips, beating until everything is blended.
Spray a Bundt pan or tube pan with cooking spray. If you use a solid pan, the center will take too long to cook. That's why a tube or Bundt pan works best.
Add the batter to your prepared pan.
Set the cake on the grill, cover, and smoke for 50 minutes to an hour. A toothpick should come out clean.
Take the pan off of the grill, for 10 minutes cool the bread. Remove the bread from the pan carefully and then drizzle it with some melted butter.

Nutrition: Calories: 148.2; Protein: 3.7g; Carbs: 26.8g; Fat: 2.8g

Recipe Index

269.	Cheesy Jalapeño Skillet Dip	119
63.	Chicken Drumsticks	40
51.	Chicken Sandwich	35
96.	Chili Sweet Smoked Pork Tenderloin	51
263.	Chimichurri Sauce	118
109.	Cider Pork Steak	55
127.	Cider Salmon	62
264.	Cilantro-Balsamic Drizzle	118
84.	Cilantro-Mint Pork BBQ Thai Style	47
166.	Cinnamon Apricot Smoked Chicken Thighs	79
72.	Cocoa Crusted Pork Tenderloin	43
283.	Coconut Chocolate Brownies	125
37.	Corned Beef Pastrami	29
36.	Corned Beef with Cabbage	29
151.	Crazy Greek Lamb Gyros	72
160.	Crown Rack of Lamb	76
112.	Cuban Pork	57
195.	Cured Turkey Drumstick	91
259.	Dill Seafood Rub	117
266.	Dry Rub	118
260.	Espresso Brisket Rub	117
286.	Exotic Apple Pie	126
55.	Fajita Chicken Kebabs	37
42.	Feta Spinach Turkey Burgers	31
147.	Filet Mignon with Pineapple Salsa	71
117.	Finnan Haddie Recipe	58
115.	Fish Recipe	58
237.	Garlic Parmesan Wedge	110
135.	Garlic Salmon	65
118.	Garlic Shrimp Pesto Bruschetta	59
60.	Glazed Chicken Drumsticks	39
148.	Glazed Lamb Chops	71
253.	Gorgonzola Dipping Sauce	115
54.	Greek Chicken and Veggie Kebabs	37
154.	Greek Leg of Lamb	73
27.	Green Burgers	26
71.	Grill Pork Crown Roast	43
216.	Grilled Artichokes	100
136.	Grilled Aussie Leg of Lamb	67
274.	Grilled Banana Split	122
45.	Grilled Beef Burgers	32
240.	Grilled Broccoli	111

3.	Grilled Butter Basted Porterhouse Steak	17
275.	Grilled Cheese Crackers	122
272.	Grilled Cheese Sticks	121
59.	Grilled Chicken Cutlets	39
178.	Grilled Chicken Salad	84
273.	Grilled Chicken Wingettes	121
239.	Grilled Corn	111
211.	Grilled Eggplant and Pepper Goat Cheese Sandwiches	98
212.	Grilled Fava Beans with Mint, Lemon Zest and Sumac	98
205.	Grilled Flounder with Banana Leaves	95
243.	Grilled French Dip	112
33.	Grilled Hanger Steak	28
99.	Grilled Honey Pork Loin	52
131.	Grilled King Crab Legs	64
156.	Grilled Lamb	74
52.	Grilled Lamb Burgers	35
165.	Grilled Lamb Chops	78
163.	Grilled Lamb Loin Chops	77
162.	Grilled Lamb with Brown Sugar Glaze	77
128.	Grilled Lobster Tail	63
279.	Grilled Maple-Glazed Acorn Squash	123
7.	Grilled New York Strip	18
50.	Grilled Pork Burgers	34
97.	Grilled Pork Chops	51
101.	Grilled Pork Chops	53
276.	Grilled Pound Cake with Meyer Lemon Syrup	122
121.	Grilled Red Snapper	60
213.	Grilled Romaine Salad with Maitake Mushrooms	99
129.	Grilled Salmon	63
215.	Grilled Salmon Salad with Avocado Cucumber Salsa	99
206.	Grilled Salmon with Lemon-Pepper	96
18.	Grilled Steak	22
277.	Grilled Strawberry Shortcake Kebabs	123
74.	Grilled Tenderloin with Fresh Herb Sauce	44
130.	Grilled Tuna	64
214.	Grilled Zucchini with Zaatar	99
152.	Ground Lamb Kebabs	73
49.	Ground Turkey Burgers	34
125.	Halibut in Parchment	61

255.	Hawaiian Mojo	116
23.	Herbed Beef Eye Fillet	24
149.	Herbed Lamb Chops	71
12.	Herbed Rib Roast	20
181.	Herbed Smoked Hen	85
24.	Herbed Steaks	25
157.	Hickory Rack of Lamb	75
173.	Hickory Smoke Patchcock Chicken	82
32.	Homemade Meatballs	27
91.	Honey Glazed Ham	49
17.	Honey Glazed Smoked Beef	22
194.	Hot Sauce Smoked Turkey Tabasco	91
288.	Ice Cream Bread	127
203.	Italian Grilled Shrimp	94
192.	Jalapeno Injection Turkey	90
123.	Jerk Shrimp	61
68.	Juicy BBQ Chicken	42
270.	Juicy Loosey Cheeseburger	120
271.	Juicy Loosey Smokey Burger	120
31.	Kalbi Beef Ribs	27
83.	Keto Parmesan Crusted Pork Chops	47
10.	Korean Beef Rib Eye	19
25.	La Rochelle Steak	25
39.	Lamb Burgers	30
155.	Lamb Chops	74
153.	Lamb Rack Wrapped In Apple Wood Walnut	73
138.	Leg of a Lamb	67
142.	Leg of Lamb with Salsa	69
174.	Lemon Cornish Chicken Stuffed With Crab	82
65.	Lemon Mustard Chicken	41
66.	Lemon Pepper Chicken	41
93.	Lemon Pepper Pork Tenderloin	50
88.	Lemon Pepper Wings	48
198.	Lemony Lobster Tails	93
26.	Lemony Mustard Crusted Veal	25
124.	Lobster Tails	61
232.	Mac & Cheese	107
197.	Mahi-Mahi	93
265.	Mandarin Glaze	118
187.	Maple Bourbon Turkey	88
182.	Maple Glazed Whole Chicken	85
57.	Maple-Glazed Chicken Wings	38

64.	Meatballs Kabobs	41
145.	Middle Eastern Lamb Stew	70
231.	Mushroom Barley Soup	107
38.	Mushroom Beef Burgers	30
234.	Mushrooms Stuffed With Crab Meat	109
11.	Mustard Beef Ribs	20
217.	Nicoise Salad with Grilled Fish	101
250.	North Carolina Barbecue Sauce	115
242.	Nut Mix on the Grill	112
278.	Nutella Grilled Cheese	123
184.	Orange Chicken Wings	86
80.	Panko-Breaded Pork Chops	46
179.	Parmesan Chicken Wings	84
100.	Parmesan Roast Pork	52
199.	Parsley Prawn Skewers	93
108.	Pineapple Bourbon Glazed Ham	55
113.	Pineapple Maple Glaze Fish	57
107.	Pork Loin Roulade	55
89.	Pork Shoulder	48
81.	Pork Tenders with Bell Peppers	46
209.	Potato Gratin	97
241.	Potato Roast	111
30.	Prime Rib Roast	27
77.	Pulled Pig Pork	45
221.	Pumpkin Quesadillas	103
256.	Queen Spice Rub	116
86.	Raspberry Pork Ribs	48
233.	Red Beans Rice	107
2.	Reverse Seared Flank Steak	17
8.	Rib Roast	19
29.	Roast Beast	26
196.	Roast Turkey Orange	92
143.	Roasted Leg of Lamb	69
183.	Rosemary Chicken	86
144.	Rosemary Lamb	70
90.	Rosemary Pork Tenderloin	49
120.	Salmon Cakes	59
76.	Sausage Hash	44
186.	Savory-Sweet Turkey Legs	87
116.	Seared Tuna Steaks	58
201.	Sesame Seeds Flounder	94
246.	Shrimp Cocktail	113
207.	Shrimp Kebabs	96

122.	Shrimp Scampi	60
119.	Shrimp Tacos	59
70.	Simple Smoked Pork Ribs	43
230.	Slow Cooked Vegetables	106
34.	Slow Roasted Shawarma	28
1.	Smoked and Pulled Beef	17
248.	Smoked Asparagus with Parsley and Garlic	113
102.	Smoked Bacon	53
6.	Smoked Brisket	18
176.	Smoked Chicken Breasts in Lemon Marinade	83
177.	Smoked Chicken Burgers with Feta Cheese	83
175.	Smoked Chicken Patties	82
134.	Smoked Crab Legs	65
245.	Smoked Guacamole	112
78.	Smoked Honey - Garlic Pork Chops	45
244.	Smoked Jerky	112
158.	Smoked Lamb chops	75
137.	Smoked Lamb Shoulder	67
79.	Smoked Pork Chops with Tarragon	45
104.	Smoked Pork Cutlets with Caraway and Dill	54
105.	Smoked Pork Ribs with Herbs	54
15.	Smoked Pulled Beef	21
159.	Smoked Pulled Lamb Sliders	75
140.	Smoked Rack of Lamb	68
21.	Smoked Roast Beef	24
247.	Smoked Russet Potatoes	113
132.	Smoked Sardines	64
114.	Smoked Sea Bass	57
106.	Smoked Spicy Pork Medallions	54
249.	Smoked Sweet Pie Pumpkins	114
20.	Smoked Tri-Tip	23
170.	Smoked Whole Chicken with Dry Rub	81
190.	Smoked Whole Turkey	89
188.	Spatchcock Smoked Turkey	88
61.	Spiced Chicken Breasts	39
58.	Spicy Barbecue Chicken Drumsticks	38
62.	Spicy Chicken Thighs	40
202.	Spicy Filet Mignon with Sweet Onion	94
35.	Spicy Grilled Beef Steak	28
139.	Spicy Lamb Shoulder	68

268.	Spicy Sausage & Cheese Balls	119
133.	Spicy Smoked Shrimp	65
252.	Spicy Thai Peanut Sauce	115
218.	Sprouted Lentil Burgers	101
220.	Sriracha Roasted Potatoes	103
126.	Sriracha Salmon	62
47.	Steakhouse Burgers	33
40.	Stuffed Burgers	30
222.	Stuffed Mushroom	103
225.	Stuffed Pepper	105
103.	Stuffed Pork Crown Roast	53
223.	Stuffed Squash	104
208.	Stuffed Tomatoes	97
261.	Sweet and Spicy Cinnamon Rub	117
267.	Sweet and Spicy Jalapeño Relish	119
92.	Sweet Bacon Wrapped Smokes	49
167.	Sweet Smoked Chicken Breast with Celery Seeds	79
67.	Sweet Tangy Orange Chicken	41
28.	T-Bone with Blue Cheese Butter	26
5.	Teriyaki Beef Jerky	18
172.	Teriyaki Smoked Drumstick	81
251.	Texas Brisket Sauce	115
19.	Texas Style Brisket Flat	23
9.	The South Barbacoa	19
257.	Three Pepper Rub	116
219.	Toasted-Baked Tofu cubes	103
210.	Tofu with Orange Sauce	97
75.	Togarashi Pork Tenderloin	44
224.	Tomato Green Bean Soup	105
53.	Tuna Burgers	35
185.	Turkey Breast	87
262.	Turkey Brine	117
41.	Turkey Burger	31
189.	Turkey Jerky	88
204.	White Bean Grilled Salmon and Arugula Salad	95
191.	Whole Turkey	89
141.	Wine Braised Lamb Shank	69
164.	Wood pellet grill Lamb	77
4.	Wood Pellet Grill Prime Rib Roast	17
161.	Wood Pellet Grilled Aussie Leg of Lamb Roast	76
169.	Wood Pellet Grilled Chicken Satay	80

168.	Wood Pellet Smoked Chicken Breasts	80
171.	Yan's Grilled Quarters	81
56.	Zesty Garlic Grilled Chicken	37

Made in the USA
Middletown, DE
15 October 2023

40857876R00077